SPEAK UP!

EDDIE "PIOLÍN" SOTELO

SPEAK UP!

FINDING MY VOICE THROUGH HOPE, STRENGTH, AND DETERMINATION

A CELEBRA BOOK

Celebra
Published by the Penguin Group
Penguin Group (USA) LLC, 375 Hudson Street,
New York, New York 10014

USA | Canada | UK | Ireland | Australia | New Zealand | India | South Africa | China
penguin.com
A Penguin Random House Company

First published by Celebra,
a division of Penguin Group (USA) LLC

First Printing, March 2015

ISBN 978-0-451-47274-8

THE LIBRARY OF CONGRESS HAS CATALOGED THE SPANISH-LANGUAGE EDITION OF THIS TITLE AS FOLLOWS:

Sotelo, Eddie.
¿A qué venimos? ¡A triunfar!: cómo encontré mi voz entre la esperanza, la fuerza y la determinación/Eddie "Piolín" Sotelo.
p. cm.
ISBN 978-0-451-47275-5
1. Sotelo, Eddie. 2. Radio broadcasters—Mexico—Biography. I. Title.
PN1991.4.S62A3 2015
791.4402'8092—dc23 2014042061
[B]

Printed in the United States of America
10 9 8 7 6 5 4 3 2 1

Set in Utopia
Designed by Sabrina Bowers

PUBLISHER'S NOTE
Penguin is committed to publishing works of quality and integrity. In that spirit, we are proud to offer this book to our readers; however the story, the experiences and the words are the author's alone.

To those who wake up every morning ready to move forward, no matter what obstacles may stand in your way. Keep hope and faith alive.

To Edward and Daniel, my sons and greatest joys.

To María, the light who shines upon me.

SPEAK UP!

PROLOGUE

Throughout the history of the world, there are people who stand out because their mission in life is to inspire and touch the lives of many. These are human beings who do not expect life to take them on an uncertain journey: they are the ones who shape their own destiny through hard work and perseverance.

One of these people is my friend Piolín. Eduardo Sotelo was born in Ocotlán, Jalisco, Mexico, and at a very young age, he made the difficult decision to leave his family and friends behind and to forge a new destiny by traveling to the United States. Like many of our immigrant brothers and sisters, Piolín worked very hard once he got to this country, while at the same time continuing his studies and completing his high school education. With such a desire to succeed, it's no wonder that he has held so many jobs. Among them, one of his favorites was being an emcee at quinceañera parties. That's where he discovered his passion for expressing himself, and he decided to pursue his calling. Cultivating his talents, he started from the bottom of the ladder, reading the news on an AM radio station. But gradually he began to climb the ladder and move on to bigger and better opportunities. His great talent and dedication led to him attaining the most coveted position for a radio host: having your own morning talk show in one of the most competitive markets in all of Spanish language broadcasting, the West Coast of the United States. Thanks to his popularity and the large audience he drew, he managed to have it broadcasted on more than sixty stations coast to coast. This is a great moment in his career. But beyond his success, what impresses me about Piolín is that he decided to use his voice on the radio and his convening power to support immigrants. He became the champion of all Latinos, he fights daily to expose the injustices suffered by immigrants, and he advocates with personalities and politicians to raise awareness and bring about meaningful change. Thus, he has become not only a citizen of Mexican origin, but a true representative of the entire Latino community, and an example to all immigrants who come here to make positive contributions to this country. During his career, it is worth mentioning that—in addition to interviewing important artists and celebrities—he has also hosted President Barack Obama and the First Lady Michelle Obama on his program. Visits like these establish the level of importance that Piolín has as a leader of our community. Comprehensive immigration reform may still be far away, but it still has supporters behind it: people like Piolín, who know how to reach the heart of the people not only through political messages, but also with a good sense of humor that alleviates the harsh realities of life led by immigrants who struggle daily to get by in this country.

I, who have had the opportunity to get to know Eddie "Piolín" Sotelo, can attest to the fact that he is a man with faith in his heart. That inner peace is what helps keep him going despite the many changes that life throws his way. He, with his great sense of humor, knows how to find the silver lining in any situation. I wish my friend all the best as he embarks on this new stage of becoming an author, and hope that through this book, you—his audience—can learn more about his life and career. Stories of surmounting all odds, like the ones Piolín tells here, are how you win the battle for immigration reform, while at the same time setting a positive example for a new generation of immigrants all around the world.

With much respect,
EMILIO ESTEFAN

INTRODUCTION

When I look back on the path I've traveled, I am amazed by the places I've been, the obstacles I've had to overcome, and the many joys that God has given me. But most important, I have learned from the experiences I have lived through. That is what I want to share with you in this book, and that is what made me decide to write it.

The lessons I have learned in life have helped me to be clear about the values that guide me: my faith in God, the solidarity I feel toward others, the value of an education, and the relentless pursuit of my dreams. I always consider these priorities when I have a decision to make.

From my family, I learned the value of togetherness. Through our daily lives and from knowing the sadness of being separated for long periods of time—first, when my dad and older brother decided to come to the United States, and then later, when I followed in their footsteps, leaving my mom and little brother behind—I learned just how important the concept of family is in each of our lives.

My faith has always been present in me. But it was only through the truly tough experiences, the ones I endured here in this country, that I finally understood the immense love God has for me and I could feel His constant presence. So, little by little, I grew closer and closer to Him, until I finally accepted Him into the depths of my heart. And it is thanks to God, the values that I learned from my family, and the sincere, unconditional love I have for my wife, María, that I now have a family of my own who makes each day fulfilling and makes me want to get better each and every day.

The challenges I experienced when I first arrived in the United States only made me stronger and drove me to pursue my dreams with an even greater intensity. But they also taught me how important it is to be informed so that you're not easily deceived, and about the enormous challenge the majority of the immigrants in this country are facing, and how important it is that we stand firm to improve our situation. Immigrants are people with a powerful desire to succeed and to contribute each and every day to the greatness of America through their hard work.

The time I spent filled with anxiety and stress, when I was very nearly deported for having used false documents, made me realize just how important it was to share my experience with others. I wanted people to learn from what I'd gone through, so they might avoid the same problems that I had. And that is why, once my immigration status was resolved, I began using my radio show as a means for sharing what I'd learned and seeking experts to help others with immigration issues.

That same desire to share my experiences is what made me want to write a book. I'd been thinking about it for several years, driven by listeners and even some friends and relatives, but I didn't have the time or even an idea of where to begin. But in 2013, I finally decided to do it: to face this new challenge, to remember my past, to write it down, and to share it.

The result of all my experiences is in this book, which you have in your hands. I hope that what you read in these pages inspires you to keep moving forward, to find the answers that you need, and to never, ever give up.

CHAPTER 1

"YOU WILL BE A NOBODY IN LIFE!"

No matter how hard I ran, I still missed the bus. It had been a rough day, like almost every day since I started, but I didn't normally miss the bus to work at the photography studio, one of the several jobs I had. Maybe, if I hadn't spent those extra minutes talking to my friends, telling them that I really had to go, that I couldn't stick around talking about soccer practice, I would have made it.

Oh, man, I missed it, was the first thing I thought when I saw the bus pulling away. I had a long wait before the next one arrived, so I decided that the best thing for me was just run to the photo lab, which was located on Main Street in Santa Ana, not too far from where I was. That way, I'd get there faster than if I just waited. It was raining, but I didn't care; it was better to get there as fast as possible. But as hard as I ran, I still showed up a half hour late to work. I misjudged the distance, and to make matters worse, I was soaked.

My dad was going to be furious! He worked with me there at the lab, and so I decided to sneak in through the back door into the darkroom so nobody would see me showing up late. Or that's what I thought. As soon as I closed the darkroom door, there was a hard knock on the other side. It could only have been my dad. It was all but impossible to open the door to the darkroom without making noise, because blinds were hanging on the back side of it. I did everything I could to make sure it swung as quietly as possible, but I wasn't successful.

"What's up, Dad?" I asked.

"Come out," he immediately replied. He sounded really upset.

Unwillingly, I stepped outside.

"What time did you get here?"

"Well, I've been here awhile."

"No. No, you haven't," he replied, very firmly, and then he began to shout: "You know what? With all the things you are doing, you will be a nobody!"

"What are you saying?" I asked, confused.

"I'm saying you will be a nobody!"

He was so angry that he looked as if he was about to hit me. He didn't, but his words hurt so much that I would have preferred that he did.

It's true, at that time in my life, I was juggling many things at once, a bunch of different odd jobs that seemed to have taken all the hours in the day. But what my dad didn't realize—or didn't want to realize at the time—was that I was trying to find something, a direction, the best way to help my family. I even worked through the weekends, and my only distraction was going to the Laundromat on Saturdays. There, I'd also check out the bulletin board to see if any job opportunities had been posted, and make friends with anyone who could offer me work. I was seventeen at the time, and all I wanted was a way to make ends meet. My dad was fully aware of that, and I just couldn't believe what I was hearing from him.

"You know what?" I shouted, though I really wanted to shove him, hit him because of the pain he was causing me. "I'm gonna make you eat those words! I'm gonna be somebody!"

As I said that, the tears started to flow, and since I didn't want him to see me cry, I turned around and went back into the darkroom. I slammed the door behind me and bawled my eyes out. I lay down on the floor and turned off the light. *What a nasty thing to say to me,* I thought, over and over again. *Maybe it's true, maybe I never will make something out of my life,* I said to myself, once I had calmed down. But then I realized that wasn't true. Even though I was doing a thousand things at once that didn't seem to be going anywhere, deep down in my heart, I believed that I could achieve many things in life, even more than my father—or I—could imagine. I can't explain it, but at that moment I felt that clarity and that conviction. So I dried my eyes, opened the door, and went to see my dad.

"I'm sorry I yelled at you," I said. "I think we need to talk." But I couldn't even begin to speak before I hugged him and we both started to cry.

"I'm sorry I missed the bus," I explained.

"I'm sorry too, *m'ijo*," he replied, "but we have so much work to do. The owner is always complaining because I can't get it all done myself."

And with that, we began working immediately. There were photos that needed to be enlarged, and there was no time to lose.

My father had been upset because of the pressure he had on him. He needed to do things right at work and provide for his family. And while his words were hurtful at the time, I will always be grateful for what he said to me that day in the darkroom, because ever since that moment, I knew I'd be putting all my efforts in what I was doing to become someone in life. *I'll always remember what he said, for the rest of my life,* I said to myself. I was convinced. What my dad told me then was no longer something negative, but had become something eternally positive. It pushed me to get better each and every day. I still remember it, and it continues to be a source of strength.

Every time I'm faced with a difficult situation, every time I feel afraid or uncertain when dealing with a new or unfamiliar challenge, I remind myself of what my dad said to me that day, and that helps me find the self-confidence and desire that has allowed me to get to where I am today.

Despite all the challenges and obstacles I've encountered in my life—and there've been more than a few—this belief that I'll be able to succeed helped me find the wisdom to overcome them. At the end of the day, that's what life is: a series of challenges that we need to overcome, that we can learn from, and that give us an opportunity to better ourselves each and every day.

That's why I came to this country, to this world. Better yet, that's why we all came to this world: to succeed!

PART ONE

MEXICO

CHAPTER 2

KNOWING IT'S RAINING WITHOUT LEAVING THE HOUSE

When we were little, my older brother, Jorge, and I spent a lot of time playing together. We were good friends with big imaginations. Sometimes we'd take Popsicle sticks and pretend they were airplanes.

"Ay, let's go to the United States!" we'd say.

To us, the United States was the place from where people came back with new sneakers we'd never seen before. Everything was there and everyone who lived there had the money to buy whatever they wanted.

From the patio, we'd watch planes flying in the sky, and asked ourselves, *When will we be able to go to the United States?*

The house where I was born was a rental. My parents, my brother, and I all lived under that roof. It was a simple brick structure located in Riveras de Sula, a humble neighborhood near Ocotlán in the state of Jalisco, Mexico. To get to school, we had to walk along the side of the road, where there were normally more people than cars, but the few that did come flying by kicked up so much dust that I thought, *Why bother taking a bath if I'm gonna end up this dirty?*

Our house was an adobe structure with a tile roof, like most others in the neighborhood. Not far away was a eucalyptus forest, a nursing home, and a brickwork yard, and the passersby had to contend with stray dogs and horse-drawn carts delivering milk in enormous metal containers. The street right in front of our house was on a public bus route, and every time one drove by it spit out a cloud of smoke that engulfed everything and kicked up so much dust that it was impossible to keep it from getting everywhere. However, my mom went about cleaning everything just the same, and I remember saying to her once, "Why do you spend so much time cleaning if more dust is just gonna come in? It doesn't even matter if we close the door, because it's gonna find its way in somehow."

Not far from the house were a few dirt soccer fields where I'd play with my friends, and just beyond them—near Lake Chapala—was a neighborhood that was home to many fishermen and known as *Cantarranas* because it lay along a river from which frogs would emerge every night and start to sing. This same river passed behind my house, and since the neighborhood streets weren't paved, every time it rained, the house would flood. Many of the storms came during the night, and I don't know if it's because I got used to them or if I'm just a heavy sleeper, but I remember from time to time that I wouldn't know that it had rained until after I'd woken up. I didn't need to look out the window or leave the house to confirm it because the water was almost level with the bed.

Now that I think about it, I have no idea how we didn't all drown in our sleep! But back then, it never seemed to be a concern. On the contrary, that much rain was a fun thing, because every time the neighborhood flooded, Jorge and I would go out to splash around with the other kids on the block. We spent the day splashing in the water, jumping and swimming and covering ourselves in mud. The fact that the street wasn't paved didn't matter much to us because we knew how to take advantage of such a benefit. Plus, we were children. And we were happy.

Sometimes, when my dad saw us splashing around in the puddles, he'd say, "When we have the money, I'll take you to an awesome pool."

If at the time, someone would have told me about everything I would later go on to do, I would have laughed. Me, a poor kid from Ocotlán, hosting a talk radio show with people listening in from all over the world? Impossible!

But nothing is.

As is the case with the vast majority of the immigrants in this country, I grew up in a rather poor family that didn't have much in the way of resources, but what we did have was a strong work ethic and a great family spirit. My dad worked for Celanese Mexicana, a textile factory that had a plant in the city at the time, while my mom was in charge of taking care of the house and of us. Their attitude and outlook on life taught me that you have to really make an effort if you want to progress, and that you can't be afraid of challenges and problems.

The house we grew up in had a back patio, where my parents liked to keep plants and trees. I still have a picture of me with one of my cousins sitting out there.

When I show this photo to my children, they ask me: "Papá, why are your shoes all worn-out and with holes?"

"Because that's all we had," I reply. This always brings out a bit of a laugh, because despite my worn-out shoes, I look quite happy in the picture.

Of course, because to be happy you don't need new shoes or lots of money.

I guess another reason why my shoes looked like that was because I was the second child to be born, which isn't always a good thing since you tend to get hand-me-downs. The shoes had obviously once belonged to my brother.

I distinctly remember that as soon as my mom saw a hole in my brother's pants, she automatically gave them to me, after fixing up the hole with one of those iron-on patches.

"But I don't want these old pants, Mamá. Why are you giving them to me?" I would ask, a bit disappointed.

"It's okay. Just put them on," was her only answer.

So I had no choice but to walk around with more patches than an old tire, because that's how it was: I got shirts, shoes, and everything that came along with them . . . even the bangs my brother had to endure years before. Thanks to the practice my father had gotten with my brother, the smacks I got were even more severe, and maybe that's why I'm more resistant to such things today. At least, that's my theory!

I always thought that when I had my own children, I wouldn't do to them what was done to me: be forced to wear my older sibling's clothes. Fortunately, I was able to fulfill my promise, though it might have something to do with the fact that they're so far apart in age that handing down clothes wouldn't make any sense.

When we were in elementary school, my brother, Jorge, was very studious. He always got good grades, and my parents rewarded him for it. And as if that weren't enough, he was a great soccer player as well, and everyone at school respected him. I also looked up to my older brother back in those days; I wanted to do everything that he did, and I always tried to do things that would make him proud of me.

But all that changed when he started high school. He began hanging out with the wrong crowd and started drinking. Little by little, he forgot about his schoolwork and even soccer, to the extent that for his entire senior year, he was skipping classes to go drinking with friends, either at a liquor store near the school or at a pool hall. One day, our dad saw him staggering down the road, completely drunk, when he was supposed to have been in class. And that was it, because our dad gave him a lashing on his back to teach him how to behave himself. But it didn't work, because my brother didn't change his ways, and his grades started to drop. To try to hide this, he got together with some of his friends with the idea of bribing their teachers. There was one who liked to drink tequila, and together—between the money they had from working plus whatever they were able to gather—they were able to buy a couple of bottles. But the plan quickly fell apart when our dad found out what my brother was planning to do, and although he disciplined him again, by then it was too late: He barely finished high school after passing a set of special exams that took place during the holidays. It was a true shame, because despite his great athletic talent, my brother lost his chance at pursuing a career as a professional soccer player that might have carried him as far as Guadalajara and to one of the club teams there, Atlas. It was truly sad to see how alcohol wore down his strengths and abilities drink by drink.

Despite being so young, I was well aware of everything that was going on with my brother. I could see how my parents were suffering. And also, during that same time, I watched how alcohol damaged my dad, who drank excessively throughout my childhood. Oftentimes he wouldn't come home at night, choosing instead to go drinking with my maternal grandfather. Despite his drinking too much and losing his composure, I know that he was always true to his principles, because on some of these drunken occasions, my grandfather would bring women over to see if he would succumb, but my dad always remained faithful.

All I can say about my dad's drinking is that it truly hurt me to see him like that. Especially when our mom wouldn't let him in the house and he had to spend the night outside. And when he would show up drunk, he would often become aggressive and physically attack us, something which hurt less in the body than it did in the heart. But he was my dad, and I loved him a lot.

When I finally confronted him, he promised me that he would stop drinking. He used to swear to it, especially during Holy Week. Sometimes he succeeded in keeping his word, but other times he didn't, and that made me feel betrayed. I think that was the moment when I learned how important it is to fulfill the promises you make, because every time he promised me something, I would feel a sense of peace and serenity in my heart that let me know that everything was going to be all right. But then, when he broke his promises, I'd feel a deep sense of pain, and my whole world would start to crumble.

Alcohol can take control over you, and sometimes my dad would try to conceal it so he could continue to drink. Sometimes I'd go up to him, take the glass of whatever from his hand, and smell it.

"Is there alcohol in this, Dad? Are you lying to me?"

"No, look, I have the soda can right here."

"No, Dad, this smells like alcohol."

My dad would feel embarrassed, but sometimes he would get angry enough to hit me. "Mind your own business!" he'd say.

This isn't life, I thought. It doesn't make sense to work so hard just to end up wasting the money you earn on getting drunk. During times like these, I'd usually hole up in my room and pull my hair out in frustration at feeling so helpless.

In time, my dad's taste for alcohol began to decrease. Drinking gave him horrible headaches, and one day he said, *God, my family and I can't continue to suffer because of my habit.* And with conviction and discipline, he was able to cut down on his drinking.

Even though I was only seven, I had learned a valuable lesson: There's no logic in wasting your life on alcohol. Or any vice, for that matter. The pain and disappointment I suffered as a result of my dad's and brother's alcoholism was so powerful that I knew, even at that age, that such a life was not for me. I saw no benefit in it. I just couldn't understand why they liked to drink so much if all it did was make them angry and short-tempered, as if they were always having a tough time about something. For that reason, to this day, I neither drink nor smoke. So far, thanks to God and to exercise, I've been able to keep that promise to myself and my family.

I remember, back behind the house I grew up in, there was a lime tree that had a special significance for me: the possibility of helping the family. When I was old enough to understand the economic needs we had, I decided to pick the limes and bag them up, five at a time, and set them out on a little table that I'd set up in front of the house. There, I'd set up shop, and sell the limes to people passing by.

Sales weren't great, but they came. As time went on, I started to think about ways to make my little business grow, until one day I thought, *Why don't I also sell bags of ice?* So that's what I did: I put bags of water in the freezer—one of the few luxuries we could afford—and when they froze, I'd set them out on the table with the limes. Now that I had more to offer, I could attract more clients. Finally, my mom suggested, "Put the lime and the ice together."

And so I started selling bags of lime-flavored ice. While it didn't make me a millionaire, the sales did increase a bit. That was my first experience as a businessperson, as well as my first opportunity to help my parents out economically.

Getting interested in helping the family was something I learned from my parents, aunts and uncles, and grandparents. Both sides of my family are hardworking and enterprising people, besides being generous. It didn't matter that they came from an economically disadvantaged situation; they all worked hard and never hesitated to help one another when needed, especially when it came to other family members.

In school, I had a few friends whose parents had lost their jobs, and they dealt with it by sitting around the house, wasting time. That really bothered me, because I couldn't understand how someone could lose their job and just sit around idly, playing with their thumbs. Why not go out each and every morning and look for a new job? Or why not just invent one?

I was used to seeing the opposite in my own family. Each day, I'd see my parents get up early, ready to start the day. My mom got us ready for school and my dad went off to work, regardless of whether it was raining or whether he was tired or things weren't going well at his job. That's how it had always been, and so every morning he'd head out the door with the belief that one way or another, his efforts would yield results.

He got his first job at the age of nine. Every morning before school, he'd go out into the street to sell Jell-O squares. He'd walk up and down the street yelling, *Jell-O! Jell-O!* and the people who wanted some would come up and buy it. He was very young, but that didn't stop him from looking for ways to make a living. Later, he found work at a photography studio in Ocotlán, and when that job didn't work out in the end, he moved to other places throughout Mexico where there were photography studios willing to hire him. That's how he ended up spending time in places like Tepatitlán, Mexico City, and Tijuana. After that, still fairly young, he crossed the border in search of new opportunities, which is how he found himself in Cupertino, California, hard at work in the fields picking—or as we say in other parts of Mexico—harvesting apricots and, later, vegetables.

His initial plan was to stay there for about three years to earn enough money so he could get married, because he'd realized that he could make more money working in the fields in the United States than he could as a photographer in Mexico. Besides, by that time, he had already met the woman who would later become my mom. He'd fallen in love with her, and they were a couple. She was still living back in Ocotlán, and they kept in touch by sending each other letters, which was more common back then. E-mail obviously hadn't been invented yet, and phone calls were all but impossible. It cost a fortune, and you had to have a phone in your home, or use your friend's.

For my parents, distance and slow correspondence proved to be no barrier to maintaining a loving long-distance relationship. But of course, my mom would have liked to have him closer. She didn't like the fact he'd planned on staying in the United States for so long, and didn't care about the money he wanted to earn before returning to Mexico. All she wanted was for him not to be so far away, and so one day she decided to stop writing letters to my dad. That made him nervous. He kept on writing to her for some time, but as the weeks and months passed without a response, he knew that something was wrong and didn't have to think long before making a decision. He clearly knew what his priorities were and went back to Ocotlán earlier than he'd planned: He didn't want someone else to win over my mother's heart, or for her to simply lose interest.

I don't know what the reunion was like or what was said when they finally saw each other again, but I imagine it was full of emotion and affection. There's a reason they're still together, and have built a family together that has survived a number of ordeals throughout the years, and that inspires me to keep on going whenever problems come up in my own life.

After my father asked his future father-in-law (and my grandfather Don Bartolo) for his daughter's hand in marriage, Don Bartolo asked my dad what his plans were going forward. My dad replied, "Well, Don Bartolo, if I can't find a job here in Ocotlán, I'm going to have to go to Tijuana or even try to find a job in the United States."

Apparently my grandfather didn't like my dad's answer at all, because the very next day he handed him a letter requesting my dad's presence at the offices of Celanese Mexicana, a factory with a longstanding presence in Ocotlán that produced linen for making clothing. My grandfather Bartolo had worked as an electrician at the factory for many years, and used his connections there to get my dad a job interview. When he showed up at the offices, they gave him an aptitude test, and hired him shortly thereafter. And that's the story of how Papa Tolo (which is how we lovingly referred to our grandfather Bartolo) gave him his daughter's hand, along with a job, so they could move forward together.

My grandfather loved his daughter very much, and he wasn't

happy about the thought of having her move far away from him. My mom was his favorite daughter, because she was the one who was the most attentive to him and my grandmother. I remember, on more than one occasion, having to spend hours and hours in the hospital with my mom because no matter what else was going on, if her parents needed her, she wanted to be there for them.

As a worker for Celanese, my dad was able to join a labor union that helped people with limited resources get a home through Infonavit, the Mexican federal institute for workers' housing. I was always struck by this, because I couldn't understand how my dad could be spending so much time helping other people when, to me, it looked like we needed help ourselves.

"Hey, Dad, how come we don't have a house and yet you're helping other people get theirs?" I asked him once. I really didn't understand it at the time, especially when I thought about our family's economic difficulties, and the torrential rains that flooded our home every winter. The houses built by Infonavit certainly weren't big, but I remember they did have a few amenities, like a finished bathroom, a kitchenette, a living room, paved streets. . . .

"Yes, son," my dad replied, "but there are people who have greater needs than we do. At least we have a place to live, even if we have to pay rent. These other workers have no place at all."

His explanation helped me understand an important truth, one that guides me to this day, and which I would practice years later, when I started working in the radio business: You have to help those who need it the most. No matter what you might be lacking in your own life, there's always someone who could use your help. Always.

This outlook on life was something I learned not only from my dad, but also from my grandparents.

Whenever a neighbor was sick, my dad and grandparents would tell me, "Son, we made chilaquiles. Take them over to the neighbor who's sick."

My first reaction was, *Great, that's less for me,* but I never refused and I did as I was told. I was too young at the time to fully understand what they were doing, but bit by bit I began to realize what it was they were teaching me: Always share my blessings with others. That lesson would echo throughout my entire life, and to this day it's one of the guiding principles by which I live.

Whenever we'd go to the market, Papa Tolo would buy two or three extra tomatoes, and when it was time to head home, he'd say to me, "Okay, son, go knock on the neighbor's door."

It could have been any neighbor. I didn't understand at the time, but I now know that it was someone who was sick or out of work.

"My grandpa sent me over with this," I'd say when the neighbor would open the door. They were always quite surprised and very grateful.

But my grandpa's generosity wasn't limited to just friends and neighbors. I remember one Christmas in particular very well: I was around eleven at the time, and for months had been wanting a goalkeeper's jersey, but when Christmas Day came, the jersey never arrived. Maybe Santa forgot, or had problems with his budget, but whatever the reason, I was crushed. The next day, I told my grandfather, who listened attentively.

"Come on," he said. "Let's go get some juice together."

Normally he'd invite me to sit down for some juice after exercising, but this time was different. In any case, I accepted the invitation, figuring we'd have some juice and continue talking.

The juice stand we liked to visit was located in an outdoor market that was open every Saturday and Sunday. On our way, we passed a stand selling clothes, and among them was an amazing jersey. It was blue with orange sleeves, much like the one worn by Jorge Campos when he was the goalkeeper for the Mexican national soccer team.

"I wanted one just like that," I said. My grandfather stopped.

"Hey, can you take that one down for us, please?" he asked the guy running the stand.

"Whoa, yeah, just like this one," I repeated, my eyes wide with excitement.

My grandfather asked me to try it on. In all honesty, I wasn't looking for him to buy it for me. That wasn't my intent. I just wanted to know what it felt like to wear it. I can't lie. It felt good, though it was a little tight, and when I went to take it off, he said: "No, leave it on. It's yours."

Not only did I leave it on. I never wanted to take it off ever again! If a food stain got on the sleeve, I'd turn it inside out so nobody would notice. I even slept in it.

I don't know if he'd intended to buy me the jersey when he invited me out for juice, or if it all just happened spontaneously. What I do know is that he made me very happy, and I'll always be grateful for that unexpected gift.

But on my father's side of the family, my grandparents were much poorer. I remember that at their house, there was no bathroom; instead, there was a latrine in the back. It was an adobe brick house with a *tejabán*—a tile-covered roof. The key to the front door was a massive antique key, and they hid it up under the edge of the roof. When we left school and went to visit them, we had to jump to reach the key. When you opened the door, you realized that it was just a one-room home with a dirt floor. I remember my grandmother Cuca would sweep and wet the floor to keep the dust down. The kitchen was separate from the house, and instead of a gas oven, it had a kerosene one. The light in the house also came from oil—in the form of lamps—because there was no electricity. It wasn't until my dad eventually bought them one that my grandparents had a gas stove to cook with.

Behind the house, my grandmother had a small cornfield, and from time to time, we'd help her water it. And the latrine was right there in the middle of it. That's how you go to the bathroom in the country: with chickens clucking all around you, giving you a bit of cover while you're doing your business.

When I think back about the way my grandparents lived, and how hard they worked to make a better life for themselves, I better understand the great sense of dignity born from such a lifestyle. They've always been an inspiration to me, as are all people who get up every morning and—however difficult their situation may be—make an effort to better themselves and achieve their dreams.

My grandmother Cuca was fond of needlework, and would knit us sweaters and scarves. Sometimes, with spare fabric from Ocotlán Industries, she'd weave and sell floor mats. She never studied dressmaking; she just taught herself to sew by doing it. I remember, since her eyesight wasn't so good, she'd ask us to help her by threading the needle. And there we sat, trying to stick that piece of thread through the tiny eye of that needle, until we managed to succeed.

My grandfather Chuy rented a plot of land to cultivate. Despite their poverty and the harsh difficulty of working in the field, he always had a snack for me when he saw that I was hungry. He was just as generous as my other grandfather, Bartolo.

Going to my dad's parents' house always made me happy because they were always so kind to me, and taught me the value of hard work.

Education is vital. It's the key to making us better people. But when I was a kid, I wasn't really into studying. I just wasn't a good student. As I mentioned, I was always ready to work, but I was far from the hardest-working student in the classroom. I talked too much during class, and I was punished and the school would call my parents all the time. I guess I must have had my teachers at the point of desperation, because one day one of them hit me on the arm—right on the *conejo* (a slang word for biceps)—with a switch from a tree. It hurt like crazy, and ended up leaving a scar that I still have today. On that occasion, my mom went in to talk with the teacher because, while she supported the school's mission and agreed that I needed to be reprimanded if I did something wrong, she was shocked by this and thought the teacher had gone too far. When she asked for an explanation for what had happened, the teacher replied: "It's because he won't shut up."

But I couldn't help it. I liked seeing the other kids laughing loudly at the things I said. I still like it, and that's why I spend a good part of my radio programs telling jokes. I love to hear people laughing.

Some time after that, the same teacher, exasperated again, hit me with another switch, right dead center in the middle of my back. I had trouble walking for several days. Today, it seems a brutal form of punishment, but that's how it was at the time. And in the end, their strategy of spare the rod and spoil the child didn't work, because I still love to talk to this day. And I think to myself, *Whew!*

I guess this facility for chatting with people is another thing I learned from my dad, who was also quite talkative and could make friends with anyone. And while I was just like him in that regard, I found it annoying when my dad did it, so much so that I didn't even like going to places with him.

"No, I don't want to go to the market with Dad! He'll stop and talk with anyone!" I complained to my mom whenever she asked me to accompany him. Sometimes, he'd even change his entire schedule around so he could go and help someone, taking me with him.

I think the same thing is going on with my own children now, because they'll also say they don't want to go to places with me because I'll stop and talk to just about anybody. And ironically, it even happened with my dad and me. Not long ago, when I went back to Ocotlán for a visit, we were driving back to the house in my uncle's car, and I'd stop time and again to greet people I knew, including an old friend of mine from Valentín Gómez Farías Elementary School, which I attended when I was younger.

"You know what?" he said. "I'm stopping the car. You can bring your uncle's car later." And he got out and started walking away.

"Dang!" I thought. "If my dad got tired of so much socializing, and he used to tire me out when I was a kid, I guess I'm over it now!"

In the end, when it came to school, the only A's I got were when my mom made alphabet soup. And I really did look for ways to be a better student, but I never found one that suited me. In the evening, when it came time to do my homework, I focused on the task at hand, on understanding what I was doing and doing it well. I sat there with my notebook and tried to work on the exercises that the teachers had asked us to complete, but something in my head prevented them from turning out correctly. It was as if the two of them—my brain and my homework—had gotten into an argument and were no longer speaking with one another. But I tried hard . . . that much I know for a fact.

And I have to say that not all of my teachers scolded me or beat me. One of them in particular, Ms. Blanca, whom I remember fondly, was always there to help me; she was very patient, and explained things to me slowly and calmly. To teachers like her and the others who were willing to spend hours after school working with me, I'll be forever grateful, because thanks to them, I was able to pass the subjects that I struggled the most with, especially math. Actually, I have to admit, most subjects were difficult for me, and probably the only one that I really enjoyed was phys ed . . . and recess. When it came to those two, I could run around, exercise, and just have fun playing around with my friends.

And yes, I loved getting involved with every extracurricular activity that Valentín Gómez Farías Elementary School had to offer. I participated in folk dancing, choir, miming, school plays, and whatever other offering they had. It might have been something I got from my dad, because he loved the theater and always participated in church performances during Easter or Christmas. Now, whenever I'm standing in front of a microphone, a group of people, or one of the events that we've organized, I realize how useful it was to have participated in all those festivities: It took the edge off the stage fright that often affects people in those sorts of situations. And most people don't know this, but I'm actually a really shy person. Nonetheless, it's something I enjoy very much.

I remember quite well how, every day at lunchtime, I would buy a tostada—a fried tortilla—covered in red hot sauce from a bottle. And during recess, not having much money, the best I could hope for were some saltines with slices of tomato and onion. The other kids, especially those who were better off, ate their saltines with tuna. Their snacks looked tastier than mine, but deep down it didn't matter much. And since we didn't have much in the way of resources, the school gave us a free bottle of milk to drink during breakfast. Now, when I see the lunches available to my kids at school, I think about how different things are from what I used to eat when I was their age. We've come a very long way since then. I know that many other first-generation immigrants experience something similar when they think back to the way things were in our countries of origin. Oftentimes, the games we played were different, the schools are bigger and more advanced, and the food has a new, distinct flavor.

When it came to recess, like all children, I was ready to play. Especially soccer and *capirucho,* a game in which you dig a hole in the ground and place a small stick on top of it, which you then have to lift up with a larger stick. We also like to play a game called *los quemados*, where you'd make five little holes against the wall and throw a bean-bag to see which one you could get it to land in. If the ball landed in a hole that corresponded to one of your friends, he had to go grab it and throw it back at us.

Soccer wasn't just something we played during recess. We'd organize games among our friends and family members and play after school, or on the weekends. Nowadays, it's a bit more complicated for the kids, because the streets are becoming busier with cars. But back then, in Ocotlán, playing in the streets was normal, and my friends and I would meet up in an empty lot near home or the school and clear away the weeds and trash. We'd use tree branches to mark the goals, and if a neighbor happened to be doing some sort of construction, we'd offer to help unload supplies from the trucks in exchange for a little lime with which we could paint white lines on the field. It took a lot of time and effort to do all of this, but in the end we weren't even tired; instead, we were excited and proud of what we'd accomplished. But most important, we immediately got down to playing soccer, and boy, did we enjoy it! We'd spend hours there in that lot, scoring goals and trying to outdo the other team.

I started out playing goalkeeper, but since even the neighborhood dogs were taller than me, I switched to midfield, because I liked to run and go after the ball. Today, when my kids are playing soccer, I always tell them, *Don't just stand there; get moving and go after the ball!*

Although playing in the streets was fairly common among the kids in Ocotlán, my mom didn't like the idea, because—like any good mother—she was worried about us and didn't want anything bad to happen. We always had to bundle up even when it was hot. Not once did I go out to play without hearing her calling after me, *You're going to get sick! Put on a sweater!*

Similarly, whenever we'd walk to the creek, she'd supply us with at least three sandwiches in case we got hungry. We always grumbled and complained, because that seemed like too much, but there was no debating it with her. But of course, in the end, she always turned out to be right, because we ended up devouring everything she'd fixed for us, and now that I have children of my own and have to look after them to make sure they're safe and sound, I understand her even more. In fact, I occasionally find myself doing the same things that she did, like when I tell them to put on a sweatshirt when it's not even cold outside. And María, my wife, does the same whenever we go on a trip or some other excursion: She packs nuts, oranges, and granola in case someone gets hungry on the road.

At the time, I had no idea how much I would miss my mom a few years later, when I had to say good-bye to her.

As I write this book and look back over my childhood, playing with my friends, what I saw going on at home and the good and bad examples set by my family, I realize just how much it all meant to me and how much it contributed to the person I am today. My family taught me to be generous to others and to work hard. I also saw what alcohol can do to a person, which is why I've always tried to avoid it in my own life. The soccer games with friends and the way we "constructed" our fields helped me learn to be resourceful. And in school I learned not only basic skills, but also how to channel my inner strength and be at ease in public, giving me the first opportunity to realize how much I enjoyed talking with people and making them laugh.

CHAPTER 3

"IT MUST BE WHERE YOU LEFT IT"

One of the hardest lessons I've had to learn came from a bicycle.

You always imagine that achieving your dreams will be a wonderful moment of satisfaction and peace. That's normally the case, at least until you start imagining new dreams and setting new goals.

But on this particular occasion, I learned that's not always the case. And everything doesn't always come out like peaches and cream.

I really wanted a bike, because it was so cool to watch other kids riding all over the place. Whenever we finished up a soccer game, some of my friends would hop on their bikes and leave. I remember thinking that a bike was something of a luxury for a kid, whereas for an adult, it was more normal: it was a means of getting to work, or transporting his family from place to place. The point is, I became obsessed with the idea of owning a bike so I could ride all over Ocotlán to play with my friends. But since my parents couldn't buy me one, I had to settle on dreaming about it.

That was around the same time that my dad managed to buy a little plot of land so he could build his own home. It was north of Ocotlán, a little closer to the city. I was about eight years old, and I remember Uncle Toño and Uncle Chuy, who was a master bricklayer, helped us with the construction. It was an all-brick house, with no plaster or paint, and at first, the floor looked the same as it did at my grandparents' house: dirt. Later on, my dad saved up enough money to buy some flooring materials, but it would be some time before that happened.

Around the time the house was built, or perhaps a little before, I was working at a body shop owned by an uncle whom we lovingly called "El Chanclazo," and I'd spend all day there helping him fix cars and doing other repairs. Working as a mechanic means getting your hands filthy with oil and dust, so after spending a full day's work there, I'd come home covered in grease.

"With what your uncle pays you, there's not even enough to buy soap," my mom used to say because of how dirty I would get.

I remember my older brother would also sometimes work at the shop, but my uncle preferred to work with me.

"I'd rather you send Eddie over," my uncle used to tell my dad, "because when Jorge is there, I get sleepy just looking at him."

My brother probably wouldn't have found that funny, but it was the truth. I seemed to have a gift for mechanics, while my brother was just so lazy that it would take him hours to finish whatever they asked him to do. For example, if they asked him to fetch a particular tool, they'd end up waiting forever, and sometimes he wasn't even able to find it. Knowing that my uncle would rather work with me was something I felt proud about. At least there was something I was better at than my older brother.

After working with my uncle for a while, I started working at a bike shop called Martín, which still exists today, though not only in Ocotlán, but in Los Angeles! The owner, my former boss, later immigrated to the United States and reopened the same bike shop that he had owned and operated back in Mexico.

In Ocotlán, the bike shop was just down the street from the house my dad had built, so of course I would pass by it all the time. At first, I'd just see all the bikes there, and keep dreaming of one day having one of my own.

When I was about eleven, I decided to start getting to know Martín. I was still obsessed with owning a bike, and I thought it would be a good idea to become friends with the shop owner. Even though he was a few years older than me, I invited him to play soccer with us, and eventually he joined the group. Sometimes we'd get into fights during the heat of the match, but we always ended on a happy note.

And then one day, I went up to the shop to put my plan into action. Martín was there, fixing a bike, as always.

"Give me a chance to work for you," I sad. "I wanna buy a bike."

"And how am I supposed to pay you?" he replied. The repair shop was a tiny one-room operation. It was so small, in fact, that every morning Martín had to roll out the bikes that needed fixing, because there was only room inside for either the bikes or him, but not both.

"Well, how about you pay me in parts?" I said.

"Okay," he said, after giving it some thought.

I don't know what was going through Martín's head at the time—probably wondering whether or not I could actually be of some help—but I went home happy that day. My dream of owning a bike was still a ways away, but working in the shop was a good place to start.

From then on, every day after school, I went to work with Martín. I was responsible for patching tires, washing the bikes, sanding them so the owners could later repaint them, and whatever else was needed.

Just as we'd agreed, Martín paid me piece by piece: One day I got the pedals, then came the handlebars, the frame, the rims, and the spokes. Bit by bit, just like that. I loved watching my bike coming together, and seven or eight months later, I finally had all the pieces I needed.

Since I couldn't contain my excitement, I decided to put it together right after work. When I finished, I stepped back to admire it: it was red, with gear shifters, chrome rims, and black handlebars. I'd bought some Bimex stickers, which was a very famous bicycle brand in Mexico, and decorated the frame with them. And last but not least, the bike had a rack where I could store the water bottle bearing the shop's name that Martín had given me.

It was dark by then, so I decided not to ride it home to avoid getting it dirty. Instead, I walked it down the street, planning on taking my first ride the next day when it was light out and I could see where I was going. I was super happy. Finally I could get to the soccer field, or anywhere else in Ocotlán, faster than ever.

I remember that in front of our house and all down the street ran a drainage ditch where water flowed when it rained. A tree trunk had been laid across this ditch to serve as a bridge so people could cross from one side to the other and get to Don Toño's grocery store, which was just across the street. That was the ditch we'd go swimming in during the rainy season when the streets flooded. But we didn't swim alone. We were always accompanied by *tepocates*, the little tadpoles that cropped up as the season went on.

Knowing that the ditch was there, that it could be full of *tepocates*, and that I couldn't see very well in the dark, was reason enough for me to decide that it'd be a bad idea to risk falling in with my new bike. So when I finally got home, I parked it in the yard and covered it with one of my mom's towels so it wouldn't get dusty overnight.

The next day, I had to go to school, so my first ride on my beloved bike, which I paid for in hope and excitement, would have to wait until later that afternoon. I spent all day thinking about that moment, and what it would be like. And while I don't remember the details, I'm sure I had it all planned out in my head.

When school let out, I sprinted back home. As usual, a bunch of my friends invited me to play soccer, but I said no, I had a new bike I'd just put together, and I wanted to go for a ride, all by myself. I wanted to check out how it rode, and make sure everything worked just right. Even though I already knew how to ride, sometimes friends would lend me their bikes.

But my hopes were crushed when I got home and saw that my bike was not in the yard. I couldn't believe my eyes. I went to my room, but it wasn't there either. And the living room? Nothing.

With my heart in my hands, I went to my mom and asked her, "Where is my bike?"

"Well, where did you leave it, *niño*? It should be wherever you left it," she replied, without giving it much of a thought.

"But it's not there," I said, my voice barely a whisper. Again, I asked, "Where's my bike?"

I was getting nervous. I couldn't believe it had disappeared just like that, as if the earth had swallowed it up, or someone had just taken it away from were I left it. I went around and around the house, but it wasn't there. I was getting hopeless. Hours went by, and I still couldn't figure out what in the world had happened. Then my older brother, Jorge, came home—he was no saint—and when I asked him if he'd seen my new bicycle, he burst into tears.

"I took your bike," he said.

"So where is it?"

"Someone stole it from me. . . ."

The force of his words was so heavy that I can't remember what I said or even did next. It was such a shock, and it hurt so much to learn that my own brother had taken my bike without asking me, and that I never even had the chance to ride it myself. I felt crushed and betrayed, and it took me a long time before I could erase that pain from my heart.

Especially because later, some of his friends told me that the bike wasn't stolen, but that my brother had sold it. I asked him time and again to tell me the truth, but my brother always insisted that it had been stolen. Years later, when we were living in the United States, something very similar would happen, and again I never knew what really took place. Whether it was stolen or sold, it was a long time before I could forgive my brother for what had happened.

In the end, it's not the truth that matters. It's what I learned: Sometimes, even when you achieve your dreams, they don't always last long. Or they don't last at all. And that makes us wonder why. What's the point of having reached your goal? Why put so much effort into it? So many sacrifices? So many hopes and dreams?

But fulfilling a dream is so much more than just achieving a goal. It is, as I said, about learning from the journey, taking satisfaction in knowing what we did, finding out about ourselves, and of course finding opportunities to set new dreams and new goals. That's why, for me, the most important memory is of the work I put into building that bicycle, setting a goal and achieving it by myself, with my own ingenuity, my own resources, and the help of a boss and friend who could see the enthusiasm and desire to do something meaningful. Looking back, that journey mattered more than the short-lived sadness of having lost it so quickly.

CHAPTER 4

DISCIPLINE WITH TIN CAN WEIGHTS

I never miss an opportunity to go to the gym, and I always encourage my own kids to exercise every day. When I work out, I feel better: My mind clears and I can think more effectively with the blood rushing throughout my entire body. Exercise helps me maintain a sound mind and a sound body, which is why it's one of the fundamental values of my life.

I learned about the value of exercise from my grandfather Bartolo, who not only taught me a lot about generosity and solidarity with those who need it the most, but also about the importance of fitness.

I was born with a heart murmur. The doctor told my mom that I could die at any moment, and that there was little hope that I would live and grow. My parents suffered a lot of grief when they learned this, and devoted themselves to taking care of me and making sure that I had everything I needed to live and survive. And they did it so well that the weeks became months, the months became years, and I grew up sound and strong. Aside from the occasional cold, I had a healthy life with no evidence of heart problems, and I never had trouble exercising. But because of the doctor's warnings, my mom always took great care to see that I didn't get too worked up, and to make sure that I took things easy. Knowing that her child had a heart murmur also had another effect on her: It brought her closer to God, and she started going to church more regularly so she could pray for me.

One day, when I was about six years old, my grandfather Bartolo came home and asked me if I wanted to exercise with him. He wanted us to go walk up and down a nearby hill. My mom didn't want me to go because, as you might expect, she was still worried that I might die—a concern that I don't think ever completely went away—even though I felt perfectly healthy. I couldn't fully understand why she didn't allow me to do fun things.

"Please. Let me go," I begged. I really wanted to go exercise with my grandfather, and I didn't think that anything could happen. But there was no convincing my mom, who was not about to put her son's health or life at risk.

This happened several times, and I would always latch onto my grandfather's leg and wouldn't let go. I begged and pleaded but my mom refused to yield, until one day when my grandpa's arguments finally drowned out my mom's objections. And it wasn't the only time; in fact, it eventually became something of a routine: He'd come home, invite me to go for a walk, my mom refused, I begged her and told her that nothing was going to happen, she continued to refuse, and I would cling to my grandfather's leg until she conceded and I got to go with him.

Of course, Grandpa Bartolo knew the risks involved, and when I started going up the hill faster than he was, he'd get nervous.

"*M'ijo,* settle down! Don't run! Come back here, *m'ijo,*" he would yell.

"It's okay, Grandpa. Nothing's gonna happen to me," I'd call back, and then I kept on running, ignoring him. And honestly, nothing bad ever did happen to me. I didn't even feel tired or have trouble breathing. On the contrary, hiking up that hill with my grandfather made me very happy.

Behind his house was an awning made from corrugated zinc, and when it rained, it seemed like the world was coming to an end! One afternoon, sitting under that awning, Grandpa Bartolo started making weights by taking empty powdered milk cans and filling them with cement and sand, or even gravel, if he wanted them to be heavier. Then he'd weld two cans to the two ends of a long metal rod. By the way, my grandpa was an excellent welder: Not only did he make the bar bells; he also made the workout bench.

I would go over to his house all the time to work out with him and my uncles. Grandpa Bartolo was very disciplined and never missed a weight lifting session, hike, or soccer game. Plus, he'd been a boxer when he was younger, and a few of my uncles wanted to follow in his footsteps and become boxers themselves, but after trying it for some time, they just couldn't devote themselves to the sport.

I really liked working out with Grandpa Bartolo. We had fun talking while doing hill work or lifting weights, and I was also able to see just how healthy he was, and I found that we were always in a better mood after exercising. That was when I began to realize just how important the benefits of fitness can be.

I also learned about the value of exercise from my dad, who played baseball, and often invited us to come to his games. I tried my hand at baseball too, but I would have needed a bat the size of a tennis racket to hit the ball! Well, at least I can say I tried. And I wasn't quite as bad at soccer.

It was my dad and my grandfather—as well as my uncles, who also encouraged me to play—from whom I learned how important it is for parents to instill a sense of fitness in their children at an early age. If children don't see an example being set at home, they may never gain an interest in it. And that's not good, because you can't live a healthy lifestyle without exercise. When the body is neglected, the mind suffers as well. And when your body and mind aren't in top form, you feel depressed and can't perform to the best of your ability in whatever you do. That's why I find it's important to always keep your body in motion, get the blood pumping in your veins, and keep the oxygen flowing to your brain.

So I have always tried to motivate my kids to exercise, to go play basketball with them, go for a run or a bike ride, or whatever other activity may come to mind. Sometimes we even organize competitions between us, and we have a great time.

In fact, I'd say there are three things you should bear in mind in order to have a healthier lifestyle, and which you should teach your children very early on: spiritual wellness, physical exercise, and healthy eating habits. You must not lose sight of these at any point in your life. And in order to maintain that kind of focus, you need discipline: yet another value to learn, especially at home.

• • •

But I didn't just go to my grandparents' house to work out and learn self-discipline. I also went there to get into trouble, like I did with the *pila de agua* sink, a rather large sink where my grandma stored water to be used later for washing dishes or clothes, and which we also used for bathing. My cousins and I liked to pretend that *la pila* was actually a pool, and sometimes I would even jump into it from atop the roof of the house. I knew it was dangerous, but it was just so fun to jump into the water below . . . at least until I landed awkwardly one day and hit my head. I had to quit after that. Well, sometimes that's how you learn!

There were lots of temptations in that house, some of which were dangerous, which I learned one day when I was introduced to the boiler. The water was heated by a wood fire, and you could never be sure of how warm it was at any given moment, so taking a bath or shower was always a surprise.

Once, I visited my grandparents' house the day after a heavy rain. The streets were completely muddy, as were my sneakers. So before I went home, I decided to wash them. But when I was done, I discovered a new problem: They were now cold and soaking wet. I couldn't exactly walk home barefoot, so I thought to myself, *They'll dry out and warm up faster if I just put them on inside of the boiler.*

Remember when I told you that sometimes the boiler got too hot? Well, when I went back to check on my shoes, they were burned! Needless to say, I went home without them. When I got there, I made up a pretty bad story so I wouldn't get scolded: I told my mom I just couldn't remember where I'd left them. And somehow she believed me! In the end, what surprised me the most wasn't the fact that I actually thought it would be a good idea to dry them off on the boiler—I was a kid; kids don't often think about the consequences of what they're doing. It was that my mom believed me that I'd lost them, and I didn't end up getting in trouble.

My surprise was even greater, because my parents were very strict, and wouldn't hesitate to discipline me when necessary, using methods that are no longer acceptable today. When I talk about this with my dad, it makes me laugh, because he used to hit us with everything:

a fist, a belt, a hose. One time, he even threw an apple at me that exploded when it hit me in the head. That was when I realized that my dad was a good baseball player.

Virtually nobody would discipline their child this way today, but back then, in Mexico, that's how many children were disciplined.

For example, my mom always told me not to tell lies, or else she would burn my hands. And she wasn't kidding or exaggerating either, because once she held my hand to a hot griddle because she wanted to get me to tell the truth about a pot that someone had broken while playing soccer indoors. I told her it wasn't me, and that was the honest truth. But she didn't believe me . . . at least, not at first. But when she saw my story didn't change even though she was literally burning my hands on the griddle, and instead maintained that my brother—who was hiding in his room at the time—was the responsible party, she realized she'd made a mistake and went off to punish the real offender.

My dad, as I've said, was never far behind, and once, when I was about six years old, he decided to punish us in an exemplary manner. He didn't like being interrupted when he was watching a game on TV, and only spoke to us when he needed us to change the channel. We were a kind of human remote control, before the actual thing appeared in Ocotlán.

In this case, he was watching a baseball game featuring Fernando Valenzuela, and he started to narrate the game, as if he were impersonating the broadcasters.

"And now the count is two, two, and two. It's the duckling count," he said.

"Why 'ducklings,' Dad?" my brother and I asked.

"Because there are two outs, two balls, and two strikes, and the number two looks like a duckling," he happily replied, something fairly uncommon, considering he was watching a game.

"Two, two, and two . . . the duckling count!" my brother and I said in unison, and then we started cracking up.

My dad must have thought that we were making fun of him, that we thought his joke was bad . . . and yes, in fact, it was. But we had no idea what we had just unleashed. He tricked us into going to the back patio with him, under the excuse that he wanted to show us something, but instead, he tied us to a tree and proceeded to beat us until it was clear that we were never to make fun of him again. Of course, faced with such harsh measures, there was no way we would ever let that happen again.

The teaching methods my parents used were extremely painful, but I'm not judging them. They were good people who only wanted what was best for us. Besides, that's how they were raised and taught to educate and correct their children. And on the other hand, these punishments helped establish a sense of discipline in me. Now I look back on it and understand that my parents were trying to raise us under difficult circumstances because money was tight, we were mischievous and unruly kids, and we had no idea about the challenges they faced every day when it came to paying the bills, putting food on the table, and making a good life for us all.

My parents also taught us to respect our elders. Not only did we have to obey them and listen to them when they were speaking. We couldn't use any bad language in front of our parents, aunts and uncles, or grandparents. Well, actually, we shouldn't have been using bad words at all, or we risked getting an inevitable and unforgettable punishment that would leave a lifelong scar, because my mom and dad tended to use objects that would leave lasting marks: irons, frying pans, and whatever else was at hand.

We learned our lesson well, and to this day, my brother and I still hear an inner voice telling us not to swear in front of our elders, which is a sign of respect and admiration for the people we consider role models.

For example, a few years ago, I went back to Ocotlán and my uncle Raúl said to María, my wife, referring to me: "So this one doesn't talk, but he chatters like a parrot when he's on the radio?"

His comment surprised me, and I had to think for a moment before realizing that yes, I was almost always silent when I was around him.

"You know what, Uncle?" I said, finally daring to speak. "It's a blessing to hear about everything you've accomplished. It's taught me a lot, and you're a great example of hard work paying off."

Even though I meant it, saying that in front of him left me feeling almost paralyzed by the enormous sense of respect and admiration I have for him. Lack of money didn't prevent him from finding a successful career: He worked hard each and every day to pay for his education, and those efforts were well rewarded when he came to occupy a top position at Cemex, one of the largest companies in Mexico. And even with such success, he didn't get his head stuck in the clouds; on the contrary, he's a sweet and noble person, very humble and patient. He doesn't want to lavish his children with faint praise; he always makes sure that they finish what they start and that they work hard to get what they want.

Of course, he's an exception, because, as is often the case, successful parents can either spoil their children by giving them whatever they desire, or simply not care about them at all.

While on the other hand, the ways in which children are educated have changed so much, not only when it comes to discipline and obligations, but also regarding respect for your elders.

For example, just a few years ago, on another trip with María back to Ocotlán, I heard one of my cousins—who also happened to be smoking—say a bad word in front of my aunts and uncles.

"You're gonna get it," I said. But I was wrong; nothing happened at all. Nobody scolded him or told him not to swear. No one said he shouldn't be smoking. I was very surprised.

So I asked him why nobody seemed to care.

"Times have changed," he replied.

And he was right. Today, parents don't seem to teach their children how to behave in front of elders, to not do things that bother or annoy them. And while I think it's a good thing that relationships between young and old are now more direct, at the same time I feel that some level of respect has been lost.

I've also noticed that we don't teach our children as much about taking responsibility as we used to. I remember when the first job a kid had in his or her life was to run errands for the parents. Sometimes it seemed as if parents were just waiting for the children to learn to walk, and immediately they'd send them out on a task. At times, I used to think that the only reason my mom and dad brought me into this world was so they could use me to run errands. Or, to put it another way, I was their gofer: go for some tortillas, go for some beans, go for some chayote.

Yes, buying tortillas was one of the many errands my mom sent me to do. But it wasn't enough for her to have me get tortillas for the family; she also took the opportunity to ask the neighbors if they needed any tortillas as well. Luckily, I'd become friends with the vendor who sold the tortillas, so I didn't have to wait in line, and I could get back home faster.

Picking up the tortillas was not my sole responsibility. We'd usually have to help out with other household chores like sweeping the floor, making repairs, bailing water when the house flooded, and anything else that was needed to ensure things were working right. And of course there was homework and whatever odd jobs were available.

All of these things taught me the importance and value of responsibility. I didn't see it at the time, but I know that it helped me, years later, when I came to the United States with the hope of helping my family live a better life.

It's true that my own children don't run errands for us, but they do have obligations like cleaning their rooms and picking up their things. In fact, we have a sign that lays out what their daily responsibilities are. That they follow the rules is a completely different story. For instance, one day my older brother happened to look in one of my kids' rooms and saw that his clothes hadn't been put away.

"Hey, what a great sign your mom set up for you here," he said. "But apparently it's not doing any good, because you're not following the instructions!"

María overheard him, and gave our son a warning for leaving his clothes all over the place.

"Hey, Uncle Jorge, why are you so nosy?" my son said. And ever since then, every time he sees my brother coming, he'll say, "Ah, here comes my nosy uncle."

When I look back at my childhood, and the things my parents and grandparents taught me, and also how children are raised and educated nowadays, I realize just how much the world has changed, mostly for the better. But I'm very grateful for my own experience, because of the poverty I grew up in, the toughness of my parents and all the good values they taught me. They made me into the person I am today; they gave me the discipline and strength to persevere whenever things get hard. And even though I occasionally have my doubts, in the end, I always find what I need to keep on going and never give up.

CHAPTER 5

YOU HAD TO WIN THE MEDALS

Over the years, I've begun to appreciate more and more the richness of the culture and the country in which I was born, all the many manifestations of its age and complexity. Mexico's culture, like all the cultures of Latin America, is as broad as it is profound, and I celebrate it every chance I get, both through my radio program and with my family and friends.

I've always enjoyed Mexican music, and I almost always have it playing on the radio whether I am working or just relaxing at home. Sometimes I'd hum along with the melodies or sing along with the songs.

One song I really liked was "La mochila azúl" ("The Blue Backpack"), which is the same song that the actor and ranchera-style singer Pedro Fernández used as the theme for his film *The Girl with the Blue Backpack*, a huge hit in Mexico back in the early eighties. The film tells the story of a young girl who loses her parents and is taken under the wing of her alcoholic uncle, who deep down is a good person. Pedro Fernández plays the girl's friend, and is the only person who understands her and defends her from bullies in school.

Many years later, when I interviewed Pedro on my radio show, I told him that when I was little I used to sing along with that tune, and he seemed to really enjoy that. We made quite a connection, and it allowed me to get into other stories, like the one about the day he performed a concert in Ocotlán when I was about thirteen years old.

When I heard that Pedro Fernández was coming to do a show, I got really excited to see him. I loved how he sang, and I remembered the movie, plus I've always admired Pedro for the way he managed to become a success. He was born into a poor family, and his father, realizing that he had a talent for singing, encouraged him to perform at arenas. While singing at an arena, he met Vicente Fernández, who was impressed by both his voice and his presence onstage, and invited him to Mexico City to try recording a few tracks with his record company. The result was his first studio album, and despite his quick rise to fame, he always kept his feet firmly on the ground and always worked hard to earn his success.

But I didn't have enough money to pay for a ticket. So I ended up hopping one of the fences in the Arena Mexico, near Ramón Corona Street, which was where the concert was going to be held. I managed to do that without anyone noticing, and I worked my way as close to the stage as I could.

At the end of the show, before walking offstage, Pedro threw a comb into the audience, and I was the one who caught it. I always kept it with me because I saw it as something of a trophy: a symbol of everything he had managed to accomplish in life. And even though I didn't want to be a singer, I wanted to achieve what Pedro Fernández had achieved: the ability to overcome obstacles and go places in life.

By then, I still wasn't a very good student, but there were some teachers who were willing to help me improve. One of them, Mr. Varela, was known for being very demanding. With his help and persistence, I got into the Adolfo López Mateos School, which was a private school and had one of the best academic curriculums. My older brother, who was still a much better student than me, also attended the school.

I wanted to be at the same school as my brother and play on the same soccer team as him, which also happened to be a subsidiary of the Atlas team, and therefore offered a better chance of one day getting signed by the club.

Mr. Varela, who also coordinated the school's soccer team, could see my desire to play and decided it would be a good idea for all involved to help me out. But he also told me I would have to get better grades, and I promised him that I would.

At first I was able to keep my promise, but eventually my grades started to slip, and to keep my parents from finding out, I'd alter my report card. Any sixes I had turned into eights, and sevens became nines, until one day I got caught. Aside from a good beating, I got grounded and couldn't go out and play with my friends for several days. Ultimately, between my poor grades and the high cost of tuition, which my parents couldn't continue to afford, I only made it through one year at the school before being expelled. With that, my dreams of becoming a professional soccer player and getting a better education vanished into thin air.

I had to go back to public education, and so I enrolled at Escuela Secundaria Técnica 42, where I continued to be a rather poor student. Fortunately, I learned I could do extra credit work to improve my grade point average and keep me from flunking out. Never missing a homework assignment earned you points, so I started doing that regularly. Perfect attendance also earned you points, so I stopped cutting classes. Helping out the teacher was also worth a few points, so I always volunteered to clean the blackboard or pass out materials to my fellow students. So in the end, if I did poorly on a test, it didn't matter quite as much, because it would be balanced out by my extra credit, and maybe even result in a good grade in the end. The important thing was not to fail the class, even though I still wasn't all that interested in the coursework. In the end, it was even worse to retake a test, or repeat an entire school year!

Despite the changes, and the fact that I could no longer play for the Adolfo López Mateos school team, my love for soccer never slackened, and I would often meet up with my friends to play a pickup game in the street. Sometimes, during the heat of the match, the ball would fly out of the street or the vacant lot where we were playing and into a neighbor's yard, and the occasional window got broken. Whenever that happened, we shot out of there like a rocket, forgetting the fact that we lived in a small town where everybody knew one another, and eventually news of what had happened would reach my mom. The scoldings I got were tremendous, but when something really bothered her, all she would say was, "Just wait till your father gets home."

Those, of course, were the most terrifying words of all, because we all knew that as soon as Dad got home, the real punishment would begin.

Other than soccer, we liked to climb on the roofs of houses, and from the edge, we would throw water balloons at buses or shoot orange peels as people walked down the street by putting a rubber band between our thumb and forefinger and using it as a makeshift slingshot. Looking back, I realize how irresponsible we were being, because not only were we putting ourselves at risk by climbing on people's rooftops but also we could have caused an accident and really hurt somebody. Not to mention how annoying it was to pedestrians to be attacked by a bunch of teenagers armed with water balloons and fruit peels. But as kids, we found the whole thing to be very amusing.

That was around the time that I set a new goal for myself: I was thirteen, and I wanted to become a boxer and complete the unfulfilled dreams of my grandfather Bartolo. My mom, of course, was against the idea; she didn't see a future in it for me, and plus, it was a very dangerous and violent sport. I ended up sneaking out to practice. I'd fill my backpack with all the training gear I needed and secretly toss it over the back fence where a friend was waiting to pick it up on the other side. Then I'd walk out the front door, pretending to be on my way to the store or going to run some errands, when in fact I was heading to the gym to train. Even though she never caught me, she knew I was boxing, because often I'd come home looking like I'd been in a fight. And of course, she'd react pretty angrily.

As it turned out, I wasn't quite as good a fighter as I would have liked, and I gradually stopped training for the sport. But I do remember earning the nickname "The Booger," because of all the shots to the nose that I took.

Once, for example, I went behind my parents' back and signed up for a tournament in Ocotlán's main square. I have no idea how I managed to win the first fight, because afterward my eyes were swollen shut from all the blows to the face my opponent had delivered. But somehow I'd beaten him, and I was very happy and excited. I ended up losing my second fight by a unanimous decision. My opponent didn't knock me out, but my face took a beating, which you can still see today.

I remember another match, one which I was losing badly, and my trainer confronted me in the corner.

"You want me to throw in the towel?" he asked. I was really taking a pounding.

"Why would you throw it?" I replied, taking his question literally. "Why don't you just hand it to me and I'll take it over to him. We don't want him to get any angrier!"

Right around the time I was thinking about quitting boxing, I was approached by a few of the neighborhood kids who were taking karate lessons. They challenged me to a fight because they wanted to see who was a better fighter: a boxer or a karate kid. Well, to make a long story short, they too hit me with tons of punches. I couldn't even tell what direction they were coming from, and I couldn't defend myself.

These bad experiences with boxing didn't put me off from other sports. Not long after that, when I was fourteen, I decided to enter a road race that ran from the main plaza in Ocotlán to San Martín de Zula, which was almost seven miles away. I finished in third place and received a medal. It was the first award I'd ever won in my life! The road was dusty, and I remember my uncle Ramiro had gotten someone to lend me a T-shirt for the race because I didn't have the money to buy one. I was thrilled with the result, especially because I'd been very disciplined and dedicated when it came to my training: Each day after school, I went for a run, and set new goals for myself every time I ran. Still, the road race was a different experience, and the event was much more exhausting than the workouts, but boy, was it worth it!

Setting these sorts of challenges is important because it allows us to test ourselves and brings out the best in all of us. It doesn't really matter whether we accomplish what we set out to do or not; what's truly important is that we put our passion and effort into it and give it a try. That's where the satisfaction lies: in showing us our strengths and in preparing us to do even better.

With kids today, getting a medal is different. In most competitions, they give them out for just about anything, even the simple fact of having participated in the competition. When I play with my kids or watch them compete, I always tell them: "Back in Mexico, you had to win to get a medal."

It's so easy to win awards now that recently this happened to me with my kids: I had just participated in an indoor soccer tournament, and my team ended up finishing in first place. Every player on the team got a medal. I was very happy with the performance, and came home bragging about our victory. But my wife and children were having none of it, and instead were joking that surely the other team had let us win because I was Piolín.

I was completely surprised, and insisted that we had won fair and square. I even had a video of the final match, which showed me scoring a goal after faking out one of my opponents.

That play even made the nightly news! Not even that was enough to convince them. But Daniel, my younger, still had faith in me.

"I believe you, Dad," he said.

And then he took my medal away!

I still have fond memories of my time in Ocotlán, and I even managed to keep in touch with a few of my friends, like Jaime, Mario, "El Biónico," and Luis. "El Biónico" and Luis lived around the corner from my house, and now they also live in the United States. When I was working for Radio Éxitos, we shared an apartment with a few of our other friends from Ocotlán during the good old days of hanging out, turning vacant lots into soccer fields, and throwing orange peels from the roofs of houses.

Middle school was also the time when I started getting more interested in girls than before. I did whatever I could to get their attention, but they barely noticed me because I was so short. In fact, at school, whenever we had to line up in order of height, I was always at the front. Getting a girl to like me in high school wasn't a challenge; it was a miracle!

One of my strategies was to offer a fried tortilla covered with the red chili salsa I brought for lunch. To make it look even better, I'd let the tortilla dry in the sun, so the salsa would turn a deep, delicious color.

"Don't you want to try some?" I'd ask.

The problem was that some kids with more money than me would cut in and offer them crackers with tuna, tomato, and onion. The girls always ended up going with them.

So I started thinking of other techniques for attracting their attention that wouldn't leave me at a disadvantage. My solution—which I thought just might work—was to write poems for them where each line began with a letter from their name. At first, I didn't have any luck. But eventually it worked, and I got a girl to go out with me. But then I started to think, *What does she really see in me?* One day, I got the courage to ask her.

"Why are you going out with me?" I asked.

"Oh, it's because you're so ugly, it makes it look like I have a bodyguard!"

After a few hits and misses, I eventually found myself a girlfriend. She was very thin, with straight hair and light brown skin. She was also very polite and studious, and she was always helping out her parents. Sometimes she said she couldn't hang out with me because she was busy doing something with her family. It was a cute, innocent little courtship.

I remember one day I wanted to kiss her. I told her so, but she was too embarrassed that someone might see us, given the lack of privacy. We were standing underneath a light, so I took out one of the rubber bands I used to sling orange peels at people, took aim, and fired, shattering the bulb overhead. How could I miss the chance to kiss a girl for the first time on the line?

"What are you doing?" she said, stunned, before I moved in for the first kiss.

I was so happy, it was like walking on air.

Unfortunately, the relationship didn't last long after that, because a few months later, I moved to the United States. When I told her I was going to America to help my dad and brother better take care of our family, she was sad. But since it was such an innocent little relationship, saying good-bye wasn't terribly difficult. We promised to stay in touch, and at first we did, sending letters back and forth to each other. But as time went on, I had to focus more and more on work, and our correspondence gradually came to an end.

Just because I started middle school didn't mean I stopped working. One of my jobs was at a photo studio called Central Fotográfica Muñiz, where I was in charge of developing the rolls of film that customers would drop off.

On top of that, I started working at a shop subcontracted by the company where my dad used to work, Celanese Mexicana. I worked on a lathe making screws. To get to work, I rode my bike—not the one I built with my own two hands, and which somebody allegedly "stole"—but a different bike that the shop owner lent me, and which had a big basket for carrying around nuts and bolts. On the way to the job was a very steep hill, and I used to ride down it as fast as I could. I loved the feeling of speed, and being able to get to work more easily.

I was able to get that job because, at the time, some companies had opportunities for underage children like me to practice and learn different skills. This was quite useful, because it gave kids the chance to explore different careers or jobs which they later might want to pursue as adults.

That was also around the time that my dad came to the United States looking for better opportunities to provide for our family. He'd been there once, when he was younger, and so he knew that the work paid better. With what he could send back to Mexico, we could live a better life. Shortly thereafter, my older brother followed him there looking for a job to help out the family. So Jorge was the first of us to fulfill the dream we had as kids, watching planes streak across the sky, wondering when we would be going to the United States as well. A couple of years before my dad and brother left, my brother Edgar, the youngest, was born.

CHAPTER 6

"COME OVER HERE"

My dad came to the United States when I was around fourteen years old. He'd realized that things had stagnated in Ocotlán, and if something didn't change, we'd be stuck in our current situation forever. His job didn't offer many opportunities for growth, and he hadn't gotten a raise in a number of years. Also, my dad had a bit of an adventurous spirit and a tireless drive to find ways to improve his own situation and that of everyone around him, especially his family. So even though he knew he'd be moving far away from us, and it would hurt not to be able to see one another while he was away, in the end, he decided that the best way to improve our financial situation would be to try his luck in the United States. So in 1984, when I was fourteen years old, he went north, intent on crossing the border and seeking a better future for us all.

It wasn't a decision he made overnight, of course, but slowly, deep inside of him, the idea of leaving Ocotlán began to take shape. He kept it to himself, and didn't tell us that he was thinking of moving until the very last moment. First he talked with our mom, and then the two of them told the rest of us. He'd decided to go to America to look for opportunities that would offer us a better life. Honestly, I didn't really understand the reason for why he was leaving for the United States, and I didn't realize just how much I would miss him. They didn't give us a whole lot of information at the time, mostly because they didn't want to worry us or make us sad.

My dad didn't have a definitive plan for getting to the United States; all he knew was that it was easier to get a better-paying job there, and that he could start out by living with an aunt and uncle who were already on that side of the border.

Good-byes were always very sad in my family, full of emotions and tears. But bidding farewell to my dad was even more difficult, because we all knew that we wouldn't be seeing him again for a long time.

I remember going over to see Grandpa Chuy, my dad's father, so he could give him his blessing. At the time, my grandfather worked as a brickmaker, drying them in the oven until they turned that special shade of red. The brickwork yard, called La Ladrillera, was located just outside of Ocotlán.

"Well, Dad, it looks like I'm going to the States to try my luck," my dad said.

"If it's for your sake and the sake of your family, I give you my blessing," my grandpa replied, and we all knelt down to receive it. "Son, may God watch over you, and help you to succeed."

Then we all embraced and started to cry. I hugged my dad, my grandpa Chuy, and my brother Jorge, and still couldn't stop crying. Finally, we returned home.

The next day, we went to the bus terminal to say good-bye to my dad, and there, before he got on the bus, we embraced one last time.

"I love you so much, Dad," we all said. "May God watch over you."

My dad told us all to be strong, though his voice was choking up. When he boarded the bus and started waving good-bye to us through the window, we were all in tears.

As I watched the bus pull away and fade into the distance, it felt like my heart was being ripped in two.

As I mentioned, a couple of my dad's family members were already living in the United States, including my aunt Nena and uncle Manuel, who were incredibly helpful.

My older brother followed shortly after my dad left Ocotlán so he could help him earn money to send back to us. But it wasn't long before Aunt Nena sent us some sad news about Jorge. He'd started drinking again, and was doing it quite often. *Please come,* she'd say in her letters. *This boy isn't doing very well at all. He's going to lose himself.* My mom and I were crushed to know this, and to know that there was little we could do, being so far away. My brother's tendency to drink had started earlier, when he was in school in Ocotlán, and as I mentioned, it had already cost him some opportunities at a brighter future. Now that he was in the United States, it seemed the problem was only getting worse.

Hearing all of this just made me want to move to the U.S. even more, so I could look after my brother and help my father. When I finally decided to leave Mexico, my younger brother, Edgar, was about four years old, and I was going on sixteen. I was still working, turning down screws and developing rolls of film; these were just temporary jobs, and even though I was always on the lookout for other opportunities to work elsewhere, the money was never enough to really help my family. And the money we were starting to receive from my dad wasn't enough either. My mom and I would write him, asking for money, because it was becoming more and more difficult to balance our expenses.

When we would get that monthly letter from my dad, only to discover that there was no money order inside, we were still happy to hear how he was doing, but unfortunately you can't buy food with happiness alone. On those occasions where he could only send a letter, he would write things like, *I'm fine, but there's no work. I miss you.* He could be very vague in his explanations. And when the letters were accompanied by a money order, it was often no more than twenty-five or fifty dollars. My dad was working in construction, but only when help was needed, and so his paychecks weren't coming in very steadily.

Many people in Mexico and other countries think that people who immigrate to the United States automatically start making more money and can safely support both their lives here and their families back home, but that's not always the case. Finding a job and being successful in America can be a long and difficult process, and while the wages are usually higher and the exchange rate is more favorable when sending money abroad, it can be challenging and take a long time to secure a job and a steady source of income.

I remember waiting for the mailman to come down our street, and when I saw him, I'd run up to him and immediately ask if he had anything for us. In fact, sometimes, on my way home from school, I'd start looking for any mailman on any street, regardless of whether his specific route included our address. I always got excited when I saw one. Sometimes, the mailman would pass by our house without stopping to deliver a letter, so I'd run out after him.

"Excuse me, but do you have a letter from my dad?" I'd ask. "Maybe you forgot, and it's still in your mailbag."

"Well, I don't think I have a letter for you, but let me double-check." And he'd look through his bag again, just to be nice to me.

Our situation became somewhat desperate from time to time. Even more so when my dad's letters began to repeat the same, brief phrase: *Haven't found a job. Can't send any money yet.* So I started writing back to him, saying, *I want to come and work there too so I can help earn some money to send back to Mom.* I thought to myself, *I should go there, because that way, when he's not working, maybe I will be, and plus, the pay is better there than it is here. That way, there will be more money to send to my mom and little brother.* That's how I saw it, anyway: Three people looking for work, even if they only occasionally found it, would be better than two. I really wanted to help my dad and my aunt and uncle, and I wanted to get my brother out of the awful hell of alcoholism that he was getting himself into.

And sometimes I had to wonder whether my dad and my brother had forgotten about us entirely. It was a feeling that grew stronger as the letters started to come less regularly or when they sent us pictures of the two of them at a park, of my brother as a chamberlain in a quinceañera party, or of them doing something special together. I thought to myself, *What an exciting life they're living there,* and so I concluded that their memories of us were slowly fading from their minds.

When I told my parents about my idea to come, they didn't take it very well. I told my mom first, but she was against the idea because she didn't want to see another family member leave, but also because crossing the border was dangerous. My dad wasn't in favor of it either. He agreed with my mom that it was too much of a risk without documents. But on the other hand, there was no other way to do it: Applying for a visa wasn't an option, because I would have had to prove I had money, a job lined up, or some sort of financial stability, and I had none of that.

But despite their objections, and after many painful nights of thinking it over, I made up my mind. I knew I would be leaving my younger brother and my mom alone in Ocotlán, and that I might not see them again for a very long time, because crossing the border without papers would prevent me from coming back to Mexico anytime soon. Yet I felt this was the only way to help my family. I also felt that I didn't have much of a future in Ocotlán. So I worked up the courage to break the news to my mom.

"I'm going. With or without your blessing. Either way, I'm going."

But of course I wanted her blessing.

CHAPTER 7

I PROMISE YOU

Finally, she gave me her blessing. She had no other choice, seeing my determination to head north. But her acceptance didn't stop her from angrily asking me why I was going to leave them there, and what was she going to do without me. She'd be alone with a small child, and nobody to help her get through the daily tasks of running the home. Her arguments always made me think twice and feel awful, but I was still convinced that leaving would be the best for all of us.

The day of my departure came. I remember my mom and my little brother, Edgar, standing in front of me, outside our house. We all hugged and began to cry. My mom couldn't let go of me, and I couldn't let go of her.

I'll never forget that embrace.

I always think about it whenever I'm facing some difficult decision here in United States, because that memory of her always gives me the strength to keep going and find solutions, to fight defeat.

Between sobs, she said: "Don't you forget about us."

"I promise I'll never forget about you, Mom. I promise I'll work hard so we can all be together again soon."

CHAPTER 8

A LONG TRIP

As soon as I left for Tijuana, I already missed my mom and brother. I remember walking through the streets of Ocotlán with my backpack, saying good-bye to all my friends and telling them I was going *to the other side*, crossing over to the United States. While bidding my farewells, I started feeling very sad. I turned around and looked back down the street I had been walking along, and there, in the distance, were my mom and my younger brother. I was getting farther and farther away. Little by little, step by step, they were falling out of sight.

That's when I thought to myself, *Now this is for real.* And even though I'd thought about what it meant to leave my family, my friends, and my country behind me, it wasn't until that very moment when I realized how it would actually feel to embark on an adventure, not knowing the outcome. Times like that remind us that you never really know what you have until it's gone.

I took a bus from Ocotlán to Guadalajara, and there I transferred to another that would take me on a long and winding road to Tijuana. I don't remember much about the trip itself, just endless hours of watching the increasingly arid landscape pass by. And the sadness of leaving my family, which gave way to uncertainty. Would I ever see my mom, my dad, or my brothers again? That, I didn't know, but I wanted to see them again, with all my heart.

When I arrived in Tijuana, I was met at the bus station by a lady friend of the coyote whom my dad had hired to help me cross the border. To identify herself, she was carrying a picture of my dad and me. After introducing herself, she took me to a seedy hotel, a really dirty and decrepit place that smelled of rot. When we got out of the car, I saw a bunch of people peering through the windows of one particular room, while other people opened their doors and looked at me with sternness in their eyes. I didn't know any of them, and I was starting to feel very afraid.

As we entered the small room where a group of people were waiting, the coyote stood up.

"This is the boy I was telling you about," the woman said to the coyote.

"He's just a kid, and he's on his own," the coyote replied. "Does he have the courage to cross?"

"Yes," I said. "Of course I have, sir."

"You take care of him. Very, very, very good care of him," said the woman. "You know where I'll be waiting on the other side."

All I could do was follow their eyes; my head was spinning from trying to understand what was going on.

"And the money?" asked the coyote.

"Don't worry about that," the woman replied. "As soon as he makes it to the other side, the money will be given to you. I'm responsible for that."

We'd been told it would cost $300 to get me across, and as promised, the coyote got his money when he turned me over to my dad. Back then, coyotes were more trusting, but now I know they always demand money up front.

After speaking with the coyote, the woman explained to everyone in the room what we were going to have to do, what it meant to cross the border, and how we would walk through the hills. We were never to separate from the coyote at any time, and we mustn't ever let fear get the better of us: We'd be walking in darkness through the middle of the desert, doing everything we could to avoid running into *la migra*, the border patrol. But at that moment, inside the room, I wasn't as scared about the crossing as I was nervous about being in a city so much bigger than Ocotlán. I'd seen the city as we drove from the bus station to the hotel, and everything was so different, so much more hectic, with so many more people.

The woman and the coyote continued to speak to each other, arranging the secret details.

"Don't worry, kid. You're gonna be fine," he said, seeing that I was nervous.

We spent the rest of the day there, all of us piled up in that little hotel room, and when night fell, we headed for the hills on the Tijuana side of the border. Somewhere in those hills was the border with the United States. I couldn't believe I was so close.

I noticed that some of the people who were crossing with me brought bags of clothes with them. Some, the lucky ones, I guess, had small backpacks. I had a small plastic bag with a bean sandwich, which the coyote had given me.

"Eat up, kid. It's a long hike," he said when he handed it to me.

When we reached the edge of the hill, the coyote had us sit down on some rocks to rest up before we started the ascent. I remember seeing a few men selling atole and tamales, offering us the last chance to satisfy our hunger before the crossing began. I was too nervous to eat, but I remember them well, because it wasn't something I'd expected to see.

Sitting there on the rocks, I looked out over the landscape through which I'd soon be passing: the dry arid terrain with almost no vegetation stretching away before me, with the city of Tijuana behind me, as silent as the desert. Even though it had been scorching hot during the day, now it was freezing cold, though I could barely feel it through my fear.

I remember each of the faces of the people sitting there with me like it was yesterday: Their expressions mixed with hope and fear, exhaustion and excitement for what they were about to do. Some looked tired, and I wondered if they had already attempted to cross the border on other occasions, and failed. Many were hoping to reunite with family, others to try their luck finding work, but all of them seeking a better future.

My group totaled five people plus the coyote. Four were men, and the fifth was a woman. I also noticed that mine was not the only group in the area, because I could see other coyotes, each of them with his own group. We would all be crossing simultaneously, taking similar routes. Not too long ago, I went back to that place, looking for the rocky outcrop where we had been sitting, but it has been fenced off since then, so it's no longer possible to get back to the exact same spot where we were that night.

Then we started walking, and my fear began to grow, as did the thrill of soon being able to see my dad and my brother. I could feel the dry desert air penetrating my lungs and the sandy soil underneath my sneakers. I know many immigrants like me have similar memories of their arrival in this country, all mixed with emotions and uncertainties about the journey through the desert, and dreams about what awaited us at the end of the road. From these dreams, we draw the strength that drives us to keep going, despite the dangers that lie ahead.

The coyote was always ahead of us, leading the way and showing us where to go. He also gave us instructions on how to obey orders along the way.

"When I shout *Keep going,* that means start walking or running, depending on the situation," he told us. "But when I yell *Run,* that means you start running."

We had to be alert and ready for any situation that might arise. Of course, the instructions didn't make me feel any more at ease, because anything could become a challenge at any point in time. I was looking all over the place, differentiating between the path and the desert landscape, trying to get used to it all. I also kept an eye on the other people in my group: I wanted to know what was going through their minds, who they were, and why they were there.

I remember I was watching one group member in particular, a slightly older and very tall man, when the coyote began to shout, *"¡El mosco, el mosco, el mosco!"*

This guy is scared of mosquitoes, and here I am, looking to avoid la migra, I thought to myself, and continued to walk quietly, not knowing that *el mosco* was the slang term for border patrol helicopters. That hadn't been part of the coyote's long list of instructions, and we had no idea how to react.

Some ran and hid as best they could. But there was nowhere to really take cover, except for some scraggly shrubs, so I dove underneath one. But I immediately realized that it was not a good idea at all, because it left me completely exposed. I didn't have many options, and I was paralyzed with fear, so I just had to stay there, not knowing what was happening. Should I have run? Should I have kept walking slowly? Could I have covered myself in the sand? Or found a boulder to hide under? I consider these different scenarios now, but at the time the only thing that occurred to me was the most obvious reaction of all: Don't move. There I was, barely covered, halfway between my family in the United States and the ones I'd left behind.

I could feel the rush of air from the helicopter's rotors, and the sound was growing louder.

"Don't get up! Everybody, stay down!" the coyote shouted.

Panic was setting in. *Now I know why my dad didn't want me to do this without papers,* I said to myself. I broke into a cold sweat as I felt the danger closing in on me.

"If we get split up, try to run back to Tijuana, or let *la migra* catch you!" the coyote shouted again. "That's the best strategy. . . . You're in a lot of danger if another coyote grabs you."

Why would it be better to be caught by *la migra* than another coyote? I didn't have any time to think about it, because I could feel the helicopter closing in, and starting to descend toward me.

Between the fear and the blasts of air blowing dust and sand in my face, I did something very dumb: Instead of lying still, I curled up, hoping I would look like just another rock in the desert to the officers in the helicopter above.

My grandparents always told me I could pray to God whenever I needed to. So at that moment, I asked God to make me invisible. By then, the helicopter was so close that I could make out the faces of the officers on board. It was made in part from fiberglass, and they were looking directly at the spot where I was hiding: They could see exactly where I was and what I was doing. I tucked my head down, full of fear.

I felt lost. I was waiting for them to grab me, and wondering what would happen to my dad, who would be waiting for me on the other side with my brother and my aunt and uncle. Would they be worried? What would they do? What would I say to my mom when I was sent back home? What would happen to my younger brother? How could I face them? I didn't want to get caught. My stomach was tied up in knots, and I felt like crying.

Even though it was the middle of the night, all of a sudden, it felt as if the sun had risen. The searchlights on the helicopter illuminated everything, down to the tiniest detail. And I was right there, underneath it!

I remember looking up again, and seeing the officers for the second time. I put my head back down again and said to God, *Well, it's in your hands now.*

No sooner had I uttered those words than I heard them starting to pull back. Many things rushed through my mind, but one of them stood out above all others: *Don't forget about us,* I could hear my mother repeating.

CHAPTER 9

DOWN THE HIGHWAY

I'll never know what exactly happened, or why the helicopter veered away when it seemed certain that *la migra* had seen me. Did they really think I was just a rock or a bush? Was I actually invisible? Had they gone for backup or called the border patrol to detain us? All I knew was that I was grateful to God, because I'd witnessed a miracle, and now I had a second chance.

Sometimes it's easy to lose hope when faced with trouble, easy to forget that we must never stop believing in ourselves and in the strength that God grants us. In the end, no matter what the outcome may be, it is His will and it will be for our own good. All we can do is make the best of it while being guided by His wisdom.

As soon as the helicopter flew away, I stood up and started looking around for the other members of the group. I realized that I'd lost my bag with the bean sandwich, but I didn't have time to worry about that. As I walked around, I tried to shake the sand that had gotten into every inch of my clothing. But now, without the spotlights, the desert was once again left in pitch-blackness, making it all but impossible to know where I was going. Eventually I realized that nobody else was around, and I had no other option but to keep walking. The worst thing I could do would be to stay in one place, because surely the border patrol was on its way, so I knew I had to keep walking. With every passing minute, my feelings of fear increased.

It wasn't long before I realized I was lost. What direction had I been headed before *el mosco* showed up? Was I now heading back to Tijuana without even realizing it, or walking directly into an area where the border patrol would be waiting for me? I continued to wander through the desert for some time, until I heard the coyote calling out to me: "Hey, kid, I'm here! Follow me."

Without hesitating, I started running in the direction of his voice, until I literally ran into him and the other members of the group. Despite the cold desert air, I was sweating. Fortunately, we hadn't been separated by too great a distance, and we were all able to reunite again. We kept on going, taking extra precautions now, hiding from time to time behind the different boulders we saw, in case *la migra* closed in on us again, which didn't take very long.

"Take cover! Take cover! *La migra* is coming again!" we heard the coyote yelling.

But where could I hide? I looked around and saw nothing. No large boulders like there had been just a few minutes earlier. Finally we ducked under an abandoned stone gully that looked big enough to be the entrance to a cave, while others headed to some nearby bushes. I could hear the border patrol truck passing just uphill from where we were hiding. I could hear the tires skidding over the sand just above our heads, and the sound of the engine. It seemed like the same story repeating itself: that we kept running into them at each and every step along the way, and that inevitably, at some point, we would be caught. I was starting to feel run-down from the trip, the fear, the nerves . . . all the emotions and frustrations. The truck was moving slowly along, and at one point I thought it was going to stop, but once again we were safe: They kept on driving without realizing just how close they were to finding us.

Later I came to realize just how knowledgeable the coyote was when it came to the local terrain, because he knew exactly where to hide, and which spots provided the best cover. I also noticed that occasionally he would reach down and pull open a sheet plate in the ground, revealing a small cave or tunnel in which we could hide.

There were more challenges along the way, because on more than one occasion we had to jump a fence, crawl through a ditch, or slither under barbed wire, risking getting pinched. That part is all a bit fuzzy now, because I was too preoccupied with fear and hunger. What I clearly recall was feeling a huge lump in my belly. And I wasn't the only one, because when I looked into the faces of my fellow companions, I could see they were feeling the same things as me. In fact, a couple of them said they would rather turn back. We were exhausted and frightened, and our hope was running thin. Every time that happened, the coyote would try to cheer us up: "No, you've gotta keep going. Come on, we're almost there!" he'd say whenever someone said he wanted to stop. And in the end, nobody turned back.

We kept hiking and jumping fences until we reached a highway. There, he told us to stop and lie down off to the side of the road so he could tell us what to do.

"Now we're gonna cross the freeway," he said calmly, as if this were normal.

A freeway! I'd never seen one before. The only roads I'd known were the ones around Ocotlán, and the ones the bus took to get to Tijuana, and none of them was as big and wide as this one that lay stretched out before me.

We had to make it to the center, where the median separated the traffic heading in different directions, and then lie down there until we could see that it was clear to continue on to the other side.

"But how is that possible?" I remember asking. Since it was dark, you could see the headlights of the cars coming in both directions and how fast they were moving. Since it was the first time I'd ever seen a freeway, I was overwhelmed by so much speed and movement. And to top it off, this freeway was full of traffic.

"Just watch me," the coyote said, his voice calm and collected. "I'll go first so you can see what to do. After I get to the other side, I'm gonna jump that fence." He pointed across the freeway. "I have a car there. You'll see. I'll meet you on the other side."

And with that, he sprinted across the freeway. He did exactly what he said he was going to do, and the rest of us followed him, one by one. I was terrified; I didn't know if I could make it, or if I should even dare to try. I didn't want to think about getting run over by a car going at that speed. I don't think I'd ever seen cars moving that fast, and with the lights coming at me from either side, I was starting to feel dizzy. And the fatigue was setting in.

When I looked up and down the highway, seeing the speed of the headlights and the short distance between them, I understood why so many people have died while attempting to cross the border.

I was the last member of the group to make the attempt. As I walked up to the shoulder of the highway, I could feel the wind blown by the speeding cars. Finally, I mustered up the courage and started running: I picked a break in between headlights and ran as fast as I could to the median. I felt paralyzed, still terrified by the cars flying by. What I had managed to do did nothing to take away the fear and uncertainty. The lights were so blinding that, for a moment, I had no idea what to do next: It took everything I had just to listen to the voices of the people in the group, and I asked God to grant me the strength to know when I should make my move. I worked up my courage and made the decision to go, to cross the rest of the freeway, while inside of me, a little voice was saying, *What are you waiting for? Go on, you can make it!* I was terrified, but I started running, feeling the asphalt beneath my feet and the cars approaching me at full speed, distracting me, making me lose my concentration. Finally I reached the fence on the other side, safe and sound. As I started to climb over it, I noticed that my palms were sweaty, but that didn't stop me from reaching the other side.

I heard dogs barking excitedly and people coming out of their homes. Some even opened the doors to their garages. I couldn't understand what they were saying, so I assumed they were Americans and were calling the police to report us. I felt the fear welling up in me again.

That was when I noticed the coyote was changing his clothes. He'd taken off his dirty jeans and sweat-drenched shirt, replacing it with a long-sleeved white shirt and a tie. He wiped his face with a towel and said, "Okay, now what we're going to do is have you climb in the trunk."

At first, I thought it was a joke. I said to myself, *There's no way we can all fit in there.* But soon enough I realized he was serious, and that some of us would have to pile in the trunk: the four men, to be exact. It was harder than I thought it would be, because the space was very limited, even though the spare tire had been removed. I assume someone had taken it out so that more people could fit inside.

Ultimately, we realized it would be impossible for the four of us to fit. There was just no space for eight arms and legs and four heads and torsos. No matter which way we contorted our bodies, the only way the four of us would squeeze in would be if we were made of jelly, so the coyote decided that one of us would have to ride in the backseat. It was a risky solution, because it would have been easier for just the coyote and the woman to pass without attracting suspicion, posing as a couple on their way home for the night. But a couple with a man in the backseat could easily attract attention. Still, though, I would rather be the one in the backseat (or even in the front, though that was riskier still) instead of being crushed between three other people in the trunk of a car. The coyote chose the tall, older man to ride in the car with them. Maybe he picked him because the calm look on his face made him less suspicious, as if he hadn't just run across the border. Plus, the coyote had a change of clothes for those who rode in the car, to give them a cleaner and more presentable appearance.

As if things weren't nerve-racking enough, the coyote told us we still weren't safe from being discovered, because even though we were actually in the United States now, miles north of the border there are still immigration checkpoints where cars and passengers can be stopped and searched.

"When I stop, don't move. . . . Don't even breathe," he instructed us. "That will be the checkpoint."

Then the coyote closed the trunk, climbed into the front seat with the woman next to him and the older man in the back, started the engine, and the five of us embarked on the final stage of our journey. Those of us packed into the trunk were sweating despite the cold. I remember one of them had his feet firmly planted up against my face. I could feel the weight, body heat, sweat, breath, and fear of the other two people in there with me.

Between the fear I was feeling, the lack of space and ventilation, and the smells, I was starting to feel short of breath. I managed to lift up a bit of the lining, which normally would be covering the spare tire, and tried to fan myself a bit, but it did little to calm me down.

"I can't breathe! I can't breathe!" I said, starting to panic.

"Easy, just take it easy, kid," the other two men said, getting ever more nervous themselves from seeing my frantic reaction. The situation wasn't looking very promising.

At times like this, when we feel anxiety and fear sweeping over us, we can lose control of what we're doing and let our instincts take control, causing us to lose sight of the goal we're trying to reach. And on that occasion, in the trunk of that car, squeezed between the bodies of two other people, ultimately—and in spite of the despair that was starting to settle in—I managed to find the strength in myself and in God that I needed to keep me from starting to scream and cry, which would have put us all in greater danger.

Along the way, we stopped several times, and on each occasion we could hear dogs barking and people speaking English. That was when we were most afraid that a border patrol agent would search the car and find us there in the trunk, and that fear made the situation even harder to bear. I wanted to cry, to scream, to run away from it all, but instead I began to pray, just as my grandparents would do every night before going to sleep. When I was a child, whenever I'd spend the night at their house, they would always say to me, "Let's pray."

That memory came to mind, and I started doing the same thing I'd do with them: reciting my prayers like a good little boy. Little by little, I found myself starting to calm down, and connecting with God made the rest of the journey a bit more bearable. Nothing would come between me and my decision to join my dad and my brother.

Finally, after all the dangers had passed, we emerged unscathed at our destination: the city of Santa Ana, California. There, my dad and my brother Jorge would be waiting for me, along with my aunt Nena and uncle Manuel, who had welcomed us into their home, even giving us a small room in which we could start to build our future in this country.

Crossing the border into the United States was an extremely intense process, the kind that tends to form strong bonds between the people who experience it together. Yet it was likely that I'd never see these people again because once we crossed the border, everyone would be taking their own path moving forward, paths that would never cross again.

When I got out of the trunk, I started sprinting straight to where my family was waiting. I felt a huge wave of happiness and relief wash over me. I was relieved to know that I would never have to be crammed into that trunk again, struggling to breathe and not knowing if I would ever make it to see my dad and my brother. I was so very happy to be reunited with family and loved ones. I hugged my dad and said, "Now I know why you wanted to make sure I realized how dangerous this would be. But you know what, Dad? It was worth it. And I didn't go through all that just to waste any time." And immediately I thought to myself, *There must be a reason why I risked my life like this, because I could have died trying to cross the border.* Then I continued with what I had been trying to say: "Mom told me, don't forget about us. Because oftentimes, we thought you'd forgotten, Dad. That you and Jorge had forgotten all about us."

"No, *m'ijo.* Soon you'll see," he answered sadly, "that sometimes there really is no work to be done, and that's why I didn't have any money to send you. That's why sometimes I couldn't even write to you. . . . What would I say?"

We hugged for a long time, without saying a thing. I was so grateful just to be there in his arms. Like the vast majority of undocumented immigrants in this country, we had risked our lives in search of a better life for our families. A future that we would build through hard and honest work. We wanted to be a part of this country, and to give back to it for the great opportunities that it was offering us.

With everyone in tears, I told them about all the things that had happened to us during the crossing. When I finished my story, I looked at my aunt and said, "I want to start working right away."

"Well," she said, "there are some cans that need collecting."

PART TWO

UNITED STATES

CHAPTER 10

FORGING A PATH

I came to America with the determination to do whatever it took to help my family, to do whatever work I could do to start a better life. Once the fear of the border crossing had faded—which had to happen very quickly; in less than a day, in fact—I started preparing myself to do what I'd come here to do. I couldn't go back to Mexico, which is something I thought a lot about over the next few years, so the best thing for me was to devote myself to building my future here and therefore help my family, which was the reason why I decided to come to the United States in the first place.

As I previously mentioned, when he first came to America, my dad worked in construction. When I arrived in Santa Ana, he was working for a book distributor, packing boxes and loading them onto trucks for shipment. There weren't any openings there and, on the other hand, construction wasn't an option either because I was a young teenager. So, just as my aunt Nena suggested, my first job on this side of the border was collecting cans. She taught me what to do, where to find them, how to prepare them for recycling, how to collect the deposit on the cans, and everything else. She even generously provided the bags for me to collect them in.

So every day I went to parks, checked behind stores, and walked the streets, checking trash cans for recyclables. Sometimes, when I was poking around behind stores, the managers would get nervous because they thought I was trying to sneak in the back and steal something. When I would see them approaching me, I'd run because I didn't want them to call the police. When I finished collecting for the day, I'd crush the cans and head to the recycling plant. They used to pay by the weight of the cans you brought in.

My uncle distributed tortillas for Ruben's Bakery of Santa Ana, and my aunt worked in a factory. In their spare time, they collected cans as a supplement to their income. They were a great source of inspiration and led by example with their strong work ethic and extreme generosity. I will always be grateful to them for the help they offered us when we first got here. Although they had been in the United States far longer than we had and were hard workers, they lived modestly, in a small house in a working-class neighborhood.

I used to show my appreciation by sweeping their driveway or washing their car from time to time. I'd use a mixture of cola and sugar to shine up the rims; it always attracted a swarm of flies, but it gave the tires a nice dark color. I never told them I'd be washing their car, and of course I never asked for anything in return. They'd done too much for us; instead, this was my way of paying them back.

I'm especially grateful to my aunt, because she was the one who insisted that I keep going to school.

"You're too young. In this country, you can't just work," she said. "You have to go to school. Otherwise, they put you in jail."

I think my aunt was trying to scare me, and it worked! However, it wasn't the only thing that made me enroll in school again. I knew there was value in learning, and preparing yourself to be better, even if going to school was hard for me.

Once my aunt showed me the ropes of can collecting, I'd spend some time every day going to parks, shops, Dumpsters . . . anywhere I thought I might find empty soda cans. I pulled them out of the trash, crushed them with my foot, and sold them back to recycling centers. After, I sent whatever money I made back to my mom.

My aunt and uncle's house was small and modest, as I mentioned, and the room we stayed in was tiny as well. To give you an idea, just picture the bathroom being outside in the backyard. So, whenever one of us would come out of the shower, we would be freezing. It was even worse when it was raining or when I had to use the bathroom at two or three in the morning. Sometimes the hot water wasn't running, because the heating tank didn't hold very much, which reminded me of the boiler at my grandparents' house, which put out water that was either not warm enough or scalding hot. In any case, it was always best to be the first to shower at my uncle's house, because if you were the last in line, that almost always meant cold water. But that's just how things were, and it motivated me to make things better.

The neighborhood wasn't very safe. It wasn't uncommon to see parts being stolen off of cars, and occasionally, at night, I heard gunshots being fired nearby. I was glad I wasn't living on the streets, and fortunately nothing tragic ever happened to myself or my family.

Despite all of this, we were still grateful to have the support of my aunt and uncle and for the happy times we got to share with them.

We only occasionally got together, because the house was so small that the five of us couldn't fit at the table at the same time. Plus, we were each running on different schedules and would get home at different times of the day, but we never missed an opportunity to talk to one another and offer support when and where it was needed.

That's one of the great things about family: It's a group you can always lean on, where we can find love and shelter when things aren't going so great, where we can talk about our day and spend some quality time together.

Gradually, I started to get used to the reality of my new situation. Over time, things started to pick up, and it wasn't long before I found other jobs besides collecting old cans. I started washing cars at a used-car dealership on Main Street in Santa Ana, not far from our house, and as if that weren't enough, I also picked up a few hours here and there at the photography shop where my dad was working full-time.

The shop was owned by a man named Frank, and it was also located on Main Street. It was a tiny place that specialized in developing rolls of film, since digital cameras were virtually nonexistent at the time, and pictures were captured on a roll that had to be processed in a darkroom using special paper and chemicals. Mr. Frank was always very kind to me, and when I asked him if there was anything I could help him with at the shop, he agreed to hire me. I was in charge of developing the film rolls dropped off by customers, making photo enlargements, and providing customer service when needed, and when business was slow, I'd sweep and clean the windows.

With the extra money I made washing cars and recycling cans, I was able to buy my mom a couple of small dish sets, which I would give to her a couple of years later, when she came to to the United States. I remember thinking that I would buy two boxes of four settings each, so it would look like a lot. I really wanted to surprise her, and at the same time, it reminded me of the Mother's Day gifts I used to get her at a local shop where they also sold some sandwiches I loved: knives, glasses, cups. I always liked buying things that were useful for my mom.

My mom was delighted by the gift, and started using one of the sets immediately to serve dinner to the whole family. Those dishes got so much use—or maybe they just weren't that high quality to begin with—that they no longer exist. But my mom didn't replace them with the other set I'd bought; instead, she decided to keep them unused, in the box, at home. Many years later, when I married María, my mom gave them to her as a wedding gift, and told her the story behind them. María was so happy to learn the history, and so proud, that she decided to use them right away, and, well, let's just say that we used that second set of dishes so often that they're not with us anymore either.

It was in the darkroom of that photography shop that my dad warned me for being late. When he told me, in a fit of rage, that I would be a nobody, it was deeply hurtful, but it forced me to learn a valuable lesson. It strengthened my character and dedication to do something with my life, if only just to prove him wrong.

The darkroom was significant in my life for another reason: It was there that I started recording demo tapes. That was around the time I started wanting to be a radio broadcaster, and I used that time in the darkroom as an opportunity to start practicing and developing my skills.

It all began when my dad had been hired to photograph some actors at a theater in Santa Ana. That's where he met Jaime Piña, a radio announcer and someone I'm very grateful to, and since I liked talking to people and was already performing at the occasional ceremony, like quinceañeras or weddings, my dad informed him that I wanted to be a talk radio host. Jaime offered to give me some broadcasting lessons on the weekends. And so I went to his studio on Saturdays, and he would give me commercials to read aloud, after he'd finished his show for the day. The more I saw how his show operated, and how everyone worked on the set with him, the more I started to feel drawn to the radio. When I asked Jaime what he thought I needed to do to become a broadcaster, his suggestion was to create a few demos, or recordings of myself pretending to host a talk radio show. So, there in the darkroom, or occasionally in the bathroom back at the house, I would record songs by Los Bukis, Bronco, Vicente Fernández, Antonio Aguilar, Los Tigres del Norte, and other bands I liked on a cassette tape, and in between them, I would record myself pretending to be the DJ. I'd play these tapes to friends and family members; a few of them liked the "shows," while others just made a face as if to say, *Huh? What the heck is this?* But that never discouraged me. The more time I spent making up imaginary radio shows, the more I realized that this was what I wanted to do with my life. I continued to throw all my effort into making those tapes, and eventually I felt that I was getting pretty good at them. That's when I started taking them personally to local radio stations.

This was a time in my life where I felt myself being overtaken by a great need to do many things. I don't know if it stemmed from the desire to fulfill the promise I'd made to help my family get the money they needed, or if I just simply had too much energy or curiosity. Maybe it was thanks to the love and support I got from my aunt and uncle, or from the amount of dedication I saw my dad put in every day to succeed. Maybe it was a bit of everything. But thinking back on all the things I would accomplish in a single day, it still surprises me. It also reminds me that you can always find time to do all the things you want to do. All you need to do is set goals and focus on achieving them. You need *ganas*.

What I remember most from those early days in the United States is working. We lived day to day, and couldn't spend money on luxuries. My aunt and uncle would get up every morning at four to start their day, and wouldn't be home again until very late at night. I'd be up soon after them and walk to school and study before classes began. Afterward, I'd play soccer with the school team. About four in the afternoon, I'd head over to the photo shop, where I would work from six until about ten. On the way, and at every opportunity I had, even on the weekends, I would collect cans. I also had a bag at the shop, and asked all the employees to drop their bottles and cans in it. With the amount of work I put in during the week, I could easily have justified taking the weekend off, but I didn't. On Saturday and Sunday, when I wasn't collecting cans, I was washing cars at my other job.

Eventually I also started emceeing at events here and there, cleaning buildings, or appearing as an extra in movies, while still being a full-time high school student.

I missed my mom and my brother Edgar a lot, along with my grandparents and aunts and uncles who were still living in Mexico. I also missed my old buddies in Ocotlán.

The food tasted different in America, and I missed my mom's cooking. Once, my cousin Yolanda, whose parents were my aunt Nena and uncle Manuel, asked me what food I missed the most, and I said my mom's chicken enchiladas. She offered to make me some, and I ended up getting sick! They were super greasy, and my stomach ached for days afterward, but I appreciated the gesture. Things like that, even though they don't always turn out the right way, help homesick immigrants feel better, making us feel loved and cared for.

Aside from missing the friends and family I'd left back in Mexico, it was hard to live in a place where you didn't speak the language and where you didn't know your way around. I remember getting lost wandering around the same block over and over; other times, I'd start to feel déjà vu. *Dang, I think I was just here,* I'd say to myself, because all the buildings looked the same to me.

But not every experience was negative. When I went to school for the first time and saw the building, I was amazed. Even more so when I saw the lockers in the hallways, which was something we didn't have at the school in Ocotlán. I also got really excited when I learned that, as a member of the school soccer team, I got my own uniform. I was a little disappointed to learn that I couldn't keep it at the end of the season, but hey, they gave me a uniform to play in! That was something else I'd never had before.

These are the kinds of opportunities offered to us by our adopted country, and it's up to us to take advantage of them, because doing so will help us to make things better, to move forward.

CHAPTER 11

"THIS JOB ISN'T EASY, SO YOU'D BETTER STUDY"

If I were to put on my résumé all the jobs I've done over the years, you'd see that I have been a recycler, a car washer, a photographer's assistant . . . and also an emcee and a film extra. But wait a minute! How did I become an emcee? Or an extra in a Hollywood movie?

The story of how I became an emcee all began when some clients from the photo lab started to ask if anyone might be available to take pictures at their events. The shop didn't offer this type of service, but my dad—who never passed on a good opportunity—decided to volunteer. He saved up enough money to buy a used camera at a swap meet, along with all the accessories needed to shoot weddings, quinceañeras, baptisms, birthdays, and other events that required a photographer. So whenever a customer inquired, he would offer to do the job. Taking that step was simple enough, because the clients already knew my dad, and plus they could get all their photographic work done under one roof. The shop owner benefited as well, because any pictures my dad took would have to be developed there in his lab, and the customers got the benefit of an experienced photographer, since my dad had spent much of his youth taking pictures all over Mexico, and the shots always turned out quite good. So in the end, everyone was a winner.

I would help him by carrying his equipment. Other than the camera, we would need a "tripie," which is what we called a tripod in Mexico, and a couple large screens to regulate the amount of light. You'd see me hauling all of that to a church where a baptism was being performed, or to a quinceañera, or even a wedding. Moving from party to party but always working.

One day, we were hired to shoot a quinceañera, and the emcee never showed up. Immediately, my dad—again, never missing an opportunity—told the hosts that he could do the job. He had never done anything like that in the States. He drew on his experience from participating in church programs back in Ocotlán, and he would also appear on local radio, playing music. My dad had always been very charismatic, and had great people skills. And after that first performance, other offers started to come in.

Since I was often with him at these events, taking pictures while he emceed, I got a feel for introducing people, and tailoring the music to the different stages of the party, and eventually I asked him if I could try it for myself. My first real opportunity came rather unexpectedly, when my dad was working a party; all of a sudden, he turned to me and said: "Go ahead, *m'ijo*. Introduce the godparents."

And suddenly, there I was, with a microphone in my hand, pumping up the crowd, saying things like, "Get up and dance! This is a baptism, not a funeral!"

And apparently it worked, because people got up and started to dance, laugh, and sing.

I guess I did a decent job, because after that, requests to emcee other events started to roll in. I enjoyed emceeing, but there wasn't a lot of money in it. In fact, I usually didn't see a single penny since I normally got paid in food, such as birria and beans. It wasn't because I was too young or just a rookie; it was just the standard deal of the job. But I couldn't complain, since not only were they giving me an opportunity to practice and improve my craft in front of a microphone and an audience—as I mentioned before, at the time, I still had no idea I'd end up as a radio talk show host—but it also gave me the opportunity to eat some delicious food that I normally don't eat very often. I also had fun meeting new people and making new friends.

And while they are different jobs, being an emcee and being a radio broadcaster do have something in common: You're talking to an audience through a microphone. And in both jobs, it's important to be able to improvise. For example, if a guest at the party falls down while dancing, you have to be quick and say something funny to keep the party going: *"And, folks, he's surprised us with a break-dancing move!"* Unusual and unexpected things can happen when you're on the air too. Being an emcee was a challenge I was happy to accept, almost as much as I am happy when working as a radio host.

At some point, I also got interested in the idea of working in a film, because sometimes I'd be watching a movie and think to myself, *I'd like to play the part of some character and entertain people through my performance. And hey, if I could earn some money in the process, then that would be even better!* I remember seeing an ad in the paper about a studio hiring extras for a movie, and I thought it might be a good idea to try. I had previous plans the day of the casting call, so I couldn't make it, but I kept an eye out for other casting ads for films and TV and radio shows.

Of all the films in which I participated as an extra, the one I remember the most was *Terminator 2*. I was in the scene when Arnold Schwarzenegger crashes through the huge glass front of a store in the Santa Monica mall. Working next to a successful person like Arnold made me want to pursue a film career even more and inspired me to continue to improve myself and to be somebody in life. Arnold had come to the United States as an immigrant himself, full of big plans and dreams, and by working diligently, he rose to become a respected and famous actor. He was also very friendly with us extras, and seemed very comfortable and natural around us. I remember, when we had to reshoot a scene that hadn't gone right, he told us, "See, that's why you have to study. This job isn't easy, so you'd better study."

Being an extra in a film shoot took almost an entire day, and sometimes the pay wasn't very good, but man, did I like doing it. I really enjoyed it a lot. And even though I haven't fully devoted myself to movies, the desire to appear on the big screen is something I've never given up on.

I also remember appearing on a TV show in Spanish around that same time. It was called *Let's Talk Movies*, and it was hosted by Humberto Luna and Jorge Elias. Sometimes I'd give them my review of a movie I'd seen in the theater, and one time, they asked me to read it live on the air.

But working and looking for ways to make money and help out my family wasn't all I had to do. As I mentioned, my aunt Nena convinced me that I had to keep studying hard, and showed me what school district we belonged to based on the neighborhood in which we lived. Along with the fear she had infused in me when she told me I could go to jail if I didn't study, I ended up enrolling in Saddleback High School.

Since I didn't speak English, I was put in an ESL class, which didn't turn out to be much of a help, because as I've said before, I wasn't a very good student. And now, being in a different country with a different language, I was even less of one, and every year I was at that school, I had to take ESL classes with other international students . . . and not just Latinos, though we were the majority. In fact, I almost didn't graduate because I was so bad at English and the other courses.

Being an ESL student meant that I had to take some subjects like math completely in English, but could take other classes like English, history, or science with other students who didn't speak the language. In those situations, an interpreter would be there to help explain the subject matter to us. That is, there was a teacher who taught the class in English, while the interpreter translated what the teacher was saying. This made the classes run more slowly, and it took us longer to get through our textbooks—sometimes, we weren't even able to finish them—which left us at a disadvantage when it came time for final exams, especially compared to the students who were able to speak English. No wonder why we, as immigrants, did so poorly in school. Most of us arrived here under difficult circumstances and without knowing the language. Then we attended a school where we were forced to learn English in a rush, yet some of the subjects are only halfway completed, and in the end, we have to pass the final exams just like everybody else. But we were often unprepared. There were many teachers who really made an effort to work hard so that immigrants could learn, but some parts of the system need to be changed to ensure that all students can succeed, and that they don't see their opportunities being closed off because they weren't able to complete their studies.

I remember that I often didn't understand what the teachers were saying, or the concepts they were explaining. One math subject that especially stumped me was square roots: I could barely add and subtract—I hadn't even really learned this in Ocotlán, being as bad at math as I am—and now they were asking me to take the square root of a number in English! In any case, the point was not to give up but to keep trying as best I could to understand the subject matter and get good grades, even if I wasn't always able to do it.

On the other hand, ESL students had their own set of special advisers, whom I would meet with and talk to about my concerns.

"I don't know what to do with my life. I just don't know what to do," I'd confess.

They'd try to understand my situation and my doubts, and offer me advice, but I still couldn't stop worrying about my future. Although I was working hard and liked doing it, it still wasn't clear to me what the future held for me in this new country. Sometimes, it felt like I'd be washing cars, collecting cans, or developing photos forever. All I knew for certain was that I had a burning desire to move forward and do something. But what would that be?

I remember being scolded by teachers on occasion. There was one in particular who was always calling me out because I liked to talk with my classmates and even tell jokes in the middle of class. It was a habit I'd had since I was a kid in Ocotlán, and it had always gotten me in trouble. The only difference is that here, the teacher would just tell me to pay attention or sometimes write me up, but I never got beaten with a switch.

"Don't laugh!" I'd whisper to a friend while telling him a joke.

But inevitably, the teacher would catch me. If I'd been warned before, this time I'd be asked to leave the room.

"You'll see," I remember saying to my English teacher on more than one occasion. "You're gonna need me for the school play, but I'm not gonna help come up with ideas. Just so you know."

And that wasn't far from the truth, because he was also the drama teacher. I didn't just like acting; I also enjoyed brainstorming ideas and building sets.

This was also the same time I started getting interested in being on the radio. Thanks to my experiences onstage and the enjoyment I got from making my classmates laugh, my calling started to take shape.

Though, gradually, I realized the truth: My chances of graduating weren't looking good, because my grades were still so low. I felt lost and wondered what I could do instead. Maybe I could just drop out and focus on working and making money, since at the end of the day, I was better at that than I was at school. But my aunt Nena was very insistent on the fact that getting a high school diploma was an important achievement. She said it would help me find a better, more stable job with a higher salary. I don't know if I really understood the importance of a diploma back then, but my aunt Nena was very convincing, and so I did what she asked and devoted myself to getting that diploma, no matter what.

Besides the benefits my aunt had explained, there was something else that motivated me to get better grades: the soccer team. I was, of course, interested in soccer, because I was so short that if I had wanted to play football, they'd have used me for the ball! But either way, you had to maintain a decent grade point average if you wanted to be on the team.

The first thing I did to raise my grades was ask my friends to show me their notes whenever I was having trouble understanding something. Almost all my classmates were friendly enough to let me look over their notebooks. Some of them would even put tiny mirrors on their shoes so I could see their answers, and others would pass me cheat sheets that contained answers to the exam.

But I didn't always get away with cheating. I got caught on more than one occasion.

"No, I wasn't looking at anybody's answers," I'd say.

"Yes, you were. I was watching you, so don't tell me I didn't see anything," teachers argued. And invariably I'd end up in the principal's office. Being caught cheating usually meant cleaning the toilets as punishment on Saturdays.

But cheating wasn't the only way to get better grades. In fact, for me, it was a last resort, because I was also making an effort to spend any free time I had studying. I'd walk to school in the mornings, but in the afternoons I'd catch a bus and would study, whether I was on my way back home or to one of my many jobs. It didn't matter where I was going; I always took it as an opportunity to study more.

Sometimes I'd use the darkroom at the photo shop as a place to study when there wasn't much work to be done. I'd also try to get a few minutes of study time in before going to sleep at night, although with the fatigue setting in at ten o'clock after a long, hard day, I'd usually fall asleep while doing it. And in the mornings, I'd go to school early and sit in the cafeteria, going over my notes and homework assignments. I remember my aunt would arrange for me to get a carton of milk and a chocolate chip cookie there at the school, which certainly helped me to focus and understand what I was reading! I was slowly getting better at reading in English, but when it came to speaking it fluently, I still had many years to go.

But despite my best efforts, I was still at risk of flunking out. I had no choice but to do extra course work to catch up, and so I enrolled in night classes at Valley High School. There, students would review the courses in which we'd done poorly, and it gave us a second chance to pass the final exam. It was a good decision, because although it was almost impossible not to fall asleep after a full day—going to school, participating in extracurricular activities, soccer practice, and at least one job—taking those night classes was a lifesaver, because it allowed me to get my high school diploma. During the graduation ceremony, holding that diploma in my hands, it felt like a dream come true. The first of many that would soon follow.

The important thing is to never give up, no matter how difficult or unattainable something may seem. In the end, your efforts will pay off.

It was also around this time that I got my nickname, Piolín. As is common at that age, boys like to give nicknames to one another. Back in Mexico, people called me "El Sope" because I was so little.

Here, my Latino friends started calling me Piolín, because I was still small, plus I had big eyes and a big head, just like the cartoon character Tweety Bird. And the crazy facial expressions I would make only made my head look bigger. At first, the nickname made me angry, but eventually I started to like it.

• • •

Learning English was so hard for me not only because it was a new language or because I had my head stuck in so many different things, but also because in high school I tended to hang out with other Latino kids who also spoke Spanish. I missed my country and my people, and by spending time with these kids, I felt more in touch with what I'd left behind. However, what I didn't understand was that it would have been beneficial to spend time getting to know other Americans, even if they didn't know Spanish. Doing so would have helped me to better understand American culture, not to mention improve my English.

By spending time only with other Spanish-speaking Latinos, I was confining myself to a separate world from my classmates who spoke English, and that made it all the more difficult for me to assimilate.

On the other hand, not fully understanding the country could lead to misunderstandings, some of which were quite funny. At least, they're funny to me now. For example, shortly after I arrived in the United States, some friends invited me to go get some burgers. But what struck me was that most were eating their burgers . . . with silverware! I found this odd, but because this was my first hamburger experience in the United States, I assumed that was the way you were supposed to eat them. Since I wasn't sure how to go about it with a fork and knife, I waited until everyone was distracted and hid the burger in a napkin. Then, after saying good-bye to everyone, I headed for home, and on the way, I ate my burger with my hands.

CHAPTER 12

THE RADIO STARTS TO PLAY

When I was little, my dad used to drop by the studio of Radio Ocotlán and experiment with broadcasting. Sometimes they'd let him introduce a song or the next segment of the program. My older brother did that too, but neither of them pursued a career in radio. I think it was more of a hobby for them, and my dad liked the stage more than the microphone, and that's why he always participated in theater productions at his church in Mexico.

As a kid, I thought that when they played Vicente Fernández on the radio, he was actually there, live in the studio.

"Take me to the radio, Dad, take me!" I'd demand, until one day I actually got to go, only to realize that I'd been wrong all along: the band wasn't there.

Working in the radio business wasn't something I'd considered when I was a kid, but I do remember that every time I listened to the local station, it filled me with joy. Back at my uncle's repair shop, the one we used to call "El Chanclazo," we'd have the radio at full volume while we worked. The same with the bike shop, too.

I'd also listen to the radio at home in Ocotlán while doing chores. My mom always said that we could go out and play soccer with our friends under one condition: that we sweep, mop, do the dishes, or clean the bathroom. Anything to help out with the housework. So to make the task more bearable and sometimes enjoyable, I'd turn on the radio.

My favorites were Bronco, Vicente Fernández, Los Bukis, Pedro Fernández, Antonio Aguilar, practically any Mexican music they would play. The specific program that would really set my imagination flying was "La hora de las complacencias," or "Request Your Song." I can still remember the DJ's voice and the way he took calls from listeners like it was yesterday:

"Where are you calling from?"

"I'm in Jamay" (or Poncitlán or Tototlán or any of the other surrounding areas within range of that particular radio station, which—by the way—is still broadcasting to this very day).

Then the caller would say what song they wanted him to play, and to whom they wanted to dedicate it. Then the DJ would thank them for calling, cue the music, and say: "Here's Pedro Fernández singing his hit song, 'Coqueta.' This one goes out to all the girls out there turning heads as they walk down the street!"

That was when I'd get excited, thinking that the band was actually there, in person, in the studio. *How do they get so many people to come? How awesome is that!* I'd say to myself. Only later would I find out the truth.

Of course, I wanted them to play all the songs that I liked, and I called in time and time again. I guess everyone else had the same idea, because my calls never got through, but that never took away from the excitement.

When I came to America, I familiarized myself with the radio stations here, and soon enough I became a fan of Humberto Luna. I always enjoyed listening to his show. His jokes were funny, especially the ones made by one of his characters, Doña Kika, which always cracked me up.

Shortly after finishing high school, when I was nineteen, I attended an event organized by the local radio station, Radio Éxitos. I met several radio personalities such as Ricardo Manzanares, Ramón Valerio, Francisco Moreno, Renán Almendárez, Mario Fernando, and Víctor Méndez, and quickly became friends with them. Some of them invited me to drop by their respective studios to help them out and to learn, and as a sign of gratitude, I'd always come by with some food to share: burritos one day, tacos for another, maybe some bread. I knew they weren't about to offer me a job, but at least I could earn their trust, and eventually they let me help clean the studio or serve up some coffee. They often offered to pay for the food, but I always insisted that it was a thank-you gift for giving me the opportunity to learn.

"I'm hungry too," I'd tell them.

And man, was that ever true: I was hungry to learn, to grow, to become better every single day.

I met a radio host named Ramón, who also ran a cleaning business for offices and apartments. Ramón was a hardworking, motivated man whom I've always admired and from whom I've learned a lot. He gave me the opportunity to work for his company, which served Irvine, near Santa Ana and the Hilton Hotel where my brother worked as a dishwasher.

I've always been grateful to him for giving me that opportunity.

One of the ways I used to show my gratitude was by being on the lookout for things that were happening in the apartments we cleaned, like someone stealing toilet paper. I wanted to be his eyes and ears on the ground, but without negatively affecting my coworkers, so before I reported anything, I'd always try to talk them out of doing anything dishonest.

Sometimes, the problems or emergencies we encounter can make us forget just how important it is to be grateful to the people who lend us a hand or open a door for us. That's something I always tried to remind my coworkers of.

"Come on, we're working for them," I'd say. "Just ask them if you need something."

And most of us did. Ramón appreciated the honesty of asking first instead of stealing things behind his back. For example, I'd ask him, "Hey, Ramón, is it cool if I help myself to a roll of toilet paper?"

And he'd say yes. There weren't any problems just as long as I asked him first.

On the other hand, some of the people who gradually worked their way into the work rotation with Ramón's company were acquaintances of mine whom I'd brought in as referrals. I'd recommend the most hardworking people I knew, and I always insisted that they show gratitude for the opportunity being presented to them. In other words, don't do anything dishonest, and if they saw anybody doing something like that, they should go and talk with that person. If that didn't work, then Ramón would have to be notified.

I remember getting to work and being so sleep-deprived that sometimes, while loading up my cleaning cart with the vacuum cleaner, my washrags, and my window cleaner, I'd fall asleep while standing right there in the room where they kept the cleaning supplies! It was such a small space that I could barely accommodate the cart, and yet I found a way to squeeze myself in there so I could rest up a bit before putting all my energy into the work I had to do.

I'd close the door so that the lady in charge of the building wouldn't see me and stay there awhile, and when I went back out to start cleaning, I'd turn on my radio, which always kept me company, and get working as fast as possible to make up the time I spent recharging.

In one of these buildings, it was my job to vacuum the apartments after tenants had left. On one occasion, a dog had gotten into one of those apartments when nobody was looking and made a real mess of the place. When I got there and saw what had happened, I was pretty angry. I spent almost the entire day cleaning and disinfecting and getting out all of the stains. Of course, the lady in charge wanted to know why it had taken me so long to clean just a single apartment, but I was afraid of getting some formal reprimand, so I didn't tell her what had actually happened.

In that same building lived an elderly couple who always looked out for me while I waited for my brother or a friend to pick me up from work. Sometimes, especially in the summer, they'd bring me a glass of water so I could better resist the harsh Southern California heat.

They had a sky blue Buick that was bleached out from the sun after sitting out in the open parking lot for so many years. One day I asked the lady if she would be interested in selling it to me, and if so, how much would she want for it. She checked with her husband, and we settled on a thousand dollars, which I was able to pay from the money I'd saved up.

Buying the car was a good investment because I would no longer be stuck waiting for the bus or for someone to give me a ride. I could use that extra little bit of time to pick up some hours here and there, and also fix up the car a bit. I bought a new radio to replace the original, which was basically obsolete and got very poor reception. The new radio I bought wasn't a typical car stereo, but a portable one that sat on the floor of the car so I could listen to music while driving. It sounded incredible.

However, the happiness and joy of having my own car didn't last long. Remember the story about my bike? Well, I had to go through that whole experience again, all those years later.

When I discovered my car wasn't where I had parked it, I started asking around. This time, I didn't have to wait very long, because my brother was home at the time.

"I was robbed," he said.

Not again, I thought to myself.

"No, don't say that. Don't even mess with me," I answered.

"Yeah, they stole it from me."

"Did you call the police?"

"No."

"Bro, don't you care about anything? You know how hard I had to work to buy that car? Why would you do this to me?" I said, deeply hurt. I was really disappointed in him, and reeling from the loss of something I'd bought and fixed up, and which had proven to be so useful to me.

My brother continued to insist that it had been stolen, but I didn't want to hear any more of his lies or false explanations. I was so angry that I stopped speaking to him completely.

There was a moment when I thought I'd never be able to forgive my brother for what he'd done. But one day I went to church, and they preached about the importance of forgiveness, and I knew what I had to do. I'm really not the type of person who holds grudges, and not talking to my brother made little sense. I didn't wait for him to ask me to forgive him; I just called him up on the phone. I asked him how he was doing, and he said he was surprised to hear from me because he knew that I was angry with him. I don't remember exactly what we talked about, but I didn't mention the car. I just called to say hello and check in on him. And it felt good being able to reconcile. When we finished talking, I felt as if a huge weight had been lifted from my shoulders.

After all, we weren't just brothers—we were close friends, and we both did a lot to help support our parents.

Back then, my brother was lost in a deep sea of alcoholism. He was working as a dishwasher at the Hilton in Irvine, and when he got paid, he'd go out drinking with his so-called "friends." That's how he spent his money. His entire check.

I also had some "friends" who tried to get me into drugs and alcohol, but I always told them no. Mainly it was because of how I could see it hurting my brother, when I'd go looking for him at the local bars at one or two in the morning. Sometimes, when he was drunk, he'd hit me because I tried to get him to come home with me. At times like this, his friends would also get very angry and try to pick fights with me. They wanted to beat me up because I'd say things to my brother, right in front of them,

"These guys are only hanging out with you because you just got paid today, while Mom is back in Mexico and needs help. What are you doing?"

I really didn't care whether his friends threatened me, because even though I was still shorter than I am now, and not too strong, it hurt worse to see my brother like that. All I wanted to do was make him understand that what he was doing wasn't right, that all it did was hurt both him and the family.

If only things were that simple. Fighting an addiction like alcoholism is very difficult and painful, and my brother's case was no exception.

Uncle Raúl, who was on a business trip in the United States at that time, didn't want to witness my brother throwing his life away, which he strongly disapproved of, and suggested we should move to his friend's apartment where some old friends from Ocotlán were also living. That way, my brother would not worry the family with his drinking. My brother agreed since he didn't want everyone to see him drinking and call him out on it. There were six, plus my brother and me, in a two-bedroom unit. It was one of those communal living situations where you had to write your name on your jug of milk in the refrigerator so the rest would know not to drink it. Whenever my brother was drinking with his friends, I'd have to sleep on the living room floor. I was the only one who didn't drink, and I remember I couldn't sleep because they'd be blaring music by Los Freddys, Los Caminantes, Los Temerarios, Los Bukis, Vicente Fernández, Los Yonic's, José José, Ramón Ayala, Joan Sebastian, and many more. It was like a bar. The next day I'd go to school barely having slept. It was sad to see my brother ignoring my pleas to stop drinking. Eventually I was able to convince him to move back in with Aunt Nena and Uncle Manuel, but sadly nothing changed.

One thing I did after graduating from high school was to enroll myself in a commercial acting course at Rancho Santiago Community College in Santa Ana. I was only able to attend for one semester because, with all the jobs I had, I simply didn't have the time to continue. And, well, I didn't really have the money to pay for the class. It came down to whether I wanted to continue with my course or continue eating, and so the choice was clear. It's a situation I still often find myself in: I want to do so many things all at once, and I can't say no when something needs to get done or when someone asks me for help. But in any case, taking the course, even if I didn't finish it, was time well spent, because it taught me techniques I'd later be able to put into practice.

At the same time, I continued building my friendships with the radio hosts at Radio Éxitos, even though I wasn't able to do any real work yet because I still didn't have any experience. But I didn't let that discourage me, and I kept on recording my demos and sending them out to different stations.

You've gotta be kidding me. The tapes sound amazing. They're just too busy to listen to them, I'd think to myself every time I'd get turned down by a receptionist. But I never gave up and remained positive. In fact, whenever the receptionists at the radio stations in Los Angeles, Riverside, Ontario, San Bernadino, and elsewhere would say that the people I was trying to get in touch with couldn't see me at the moment because they were in a meeting or attending to some other matter, and suggest I simply drop off my demo so they could listen to it and get back to me if they were interested, I convinced myself that what they were really doing was giving me the opportunity to record a new tape that might turn out even better.

My mom and my brother Edgar arrived from Mexico when I was seventeen and still a high school student. A year later, we moved out of my uncle's house, since all of us could no longer fit there together, and moved into our own apartment. It was a better, safer neighborhood, and right in the heart of Santa Ana, near Santa Ana Boulevard and Spurgeon, about three blocks from Fourth Street. My dad had come across it on his way to the photo shop one day.

In addition to being in a better neighborhood, and having two bedrooms—a huge improvement over the one tiny room we all shared at my uncle's house—the apartment was close to where my dad worked, which gave him more time to spend with us, and kept him from running late if the car broke down or if the bus hadn't come through. We lived in that apartment for many years, until Jorge and I had saved up enough money to put a down payment on a house in Mira Loma for my parents. We all lived in the house for a year, at which point I decided to move to Oxnard for work while Jorge remained there with our parents.

CHAPTER 13

RADIO MÉXICO

I'll never forget the day I got the news. It was December 23, 1990, and I was in a barbershop near the corner of Fourth and Main in Santa Ana getting my hair cut. Suddenly my dad came bursting in through the door.

"*M'ijo*, you just got a call from a radio station in Corona. It's called Radio México," he said.

I didn't even have time to think. Instantly, I tore off the sheet and turned to the barber: "I gotta go," I said.

"Take it easy," my dad replied. "Don't leave yet. Just wait until he's finished."

"No, I'm leaving now!" I said, and took off running.

I borrowed a car from a friend, and that night, I drove to Corona. I left Santa Ana just after seven, and arrived at my destination at just before nine.

Radio México is an AM station. Back then it was broadcasting out of a small house in a vacant lot near Highway 91 and Interstate 15 with huge antennas protruding out the back. Today, the area is mostly bodegas, but back then, it was a dark and desolate neighborhood.

I pulled in and walked up to the front door. I went in, introduced myself, and said I was there to see the program director, whose name was Sergio.

"Do you have any experience in news broadcasting?" he asked me during the interview.

"Absolutely," I said, without giving it a second thought. I didn't, of course, having concentrated solely on practicing my speech so I could be a DJ on my own music show, not to become a news broadcaster. But hey, I really wanted the job.

"I need someone to cover for our newscaster for a week while he's on vacation in Mexico."

"I'll do it."

"Okay, but you start tomorrow at five o'clock, which means you need to be here by four to get the news."

"Well, sure, yeah, that's no problem. I'll do it!" I insisted.

I didn't want to drive all the way back home, because I thought, if I did that, the friend who loaned me the car might not let me borrow it again. So I called him to explain: "Bro, you know I've always wanted to do this," I said. "Give me a chance, and I'll get the car back to you tomorrow."

He thought for a moment before answering. "Sure, no worries. Keep it."

I didn't want them to see me sleeping in the car in the street outside the station, so I drove around until I found a small park nearby. I pulled in and settled down to get some rest, but I was just too nervous to sleep.

A few hours later, I got up and got ready for my first day of work at Radio México. I went to a public restroom, splashed some water on my face, and went out to buy a dozen doughnuts to win over the broadcaster running the show that morning—the headlines were transmitted during breaks in his program, at the top of every hour—and I headed for the station.

I was very nervous.

"Hi, how are you? Nice to meet you," said Damian, the broadcaster who worked at that hour at Radio México.

"I'm Eddie. I'm here to do the news," I stammered, while the broadcaster stared at me with a look on his face that seemed to say, *What the heck?* Then I went into a tiny back room where they prepared the news for the upcoming live broadcast.

"You're doing the news at what time?" he asked. "There are newscasts at five, six, seven, eight, and nine."

I was so nervous and made so many mistakes that till this day I'd prefer not to remember the details. I mixed up some words, skipped over others, and got my tongue twisted in knots. It was awful.

"Go back in the room," the host said after several failed attempts. "Maybe you're just nervous because you're here with me."

I went back into the room he'd shown me, where another microphone had been set up. I left the door open so I could watch for him to give me the signal to begin the newscast. I tried to deliver, but I was just as bad as before. In fact, it was worse, since the door was open and the host could see the look of embarrassment on my face. Then he started getting really angry.

"Where the hell did they get you from?" he said. "Who told you you were a newscaster?"

"No, don't worry," I argued. "I'll try harder. I'll get it. Just listen." And I tried again.

But the more I tried, the more I got it wrong, to the point where I finally realized that no matter how many times I tried, it was always going to come out the same way.

"You know what?" I said. "There aren't any more news feeds coming in."

And I started repeating the previous story, thinking that since I'd already been over it a number of times and knew what it was about, I'd have an easier time with it. But even then I couldn't handle it, and the newscast was a total disaster. I was sure they were going to fire me on the spot, as soon as Sergio, the program director, found out what had happened.

But that didn't happen. Sergio didn't fire me, and I can only assume it was because he could see my dedication. I stayed at the studio that day until after dusk, offering to help in whatever way I could. I ended up staying for several days, sleeping in the same car. Eventually, my friend realized he had no other choice than to let me keep it for the week. Sometimes I'd drive back to Santa Ana to clean some apartments, because I hadn't left my previous job, but I always went back to Corona, and stayed at the station as long as possible.

I can't say that I did the news very well on the second day, either. It took time, and whenever I messed up, the same thing happened: The host would get angry, while Sergio would tell me to keep going, and not to get discouraged.

"I'll stay here" was my answer. I wasn't just talking about the job, which of course I wanted to keep—and it was a decision Sergio had to make—but I was also talking about staying there as many hours each day as possible to keep practicing. And to help out the other broadcasters in any way I could, even if it meant sweeping the studio floor without being asked.

Besides volunteering for different duties, I'd always bring something with me to the studio every day, just like I'd done when I visited the Radio Éxitos studio: Mexican bread, tacos, doughnuts, whatever food I could think of. I'd also make the coffee and do whatever I could to make sure the host wouldn't get upset.

"Sorry. I just can't help myself," I'd say as a pretext. But there was no getting him to relax.

As the days went by, Sergio saw more and more how devoted I was to doing things right, not to mention the crazy amount of overtime I was putting in, doing everything I could. I even ran errands for them! For example, if someone said, "Hey, we need to get the new Antonio Aguilar LP."

I'd say, "I'll go."

And I'd fly off to the store to buy it.

In fact, most of the time, I'd pay with my own money, even though they told me the owner of the station was in charge of that.

Once I finally got the hang of things, they eventually asked me to continue doing the news every day as a full-time newscaster. The previous one had never returned from Mexico, and I never knew why. But I wasn't interested in finding out. This was my opportunity, and I wasn't about to let it go.

I started commuting from Santa Ana to Corona every day, which was about an hour each way. I remember being completely sleep-deprived, because not only was I still cleaning apartments, as I mentioned. I was also still working part-time at the photo shop.

Because of the exhaustion, there were times I fell asleep at the wheel. Before my first radio gig, I received repeated fines for falling asleep in the old Buick Regal, before it ended up being stolen from my brother. And once, I had dozed off while driving down the freeway in a rainstorm. I woke up as the car was heading straight for the median, but I was able to get it back under control, and fortunately nobody crashed into me, and I didn't hit anyone else. But it was very frightening.

Once, I even got two tickets in the same day, for riding the line. Of course, I was falling asleep and didn't realize I had drifted out of my lane.

Now, thinking back, I realize how risky it was to drive despite being so exhausted, but the joy and excitement of having gotten that job—of finally being behind a microphone—well, there just wasn't anything like it. I was willing to push my limits to work in radio.

So to keep from dozing off and being pulled over, I'd roll down the car window and stick my head out so my eyes physically couldn't close while I was driving down the 91 freeway. Someone even told me to rub chilis on my eyelids to help keep me awake. I tried it once, but all it did was make my eyes burn and tears run down my face.

I was doing everything I could to help out and learn the radio business when one day Sergio came to me and said he needed someone to do a two-hour music show, and asked me if I knew of anybody.

"When's the show?" I asked.

"From midnight till two a.m."

"I'll do it," I replied, again, without a moment's hesitation. Finally, an opportunity to do exactly what I'd been dreaming of, ever since I was making demo tapes and dropping them off at radio stations.

"How could you do that, if you live in Santa Ana, and you have to be here to do the news at five a.m.?" he asked, surprised.

"It'll be fine. I'll do it," I insisted.

He agreed, and I threw myself into it. That was the first show where I introduced myself as Piolín. It was the beginning of an adventure I never thought I'd get to experience, and which has brought me so many blessings and so many challenges that made me who I am today.

Since I had to read the news just three hours after finishing the music show, I'd lean back in the chair and nap for a little while. But after a few days of doing this, one night, I thought I was dying, because my head fell back, my throat closed up, and I felt like I was choking. When I finally woke up, I was terrified because I had no idea what had happened.

What the heck? I wondered.

Then I remembered. That night I was playing to the audience and reading some love poems on the air. Some of them were sent in by listeners, while others I'd looked up and linked to a particular song. I was trying to get in tune with the style of the program.

Someone had called in requesting an Antonio Aguilar song, and while it was playing, I decided to go out and grab the sack of bread I'd forgotten in my car. It was a really windy night, but I didn't think much of it at the time. I started heading over to where my car was parked, when all of a sudden I heard the station door slam shut. I was locked outside, all by myself, and the only thing I could think was, *Man, now they're really gonna fire me.*

But then, almost immediately, another concern came to mind: My colleagues used to tell me to be careful because it wasn't safe to go out at night, not only because of criminal activity in the region but also because of the bobcats and mountain lions that were known to roam the area.

At first, I thought about climbing on top of my car, but what good would that do? I might have been able to fend off a bobcat, but what if someone wanted to rob me? And then there was the larger issue: the show. So I decided that the first thing I had to do was find a way to get back inside of the station, no matter what. I poked around the station house for a way in, but all I succeeded in doing was getting covered in mud from the cold and rainy weather. I soon realized that my only option to get back inside was to break in through the bathroom window, so I punched the glass with my fist.

Of course, I never thought about using something to protect myself, so by the time I had gotten back inside the station, my arm and hand were covered in blood. Also, in desperation, I didn't think to clear the glass from the edges of the windowsill, so my back and neck were badly cut up as well. I didn't realize it at the time, because all I was focused on was getting back to the studio and finishing the program.

The first thing I did was pull the LP out of the record player, though it had long since finished the final track, and all you could hear was static. I switched on the microphone and blurted out, "Well, we listened to every song on Antonio Aguilar's new album; hope you enjoyed them!" I said, pretending I'd played them all on purpose. "What beautiful music!"

Then I paused for a commercial break, and that's when I realized my clothes were covered in blood. *Now what am I gonna do?* I thought. *The morning show host will be here soon. . . . What's he gonna say? How will I explain the broken window?*

I kept playing song after song while trying to clean myself up with toilet paper. But I was cut in so many places that the blood just kept gushing out. But eventually it began to clot, and since I was wearing a dark, long-sleeved shirt, I was hoping that it would cover everything up so nobody would know what happened.

When the morning host finally arrived, and before he went into the bathroom and started asking a lot of questions, I told him that someone must have thrown a rock through the window, because there was broken glass all over the floor.

"See, I told you to be careful. You'd better not go outside at night!" he replied.

Working at Radio México was really exciting. It was my first test to see if being a broadcaster could be a real career for me. And in the end, the answer was simple, because—regardless of all the hours I put in, all the late nights and hours of commuting back and forth on the freeway, and all the mistakes I made on air—I never felt discouraged, I never let exhaustion get the best of me, and I never once thought of giving up.

CHAPTER 14

PROBLEMS WITH DOCUMENTATION

The next year, 1991, Ramón—the guy who hired me to work for his cleaning company in Irvine—told me that Radio Éxitos was looking for someone to do the graveyard shift; that is, to be on the air from midnight till five a.m. Without giving it a second thought, I went to talk to Sergio.

"I need this chance," I said. "Look, it's closer to my house. I'm really grateful to you, but I need this chance. It's a bigger station, and . . ."

"Sure, yes, go for it!" he replied. There were no bad feelings between us. He'd always been very good to me, and I will always be grateful to him.

And that was how I started working at Radio Éxitos. For a few months, I actually worked at both stations, since they weren't directly competing with each other. And even then, when I was done working in the mornings, I'd still go clean apartments. After six months with Radio México, I thanked Sergio for all his support and for believing in me. It was then that I decided to focus all my efforts on the station in Santa Ana.

After two years working from midnight to seven a.m., I got the opportunity to have my own program on the two to seven p.m. shift, which was better not only because I wouldn't be up working all night, but also because there's a much greater audience during that time frame. The broadcaster who had been hosting the show had left the station, and the management was bringing in different hosts on a trial basis. In the end, they decided to keep me on for that time slot, and together we all decided to call the show *Piolín por la Tarde* (*Piolín in the*

Afternoon). It was the first show to bear my nickname, though everyone who knew me called me by that name. I went with it because I wanted to really own the show and have my name stamped across it. I had big dreams and important things I wanted to do with this show.

The program involved playing music, making conversation and jokes and breaking traffic and local news. We publicized events in the area, and gave weather reports.

The target audience for the show was immigrants like me, people who spoke Spanish and were in a similar situation of not having been in the country for very long, and who were looking for ways to get ahead.

And even though my own situation was improving, I kept on making coffee, bringing food to the station, running errands, and staying late whenever needed. I wanted to show my appreciation for the opportunity that was being presented to me, and besides, I really enjoyed being there, doing what I loved.

But most of all, it was because I believed, and still do, that you should never give less than a hundred percent effort, especially if you're doing well for yourself. Stay passionate and keep challenging yourself by knowing that you could do and be better.

It was during that two-to-seven time slot that I started forming "clubs" where singers and band members and I would prepare and sell food to raise funds to help the community. I also started a segment of the show called "The Comedy Club" where we'd crack jokes and tell riddles and launch the so-called *piolibombas*, which were inspired by the *yucateca* bombs, humorous or rhymed popular sayings pronounced during musical pauses that are very traditional and common in the Yucatán state of Mexico.

Another one of the clubs was "The Piolín Club," which we used to organize fund-raisers and get food to the hungry, or scholarships to students who couldn't afford basic school supplies. I was inspired to create this club by something my family had always instilled in me: a sense of solidarity with those who need help the most. Because when we lend a hand to others, it helps us all to become stronger and better. If we help provide a decent meal to just one person, he or she will have more energy to do his or her job better, which means better products or services for us all. If we help someone pay for his or her studies, it means we will have a more educated community that's better prepared to take full advantage of future opportunities.

Sometimes, I'd read love poems and we also had a segment I called "Piolín Is Cupid," where we'd help reunite separated couples or set two people up on a blind date live on the air. Most of the time, whatever problems caused the breakup were small enough to be fixed on air, and some of the people who called in for the live blind dates ended up getting married.

Other times, however, the issues were a bit more complicated. Once, the problem was that there had been an affair, and yes, the situation got heated. I had no idea how to calm some of these people down, especially when they started cursing on the air, which I had to quickly bleep out the words.

"You want forgiveness? Well, first why don't you go find that [bleep] you slept with and tell her she can go to . . ."

And I'd better cut it off right here before some of you readers get offended!

I also did a shout-out segment where people could call in and send greetings to friends and family members.

Besides all of that, I also dedicated some of the songs we played. For example, fast-forward to when I met María, my future wife, and was working at another radio station. I used to play the "Vida, yo te amo" song by La Mafia. I never mentioned on the air that I was dedicating it specifically to her; I just said it was going out to "a special girl." María would be listening, and since I told her beforehand, she knew that I was playing it for her. But sometimes she liked to joke around and tell me it wasn't true, that I'd probably had some other "special girl" out there on the side. But of course, we both knew that wasn't the case.

We also gave traffic and weather reports and entertainment news, but the main focus of the program was on joking around and helping out people in need, and as you can see, it was more structured than my first show back at Radio México.

I would work there at Radio Éxitos for several years, including 1994, when two events that I remember very well took place.

The first was the earthquake on January 17 in Northridge, California. It measured 6.7 on the Richter scale and it lasted for about twenty seconds, expanding rapidly and causing severe damage. It was even felt in Las Vegas, 220 miles away. Fifty-seven people died during that quake, and the overall damage was estimated to be twenty billion dollars.

After we learned the extent of the devastation, I invited people from all our different clubs to donate food to those people who had lost their homes and were now sleeping in the streets, in city parks, or in other public spaces. It wasn't the first time we'd asked listeners and other friends of the show to donate something to people in need, but this was the first time we did something specifically for a massive cause like earthquake relief.

The other thing I remember most about 1994 was the issue of immigration was gaining a lot of attention. It was during that year, on a day like any other, that the owner of the radio station asked me for my papers. I had to admit that I was undocumented.

"If you don't have any documentation, then I have to let you go. INS has been asking me for them," he said flatly. "If I don't comply, they can close down the station."

I didn't know what to say. I loved my job, but I knew I couldn't put the owner in danger of losing his business. The sad part is that I would later learn that some of my colleagues who wanted my time slot told the boss that I was undocumented, and they took advantage of the situation to argue that they should be hired instead of me. Well, they succeeded, because just like that, I lost my job and had to leave the station. No further statements were made, nor could I say good-bye to my listeners. The members of the various clubs that I'd formed even went to the Radio Éxitos offices and protested with banners and everything. They wanted me to come back, and they wanted an explanation for why I'd been let go. But the company declined to make any other statements, even though the program had developed a large following and the station was getting tons of phone calls and demands from the public.

When people would see me on the street and asked me what happened to the program, I just told them that they fired me for not having my documents in order. That explanation was a bit risky, because if that news ever fell into the hands of the wrong people, things could have gotten even more difficult for me. But all that mattered to me was that my listeners knew the truth about what had happened.

Eventually, word got around, and some of the listeners started petitioning the station owner to help me apply for a work visa. But that never happened, and I never worked for Radio Éxitos again.

The issue of not having my papers in order caused a lot of problems. I never liked being undocumented, and ever since I got to the United States, I'd been trying to legalize my status. The year I crossed the border, 1986, was the same year that President Reagan signed a law granting amnesty to undocumented immigrants. A lot of people suggested I buy an agricultural laborer card, which is a false letter stating that I had been in this country for several years, working in the fields. I was sixteen, and we were all afraid to do that. But later there were times when I'd come to regret not taking that chance, because the path to legalization for people in my situation was more complicated than I could possibly have imagined. The fact is that getting your legal papers is always difficult for any undocumented immigrant, and while there are certain options available, there are also many dangers, and it's very important to make the right decisions at just the right times.

In any case, I'd go and talk with immigration counselors every chance I got, mostly in churches, which would offer those sorts of consulting services. I'd also call immigration attorneys who ran ads on the radio, but the answer was always the same: *You don't have any options.*

And there were—as there are now—many scam artists. On more than one occasion, someone would claim to be able to legalize my status and all my papers for a small amount of money, and I ended up becoming a victim of that trap. Sometimes we get caught up by the idea of an easy fix, instead of accepting that when you don't have all your documentation in order, there's no magic solution. And in 1992, I fell into a bigger trap, because I was even more desperate to find a way out, a beacon of hope that would finally allow myself to legalize my situation. I was terrified of what might happen if I continued on as an undocumented immigrant; I didn't even want to fill out a gym membership form because I was afraid they'd find out I was undocumented and they'd report me to immigration. I didn't even want to think about the possibility of being deported, because the fear it inspired made my stomach turn. By that time, the United States had already become my country. Everything I wanted, and everything I did, was in the hopes of staying here.

As I was walking down the street, I passed an office with a sign hanging out front that read, *We fix your papers here.* Innocently enough, I decided to enter. The people whom I spoke with gave me a lot of false hope, and told me there was a way to get a work permit. All I needed to do was provide them with a few documents: the lease of the house I was living in, records of the money I sent back to my mom, proof of being employed, education records, et cetera. And, of course, money. I left the office very excited and I went straight home to collect everything they had asked for.

Soon after that, I returned to the office with copies of my paperwork and the money they needed to start my case: one thousand hard-earned dollars. They told me the process could take some time, but that I shouldn't worry, because the work visa would come and it would be well worth the wait. But after several weeks had passed and the permit had yet to arrive—and in the meantime I had started working for Radio México, which some people told me not to do without papers—I decided to go back to the office to find out what was going on.

You can imagine my surprise and horror when I found that the office had shut down and nobody knew anything about them! Reporting the fraud to the police was unthinkable, because I was worried the police would arrest me and send me back to Mexico.

That's why it's always important to be on the lookout for fake lawyers who do nothing but take advantage of the needs of the community. Before giving anyone your money or your paperwork, you must inform yourself about them to decide if what they're offering is legitimate.

After that, and against my better judgment, I gave up on trying to fix my situation, and I decided to get another set of fake documents. I couldn't believe how many problems this ended up causing, not the least of which being a job I loved and felt passionately about.

After being fired by the station, I spoke again with Ramón. There were so many things to worry about. Just a few months before that, my brother Jorge and I had bought a house for my parents in Mira Loma, and we still had many payments left to make. Jorge was still working at the Hilton in Irvine, and by that time he'd moved up to become their pastry chef. We were splitting the mortgage payments between the two of us, and my suddenly being out of work put us in serious risk of losing the house.

I didn't know how to tell my parents about what had happened. How would they handle it? What would happen to my job, my future? The fear of deportation was becoming increasingly real, and I spent many sleepless nights worrying about everything that had been put at risk: mortgage payments on my parents' house, my career that was just on the verge of taking off, my family whom I'd probably never see again if I had to go back to Mexico under those circumstances. I felt fear, anxiety, sadness, and hopelessness all at once. As I look back, I can't help but think about the millions of undocumented immigrants out there who are in danger of being deported and are living in constant fear, thinking and feeling the same exact things I was during that uncertain time of my life.

CHAPTER 15

A NEW LIGHT

Sometimes, life puts us in difficult situations, and most of the time, we aren't sure what to do. We feel trapped, unable to move, and we feel that everything we fought so hard to build is in danger of collapsing. But what we don't realize is that the solution to our problems could be closer than we think, or in the least expected places.

I wasn't dealing with a small problem. I was in a real mess: For one, I had lost a job I really enjoyed, and I wanted to continue growing in that field. And on top of that, I had lost my primary source of income. This second issue didn't concern me too much, because I knew I could get by collecting cans, washing cars, developing photos, cleaning apartments, and whatever else. Finding work and a way to help out my family had never been an issue.

What worried me the most was that I'd reached a point where my legal status in this country had become a problem. I knew it would be very hard to move forward with my dreams and my career now that the path was closed.

I even thought about changing my name as a way of hiding my identity. Maybe move to another state where nobody knew me and start again, from the bottom, in the radio business. But how far could I go before the same thing happened again? Because of the type of work I was doing, my visibility was greater than if I sat behind a desk or worked in a field or at a supermarket. It was possible that, if I became successful again, someone would recognize me, and before I knew it, I'd be in trouble again.

I felt hopeless, frustrated, and scared. During times like these, I think the best way to find guidance is to put your trust in God, surrendering to Him and His will. And you have to trust yourself, take what you've learned to heart, and be thankful. That's what I did.

Ramón helped me out again, generously lending me his cell phone so I could search for a new job, and back then, making calls on a cell phone was really expensive. I'd call radio stations all over the place, because I wanted to keep working in that industry, and before I tried another career path, I wanted to exhaust all of my possible options.

Finally, after making countless calls and visiting several different stations, I got a glimmer of hope from Óscar Gabriel, who was born in El Salvador and was the program director for a station in Oxnard, California.

"Swing on over here and we'll see what happens," he said over the phone. Immediately I went to see him.

The station was called Radio Lazer, and it broadcasted on an FM frequency, which was different from the stations I had previously worked at, all of which transmitted on AM frequencies.

When I got there, I sat down for an interview with Óscar. He asked me a number of questions, before we came to the part which I had been dreading.

"Why did you leave your previous position?" he asked.

"Well, there were some changes," I said simply. Not in a million years would I refer to the fact I had no papers. I'm sure that at the time I came across as calm and in control, but inside my heart was pounding rapidly. "You know how it goes when people start making changes."

And that was it. He didn't press the issue any further, and promised to call me if anything was available. I left there still unsure of what might happen, but thinking that at least one door could still be open. And in the end, they offered me the job hosting my own show from two to seven in the afternoon. I accepted. It was a good opportunity, and it would allow me to continue to reach out to my listeners, to create a new audience, and to continue to work hard helping my community.

But learning from my past experience, I figured I'd need a plan B in case something were to happen again. It's important to be prepared, because you never know when you might be out of a job. What if word got around in the industry about my undocumented status and they fired me again? And what if that meant that all the doors to the radio business would be closed to me forever?

I knew that computers were playing an increasingly important role in the daily lives of businesses—I was seeing more of these machines on reception desks, in office cubicles, and in every store—so I decided to take a couple of computer classes right there in Oxnard. I wanted to learn enough about computers and software to have the skills needed for an office job. That way, if I lost another broadcasting job, I'd have another set of skills to fall back on.

However, Oxnard was far from Mira Loma, where I was living. Now I had enough money to continue making my share of the mortgage payments on my parents' house and still rent a small place in Oxnard.

The place I rented was literally just one room: empty, unfurnished, and small. But since I've always believed in saving money to secure a future, I barely bought anything to put in there. I even slept on the floor! I just threw a few blankets down and wrapped myself up in them. Sleeping like that wasn't a problem for me, not only because I'd be exhausted after a hard day's work and ready to fall asleep, but also because lying down on a hard surface helped me relax and sleep better. And when I visited my parents on the weekends, I could sleep in a bed then.

There's a lot of agriculture in Oxnard, and while driving through the area, I could see people suffering and struggling to work under the sun, in high temperatures, and it occurred to me that I should start bringing them water, burritos, and tacos.

Agricultural work had always impressed me, ever since growing up in Ocotlán and seeing my paternal grandfather, Jesús, laboring hard, day after day, to cultivate the small little plot of land that he rented. While I was on my way to the station, driving through the farmland was a daily reminder of his hard work and that of the migrant workers. I thought, *That's gotta be the most tiring job there is.* Sometimes I'd stop and visit with them.

Well, I didn't just stop to talk. It also had to do with the car I had at the time, which tended to overheat and shut down. It was a piece of junk. So I'd have to pull over near a farm and ask the workers if they had water to cool down the engine, and while I waited, we'd start to talk. They told me about their experiences and the working conditions, what they were doing to raise their families, and how those of them who weren't born here had come to America. They told me about family members they'd left behind, and what they missed about home. Those car breakdowns were always great chances for nice conversations.

These talks also reminded me of my grandfather Bartolo. One of the things I missed a lot when I came to the United States was how I'd spend my Sundays in Ocotlán, when my grandpa would take us first to church and then to play at a sports facility. I remember how all my cousins and all my aunts and uncles would be there, and how he always tried to please everyone: He'd play baseball with some, soccer with others, and volleyball with the rest. Sometimes, to add to the excitement, we'd make bets with one another, and the losing team would have to buy the juice we'd drink after the games. And after all of that, my grandfather would invite all his daughters and their families over for a family potluck: pozole, carne asada, anything we could think of. We'd have a great time, and those gatherings always infused me with a sense of community.

These conversations with the farmworkers, the memories of growing up with my family, and the solidarity with those who need it made me think that it would be a good idea to organize a picnic. At first I did it on my own, but then I got the station involved in the hopes of providing even more help.

Now, when I went out to the fields, it wasn't only to get water for my radiator or to drop off some food. When I visited with the workers, I'd tell them, *Keep it up. . . . Listen, I work at a radio station, and I'm going to talk with the program director there to see if he'll chip in for more food.* They liked the sound of that and talked and nodded among themselves. I spoke with my boss, and he approved the plan to donate food, organize events, and get involved. That's how we started working together on promotions and other ways to benefit our community.

After working with Radio Lazer for a while, I found a new room to rent with a different family who lived in Camarillo, twenty minutes from Oxnard. They were always very kind to me, and we ended up becoming quite close. They saw how hard I was working to help out my parents.

I would always do extra little things for my parents, because they were the ones who taught me that you should always be grateful in life. It not only shows the people who have been kind to you how appreciative you are; it also makes you happy and gives you a feeling of satisfaction at having done it. It connects you with people, and with God.

I ended up working for Radio Lazer for only about six months, because one day, in the middle of a show, after a segment spent telling a bunch of jokes, a call came through. I never thought that my tenure at that station would end the way it did, but I can't always predict what happens in life. Several months before, when I lost my previous job, my concerns about my career were centered on my legal status in this country. But this time I would be leaving a job I loved for a reason that had nothing to do with my papers.

The person calling in between segments was José, a program director from a station in Sacramento that wanted to try some new things. Up until then, the station he was calling from, Super X, had broadcast only in English, but they wanted to flip everything around and do the broadcast entirely in Spanish.

"Hey, I was told I should speak with you. We're building a new team to take this station in a new direction," he said.

And I never could have imagined the changes that were about to happen in my life.

CHAPTER 16

"THEY'RE LYING, RIGHT?"

By this point, I'd experienced firsthand the envy and jealousy that's not uncommon among people in the communications industry. So when I got the call from José, the program director from Sacramento, I tried to remain hesitant and keep my guard up, not knowing exactly if what he was offering was legitimate.

"Well, I'm doing pretty well here," I said. "Besides, I'm close enough to my family, you know, my mom and dad, who live in Mira Loma, in Riverside County. . . . Sacramento is seven hours away, so I wouldn't be able to see them as often."

No matter how hard he tried, he just couldn't convince me. I was also afraid that my bosses at Radio Lazer would find out about the call, so I decided to talk to them about it. Yes, it's true. I had to watch my back, but the thought of moving so far away from my parents didn't sit right with me.

After the call, and shortly after the show had ended, I went to Óscar's office and asked if I could speak with him.

"I'm very grateful to you," I said, "and that's why I want to be totally honest and up front with you: I just got a call from a programmer at another station who told me there was an opportunity to work with them. I don't want to leave this job; I just wanted to keep you informed, in case any rumors started floating around, because I wouldn't want you to misinterpret anything. So whatever issue may come up, I'll tell you about it. It's important that you know."

"Ah, okay, very well," he said nonchalantly.

Even though I turned him down, the program director at Super X came down to Oxnard in person to try to convince me to leave. But his efforts failed to succeed. I was actually quite happy with where I was working; the owner of the station, Alfredo Plascencia, had always been nice to and supportive of me; the program was doing well; I enjoyed all my listeners, my team at the studio, and the people with whom I was living. I also knew that I'd been given a really good opportunity after being fired from Radio Éxitos for having fake documents. I didn't want to seem ungrateful. Nor could I overlook the possibility that this was a strategy cooked up by a competitor who wanted to get me out of the game, since I was already doing well at Radio Lazer, drawing bigger crowds to the events and driving up the ratings.

That was when I got a call from José's boss, Jeff Holden, who was Anglo and not Latino, and between English and Spanish—he didn't speak Spanish very well, and my English wasn't any better—we were kind of able to understand each other.

"I may be a gringo, but I love Latinos, the whole Latino community," he said. "I started this station in English, but I want to switch it over to Spanish."

"Well, I have to say, my family comes first," I replied. "So I'm afraid I have to say no. But thank you very much."

"Why don't we get together and talk about this? I'll come down to L.A. to meet with you, or you come here. I'll pay for your flight, and you can see Sacramento."

"Thank you, really, but no. You see, it's just that I really appreciate the people for the way they've treated me here."

Despite the failed attempts to change my mind, Jeff flew down to L.A. anyway to meet with me in person. He was blond—though now he's somewhat gray-haired—tall and thin, and he liked to exercise, which is something that connected us right from the very beginning. He's also a very educated man who dresses impeccably and is a very good listener. He also knows how and when to speak.

His arguments were very convincing, and there was good chemistry between the two of us, so much so that I decided I should meet again with my boss. I knew the owners of the broadcasting company were planning on buying up more stations soon, which I thought might turn into good opportunities for my program.

"I want to be honest. I've already met with the general manager of another station," I explained. "I really don't want to leave, but I do want to know what's the next step for me here. I've heard you're interested in buying some other radio stations, but I don't know what your plans are for them. I also know that I'll never have a morning show here, because you've already got a great one. I would never, ever want for it to get bumped, because it's just really that good. And I wouldn't want to do that to someone, because I wouldn't want that kind of thing to be done to me. And with this other station reaching out to me, I'm just not sure what to do."

He kept insisting that I stay, but he knew as well as I did that he couldn't offer me the same opportunities that the other station was putting on the table, including offering me a morning drive show. Radio Lazer had a great morning show, with a host whom I admired, and it was doing really well. I didn't want to push Óscar to replace him. Honestly, I was afraid of what might happen.

With such a difficult decision to make, I felt I should talk with my dad and my brother Jorge, but all they did was get angry because they saw it as something personal.

"You just want to be farther away from us," my dad said. "You just want to go away so you can drink and party."

"No," I stammered. I couldn't believe that he'd said that, knowing full well that I didn't drink and almost never went out to parties. Maybe he was afraid that the same thing that happened to my brother would happen to me, and that's why he'd said something so offensive. I decided not to take it the wrong way and instead explained my reasons: "I need to take the opportunity and start thinking ahead and forging a better life now so I can secure a bright future for all of us. That's always been my wish, and now I have a chance to make it happen."

I didn't end up convincing them, but by then I had almost convinced myself.

In an attempt to seal the deal, Jeff flew me to Sacramento and toured the city with me, showing me where my people lived, where all the taquerias and Mexican stores were located. I felt at ease, and finally—after the trip, and after talking with me about the specifics of the new show, including the fact that it would be in the morning—I was convinced. But I had to say: “Honestly, I’m still just a kid who is trying to help out his family. And, well, I’m also taking some computer classes down there in L.A.”

“You can do that here too,” he replied. “I’ll help you.”

I was practically sold, but first I wanted to speak one last time with Óscar back at Radio Lazer, to let him know what I was thinking, and to see if he could come up with a reason for me to stay there.

“As I told you before, I don’t want to leave,” I told him when we finally sat down to meet, “but I need to know what’s in store for me here. I don’t mean to force your hand, but I do need to know something, at least. I truly am happy with what you’ve done for me here, and the only difference with this other station is the opportunity to do a morning show for the first time.”

In the radio business, the prime real estate is the morning show, from six to ten a.m. Most of a station’s net revenue comes from that time slot, because it gets the best ratings. The better your ratings are, the higher you can charge for commercial advertising. The time slots with the lowest ratings generate less profits. The second most important time slot is from two to seven in the afternoon, which was the position I currently held at Radio Lazer.

“I don’t want you to leave either,” he said. “But the fact is I have no way to keep you.”

I didn’t want to part on bad terms, and what I had said up to that point was true, but still he seemed a little upset. I think he assumed I was trying to get something out of the situation, to play it for my own advantage. And even though I was looking for something that would make me stay with them, I wasn’t asking for anything I didn’t deserve. So his answer made me realize that my future at Radio Lazer would be a short one.

That’s what it took to finally tip the scales.

“I understand. But I’d like to leave the door open, because I truly am grateful to you.”

And ultimately we were able to part on good terms, and I could move on with a clear conscience.

Then it was on to Sacramento to begin a new phase of my life, one that would forever change me. The excitement of the move, the new prime time show, the challenge of being a part of a brand-new project and making it grow and succeed occupied my thoughts and my time.

But I still had one big problem: no papers. I hadn't shared that fact with Jeff or with anyone else at La Super X. I simply did what I'd done before: I gave them my fake green card and my fake Social Security number.

And then, we launched the new station.

Back then, we didn't have much of a budget. We were just trying to carve out a successful niche. So I'd take the company van from the studio parking lot and drive to churches, soccer clubs, parks . . . any place I could think of to help get the word out, raise funds, or organize events. I also drove out to construction sites and farms, bringing food and water to the workers.

I kept on working just as hard in Sacramento as I did in Oxnard. I continued my habit of sleeping in the office—though this time on the floor, so the bosses wouldn't find out—and I put in as many hours as possible. I'm not even exaggerating when I say my only excursion was going to the laundromat.

And even then, my lack of documentation always hung as a threat.

One day, while waiting for my clothes to be ready, I went to a nearby store where they were raffling off coffee mugs. I thought it might be fun to participate, so I drew what turned out to be a winning number. But before I could claim my prize, the person asked me for my information, including my Social Security number.

Of course, the whole point of the raffle was to get contact information from the participants so they could later send them advertisements. I wrote illegibly, making up the numbers and signing a fake name, all from the fear that they would realize that I didn't have my documents. But the manager figured it out.

"I'm sorry, but without your paperwork, we can't give you the coffee cup," she said.

"Here's your cup back. Excuse me," I said as I rushed out of there, worried they were going to call immigration on me. I remember thinking, *Wow, I can't believe they need to check my papers just for a coffee mug!* That's when I started being afraid to even leave the apartment.

At the station, I was always talking about how I liked to help out my family, and I think Jeff might have been a bit suspicious about it all and decided to find out whether it was all true, because one day he said he wanted to go to L.A. and visit my parents' house. He invited me to go with him, but I decided to stay in Sacramento, because—of course—I was afraid I'd get caught at the airport. I told him I couldn't go myself, but that my family would be happy to meet him and welcome him into their home.

That would be the first time that Jeff ever tried a *chile de árbol*. My dad plucked it straight from the plant, handed it to Jeff, and said, *Give it a try.* Jeff thought he was going to die; he turned all shades of red, and could barely catch his breath. But he enjoyed all the food they fixed for him and the company of my family, and he realized that we really are all very close, and that I wasn't exaggerating when I talked about them. Jeff was thrilled when we returned back to Sacramento.

"Wow, what a great family you've got!" he said. "Now I know why you talk about helping them out so much."

Eventually, all the hard work, heavy promotion, and overtime paid off, because the morning show I hosted became number one—first in Spanish, and then overall—in the Sacramento market. I remember going anywhere and everywhere to attract new listeners, from local events to all the clubs and organizations I could think of. I put in a lot of hours doing the programming, and if I had to choose between going out to a movie or a nightclub and staying late to prepare for our next broadcast, I always chose the latter, because I've always believed that you have to put in a little bit extra, no matter what you want to accomplish. It's essential if you ever want to get ahead.

And the extra effort reflected through the quality of the show. The listeners knew it. They could hear how well prepared and well produced the broadcast was.

Becoming the number one show was a great accomplishment, especially when you consider the fact that nobody had believed in us, since we didn't have the same level of experience as the other, better-established Spanish language stations, which had been broadcasting for years, and on stronger signals as well.

Obviously, this unexpected success was a cause for much envy, and someone at one of the competing stations reported me to the immigration authorities. A friend of mine who worked at that station told me that one of his colleagues did a little research into why I'd left Radio Éxitos, and called the authorities.

I remember being in the broadcast booth, looking through the window into the hallway, when I saw Jeff walking toward me. He came in. That was unusual.

"Hey, I need to talk to you," he said. His face was completely red. The first thing that crossed my mind was, *What did I say? Was it something bad? Maybe I made some off-color joke?* But I was wrong. What Jeff said next made my blood run cold:

"Some immigration officers are here. They're lying, right?"

"About what?" I asked, terrified.

"They're saying you have a fake green card, that it's not yours. But I have copies of all your documents on file. . . . It's authentic, right? And the officers are telling me that your Social Security number doesn't match your name."

"They're right, Jeff."

"Don't say that. How is this even possible, if you're helping your parents and all?"

He simply didn't understand what it meant to be an undocumented immigrant, the reasons and motivations for people coming into this country crossing the border through the desert in the night. Jeff knew the community, but he hadn't fully come to understand their deeper problems and concerns. He had good intentions—he was understanding and open—but he didn't know how hard it was to get the necessary papers to work legally in this country.

"How could this happen? Explain it to me," Jeff repeated.

"Look," I said, "I submitted my paperwork, but they can't issue me a work permit because there still isn't a law, a reform, nothing. So I have to wait."

"Well, they're waiting for us in the office, so let's go there. I don't want them to think you're trying to run away out the back."

I could not believe it. I was walking down the hall to his office, where two immigration officers were waiting, and they could arrest me and take me out of here in handcuffs. When we got there, Jeff started talking to them, explaining who I was and what I represented to him, to my family, and to the community.

"He's a very loving son," he kept repeating. "He takes care of his parents; he just bought them a house in Mira Loma."

"That may be true, but we're just doing our job here," said one of the officers.

"So what can we do, then?" Jeff asked. "He's a leader of the community. He's an important voice, and if you take him away, the community will lose an important member. It will be impacted, in a negative way."

The officer thought it over for a minute. "Look, we could just take him away with us right now," the officer said bluntly. "In fact, I should arrest him, toss him in the vehicle, and deport him. But we won't." Was I hearing that right? "Because, as far as he goes, he already has an order of deportation on his record." He handed me a single sheet of paper where it was stated that I had ninety days to resolve this situation in front of a judge. "But if I see him on the street, like I said, I'm taking him in, because he's got three months max to leave the country."

And with that, they left.

I started to cry. Then I noticed almost everybody in the office had stopped working because of what was happening, and most of them were crying as well.

It was the first time I'd found myself in that sort of situation, where I felt so close to being taken away and losing everything in an instant, right then and there. I had been found out and was very nearly arrested. Immediately I thought of my parents: What would happen to them? What if they lost the house? My older brother, Jorge, and I still hadn't finished paying it off.

I was lost in all these thoughts when Jeff told me I was now unemployed. It was the second time this had happened to me within the span of a single year. It was now 1995, and the issue of immigration reform was growing more and more prevalent in the media and in the eyes of the public.

"Jeff, forgive me. Please forgive me," I said again and again. "I didn't know that what I was doing was so bad. I just didn't know it was a crime. . . . I'm very grateful to you. . . . I'll find a way to get through this."

"Calm down," he replied, with no hint of reproach in his voice. "I'll talk with the owner of the company, Luis Nogales, to see if we have any options . . . but for now, you have to go."

I explained to him how difficult—how virtually impossible—it is to fix your status when you enter the country undocumented. But he insisted he would speak with his bosses to see if there was a solution.

I packed up my things at the office, and then I went to my apartment to gather my blankets, which were about all I had, since I still didn't have a bed. I had the number one show in the area, but I had to walk away and build a new future, hopefully a better one, and think of a clear goal for myself. I had saved up as much money as I could, which wasn't all that much back then. My car was ancient with a coat hanger for an antenna; I bought my shoes at Payless; and I ate instant noodles, always while thinking about building a better life. And now, once again, everything was at risk of being put on hold. The dream was fading and I didn't see a clear way out. But this time, I didn't just lose my job. I had a deportation order on my record, and three months to leave the country.

It really was a complicated situation because I had used a fake residency card and a fake Social Security card.

I said good-bye to my coworker Benito, with whom I was sharing a two-bedroom apartment, and left him with my only other belonging: an old, heavy, massive desk that I'd bought for cheap at a yard sale and that I used to study for my computer classes. I remember he tried to convince me to stay in Sacramento, that there must be a solution.

"No, man," I replied. "I've gotta go back to my parents, because if they catch me here, they'll take me. I have to think long and hard. Maybe I'll move to another state and change my name. I don't know."

"I don't know if changing your name would work. You're already pretty well-known."

And he was right. There were articles out there with both my name and my face. It was only going to get harder to stay under the radar.

CHAPTER 17

WEARING SUNGLASSES AT NIGHT

I left Sacramento at eight o'clock at night, in the darkness, because I thought it would help me go unnoticed. I was so worried about someone recognizing me that I remember putting on sunglasses and even folding down the sun visors in the car.

I cried the whole way down I-5, back to Los Angeles, my head full of questions: What am I gonna tell my parents? How am I gonna be able to help them? What's gonna happen to me? How sad is it that I was just looking for a way to do something positive for my family, and this is what happened? What have I done!?

Most of all, I was upset with myself, because I knew that somehow there was a way I could have prevented this from happening. If only I had worked in some way that didn't expose me to the public, where only a few people knew who I was, this would not have happened. But no, I'd decided to follow my dreams: I thought I could reach them, without ever considering the possibility that they might be off-limits to me. And despite knowing the risk, I decided to keep on going after them, only to run into the same exact problem yet again.

When I finally got home, it was nearing dawn, and I still didn't know what to say to my parents. I was hoping to go straight to my room and wait for my mind to calm down enough for me to think clearly.

I slowly unlocked the door and went inside, making as little noise as possible. As I tiptoed through the hallway, I saw that everything was dark except for a light that was on in my parents' bathroom. Curious, I headed over there.

I opened the door just a crack, and saw my dad putting cream on some burns that he had on his back. I knew they must have come from the excessive heat of his car, which had no air-conditioning and plastic seats. Every day my dad would drive from Riverside to Los Angeles, where he taught photography classes to people who had been severely injured and left unable to work. With those new skills he taught them, those people could at least have one more chance at success.

When I saw the bloody burns, I closed the door with tears in my eyes. "God, I can't believe it," I mutterd. My dad is one of those people who is always looking for ways to help those in need, without ever saying, "Hey, I've got this problem. . . . I could use some help." He always keeps those things to himself, and it's only when I happen to notice something that I realize that something's wrong. Why doesn't he say anything?

"Is that you, son?" I heard him say from the other side of the door.

"Yes, Dad."

"What are you doing here?" he asked.

"Hold on, Dad. Just give me a minute. I have a stomachache." I didn't want him to see me crying, both from the pain of having seen his own wounds, and the pain from what had happened to me just the day before. "Hey, I'm just gonna go to sleep now. I'll talk with you tomorrow. I just got a couple of days of vacation, that's all."

"Oh, good," he said, relieved.

Then I opened the door, though without turning on the light. I wanted to see him, hug him, tell him how much I loved him, and yet I was still just standing there.

"Okay, Dad, I'm going to lie down because my stomach is really upset. And don't turn on the light; it hurts my eyes. I could barely make it home."

"Ah, okay, then, just get some sleep," he said quietly.

I spent the rest of the night furious with myself and with God, because I couldn't comprehend what was going on with my life: the anger and frustration was taking over my mind and my heart. Don't you see what my father is going through? I said, blaming God. Don't you get it?

I started thinking again about moving to another state and starting over with a new life. And I still didn't know what to say to my parents. I couldn't sleep.

When I finally got up, they were still asleep, so I went out to collect enough cans to recycle so I could buy a jug of milk. Even though I had a bit of money saved up, I didn't want to spend it, especially now, knowing that I didn't have a job and would have to get by some other way. The other reason for bringing home the milk was to cover for the fact I had gone out to collect cans. I wanted them to think I'd simply gone out to get something for breakfast.

But my parents weren't that naive.

"Hey, son, how come you've never been able to come for a visit before this?" inquired my dad, after I got back to the house.

He knew I never liked to take a break from work, even for a moment, and that I never liked to miss work, even when I was sick. And I'm not exaggerating: sometimes I'm surprised by the number of vacation days I've built up over the years—vacations I never took and will never take—all because, for me, missing the show just isn't an option. So it struck my dad odd that I was taking time off now.

A couple of days later, Jeff called the house asking for me, something that only increased my dad's suspicions.

"Okay, sure, hand me the phone," I said, trying to sound casual, but my parents were watching me closely while I was on the phone. I tried to be discreet: "So, what's up, Jeff?"

"Well, we're talking with an attorney to see what our options are, and you'll probably have to come meet with him sometime in the next few days. We'll find a solution. But the bad news is that, in the meantime, we can't pay you your salary."

"So how can I get back to Sacramento to meet with you and the lawyer?"

"The thing is, I can't pay for any of your expenses. If they find out that I gave you any money, I could get in trouble with the law."

"I understand."

After I hung up, I turned to my dad again and explained that I'd have to go back to Sacramento for a few days, and then I'd be back in Mira Loma. Even then, a few days after my unexpected arrival, and despite the hints my parents were dropping to get me to open up to them, I still couldn't bring myself to tell them the truth. I know how much my parents tended to worry, and I was afraid I'd make them sick with anxiety.

It was quite possible—it was certain, actually—that the family would be split up once again, that they were going to lose their son, who was being deported back to Mexico without the possibility of returning to the country in which we had all put down roots, where we were established as a family and connected to our community. Surely these were the thoughts that would be passing through their minds, causing much pain and anguish.

"There's a big board meeting coming up, and I have to head back to talk with Jeff about it."

I thought that was a vague enough explanation to successfully erase any lingering concerns and buy me a little more time to find a more convincing excuse or maybe even a solution that would save me from my doomed fate.

I scraped together what little money I had, got in the car, and started heading north on I-5. At the crest of Magic Mountain, after climbing the winding hills through Grapevine, I put the car in neutral and cut the engine so I could coast as far as possible. I figured I could save a little bit of gas that way, and it was something I did each and every time I had to go meet with Jeff and the attorney.

Finally I arrived in San Francisco, where the law firm was located and where we decided to meet.

"Well, we don't have many options," the lawyer said, quite directly. "I've been speaking with Jeff, and he tells me that an order of deportation has been issued for you."

He continued to explain the situation to me. There was little hope of finding a way out of all this, but they would continue to try. I wanted to focus the case on my commitment to and my relationship with the community. I had to make about three more trips, and in the meantime, I kept collecting cans for money behind my parents' back and dodging their questions with vague excuses.

"Just forget about it, Jeff," I'd sometimes say. "I can't keep going on like this, so just forget about it. Eventually my parents are going to find out. I'll just have to go to some other state to find work. I can't thank you enough for all that you've done."

I wanted to throw in the towel and give up. But Jeff wouldn't let me; instead, he would call me on a daily basis with words of encouragement.

He'd seen that I was a good and disciplined person, that I never missed work and always acted responsibly. That also helped him understand that being undocumented wasn't just some oversight or a way to avoid playing by the rules; rather, it was a complicated problem that didn't necessarily mean I was a bad person with malicious intentions. I understand that many Americans think that undocumented immigrants come here without any respect for the law, and instead, the intent to break it. But the reasons that motivate people to cross the border without papers are much more complex: people come here because they want a better future for their families, because they want to contribute to the American dream, and because there are a lot of jobs here that couldn't be done without the help of immigrant workers. And in those cases where legal possibilities do exist, the scope and cost of the process make it virtually impossible for a farmer who barely knows how to read and write and who lives in a remote area of Mexico to come legally into this country where his labor is needed.

I appreciated the unconditional support offered by Jeff, this angel that God had sent to me. He was the one who kept me motivated and determined to move forward. And for that, I'll forever be grateful to him.

CHAPTER 18

"WHY DO WE COME?"

When people call in to my radio show, I often ask them this question.

"¿A qué venimos?" ("Why do we come?)"

"¡A triunfar!" ("To succeed!") my listeners respond.

It's a phrase that has become a motto for my program. Something that people identify with. Once, we even printed up T-shirts with that phrase on it. I still see people wearing them on the streets every once in a while.

At first, I'd mention the name of this country in the response: that we came to the United States to succeed. But one time, a caller corrected me. "No, it should be, why do we come to this world?"

And I agreed: We don't just come looking for success in this country; we want to succeed wherever we are. And that's the beauty of being in touch with people: I can learn from them.

The expression came to me when I was driving down I-5, from Sacramento to my parents' house, after having lost my job for the second time, accompanied only by the sadness and pain of knowing I was on the verge of being deported. At one point, I had to pull over and stop the car because I just couldn't take it anymore, and I had no idea how to face my parents when I arrived in L.A.

I remember sitting there in the parked car, looking at the city lights in the distance, and pondering: *This situation I'm in right now. . . . Surely there are other people out there who are experiencing the same thing. Why do people do this? Why do people come here?* I asked, looking to God for answers. And the response was almost immediate:

They, we, come here to succeed, right? That's where the saying came from, and it has inspired many people.

I found another answer during that trip as well, though it took me a good deal of time before I could fully grasp what it meant. Many times, when something is preventing us from clearly seeing our long-term goals, from understanding the significance of our actions and the love and affection from God, it's because we're refusing to see the signs right in front of us, the ones telling us that we'll find a solution to our problems, the ones giving us the answers we're looking for. At the time, I had begun going to church and learning more about the will of God.

I remember, during that drive, just before I reached Los Angeles, I started shouting and bawling and pounding on the steering wheel with rage. I was completely desperate and hopeless.

"I need to do something now!" I cried. "I need to solve this problem. I'm sick and tired of all this! God, send me a sign. Tell me you're listening. Look, I don't do drugs. I don't drink. I don't do any of that stuff. I help out my family. What more do you want?"

It was then that I saw the antenna of a radio station. There was a light at the top of it, flashing on and off. That was the sign that I needed, the answer from God that I'd been waiting for. *That light is still flashing, and that means there's hope,* I said to myself, though—as I mentioned—it would take some time for me to fully understand the significance. *It means I'm going to come back and show all those people who reported me who I really am. We will be number one again.*

PART THREE

NEW HORIZONS

CHAPTER 19

A HEARTFELT INVITATION

During the most difficult moments in life, when we're facing seemingly impossible odds, we feel compelled to seek refuge in spirituality, to look to God for the answers we need.

I know that if spirituality was not a part of my life, I would have failed many of life's tests, and that if God were not at the top of my list of priorities, then my life would be completely out of order. That's why I strive every day to learn more about the word of God for my own life and for that of my family.

But my journey toward spiritual truth came slowly, step by step, and in a way that I never would have expected.

Although I was born into a Catholic family that attended mass every Sunday, and while God had always been important in my life, He had never occupied the central position that He does today, and that has been a huge help to me as I move forward. During my childhood and teenage years, my relationship with God was something I accepted as a part of my life, but I never really considered—never truly saw—the profundity with which I would later view it, when it became a fundamental part of me, and something that accompanies me each and every day.

The story of how I got closer to God began here in the United States. It started primarily thanks to Fermín, a friend of my dad, whom he'd met a few years earlier outside the photo shop in Santa Ana where he worked. And one day I threw a tantrum.

My dad never stopped being strict with us, even as adults. After I turned eighteen, when I would ask him for permission to go to a party—yes, even at that age, I was asking for permission—he always said I had to be back by nine o'clock. But nine is when the party just starts getting good! There was no way to change my dad's mind, and since it didn't make any sense to go to a party just to leave early, I would end up staying at home.

It was one of those moments, during my senior year in high school, when I was so frustrated and angry with him because of that curfew that I threatened to jump out of a window. That's how important having a good time seemed to me. It's worth mentioning that we lived on the second floor of the building, but under the window was a garden that was soft enough, so if I did jump, at worst, I'd break a leg. I think my dad must have made that same calculation, and believed that even if I jumped, nothing too terrible would actually happen to me. But that didn't stop him from worrying, and with good reason. I was willing to put myself in harm's way if he didn't extend my curfew.

In desperation and not knowing how to calm me down, he called his friend Fermín, and asked him to come talk to me. Back then, Fermín was my dad's only friend. The rest of the family didn't like him much, because he was always talking about God and trying to convince us to see the truth. He never missed an opportunity to invite us to church and to show us the ways in which God manifests Himself in our daily lives. We also believed in God and in Christ, but we were members of a different church, and weren't used to hearing people speak so openly about their faith. And, well, we felt quite happy with the way that we were, or so we thought.

Fermín and my dad met in passing on the street, while my dad was cleaning the sidewalk in front of the photo shop. Fermín worked for the city as a street sweeper, and he often passed by the shop. My dad, being the friendly person he is, introduced himself, and eventually they became quite close.

Right from the very beginning, Fermín would talk about God, and started inviting my dad to come and take photos of church events. And my dad—as I would later do myself—began to learn more about God's will. He started going to church regularly with Fermín, and even joined the choir so they could sing God's praises. My dad really seemed to enjoy Fermín's company and all the church activities they would go to together, but every time Fermín came by the house, we all thought, *Here comes this guy again, just to bother us.* We just wanted him to leave. But eventually, we began to see his generosity.

Whenever my older brother was drinking too much, Fermín would talk to him and help him see that his behavior was hurting both himself and his family. He also spoke to me, on that day when I was threatening to jump out of that window.

My dad called Fermín and explained the situation.

"I just can't control him," I heard him say.

"Get him over here!" I shouted. "I'll break both your noses!"

At that age, I was exercising more and feeling more confident in my own physical strength. I wasn't scared by the threat of my dad or anyone else beating me. In fact, I was so angry about the whole situation, I wasn't afraid of anything.

A few minutes later, Fermín arrived. He walked calmly into the living room, where I was standing. When I saw him there, I got even angrier. I was fed up with my dad's rules, and the last thing I needed was another man coming into our house and telling me what I could and couldn't do. At the time, I didn't like him, and I certainly didn't want to talk to him.

"So you want to jump," Fermín said. "Okay, then, go ahead."

I don't know why, but at that moment I felt paralyzed. I no longer wanted to jump, but I was still angry enough that I threatened to punch him. Fermín asked me if we could talk inside my bedroom. I agreed.

"Fine. If you really want to, go ahead and hit me," he said, once we were standing there, face-to-face. "I won't even put up my hands, because I'm not going to fight with you."

"Take it easy, calm down," my dad said, trying to defuse the situation. He was standing outside my bedroom door, but could still see everything that was going on.

"No, let him hit me," Fermín said, looking directly at me.

And, well, I just couldn't do it. I guess he had the Holy Spirit and God on his side.

"Go ahead, you take the first shot," Fermín insisted. "Why are you so angry?"

"My dad won't let me stay out," I said, feeling my rage rushing back.

"I don't want you going out late because it's dangerous," my dad said, trying to be conciliatory.

"What about all my friends? Their dads let them go out late," I argued.

"Every dad is different," he said. "I want you to have a better life. I love you and I want to take care of you. That's why I don't want you to go. It's just too late."

Fermín told me that he had prayed a lot for me on his way over to our apartment from where he lived, which was about fifteen minutes away. I looked at him in disbelief, but when he started talking to me and explaining his point of view, I found myself listening intently to what he had to say.

"Why don't you value the sacrifices your parents have made for you?" he asked. "The word of God tells us that if you honor your father and your mother, you will live a long, full life in the land the Lord your God is giving to you. Many young people like you are rude to their parents: They yell at them, they talk back to them, they complain. And there are some who even beat and mistreat them. But when they lose their parents, they shed tears of blood because they remember all the evil they have done to them. And when the children become parents themselves, they pay even more for having behaved so badly. So God tells us that if you, as a son, now dishonor your father and your mother, tomorrow your own children will repay you in kind."

I looked at him in complete disbelief of what he was saying. I couldn't move or even speak because I was still so upset. On the other hand, I couldn't help but think, *Here we go again, always talking about God,* and I rolled my eyes. But then again, I was beginning to see that there might be some truth to his words, that maybe he was actually right.

"Laugh if you want," Fermín continued. "But remember that God can take your parents away from you at any time, even when you least expect it. And if the last time you saw them was during an argument like this, you'll regret it deeply. It's important to honor your parents. Honoring them means doing what they ask you to do, unless they are trying to lead you away from God. So even if they yell at you, remember how you act toward them, because that is how your own children will behave in front of you. Be patient with them and try to understand them, and ask God to help you change and improve over time. I promise you, it works, and that they—with your example—will get better. Just like you. That way, when you are a parent yourself, you'll understand why it's necessary to discipline your children. Because we love our children, as God loves us all, and because we want them to become even better."

When he finished talking, I realized he was right: It was important for me to listen to my dad and to understand that everything he did was for my own good. I also thought about the possibility that someday I could have a family of my own—an idea that was increasingly growing on me—and that I'd want everyone to be good as well.

I also understood that Fermín had always wanted good things for us, that he was not just a nosy man but a true friend of my dad's. And, therefore, a true friend of my family. What he said to me that day touched me deeply and left me thinking about my relationship with my parents and about myself. I was very grateful to Fermín because he helped me to see things differently and made me at peace with myself and with my parents.

After that, I calmed down and left the room. I hugged both my parents, and though I didn't realize it, Fermín left us alone for a few minutes to reconcile before returning. I went back to my room knowing that I didn't really want to jump out a window or punch someone's nose in. I cried there for a while, alone, before coming back out. Fermín returned, and he started talking with me about the word of God and how important it was. Then he invited me to church with him.

Or tricked me into going. He knew that I liked to work out, and sometimes he would come over to the apartment complex and invite me to use the exercise machines with him. I'd go, unless I was already working out at the time, in which case he'd invite me to go out and play soccer or something else.

"No, this is fine," I'd say, knowing exactly what he was doing. "All the weights and machines we need are right here."

"We should get some fresh air and, after that, some dinner," he insisted.

On the way back to the apartment, he'd stop outside his church.

"I need to go inside to pick up a few things. It'll just take a second," he said, and opened the car door.

"I'll wait for you here," I said.

"Come on, let's go inside. It won't take long," he promised.

And sometimes I would go inside with him, and could hear people singing praises and praying. *Ah, dang it, this guy tricked me again,* I thought. And honestly, the parishioners seemed to me to be a little bit fanatical, because the way I had learned to praise God as a child was quite different from the born-again Christian way. But I was very fortunate to have had someone like Fermín Villaseñor bring me to church, because it allowed me to grow closer to God and accept Him into my heart.

It was around that same time that my brother Jorge began to suffer from serious health problems because of all his excessive drinking. His liver was beginning to fail, and scans showed a large spot had formed on the organ, and that surgery would be necessary. We didn't have money for such a procedure at the time; actually, we didn't have money for much of anything back then. The day before the operation, Fermín came to visit us in the hospital.

Ugh, that guy's here again? Always getting into other people's business, I thought. And when he started praying for my brother, I left the room.

The next morning, before going into the operating room, they took my brother to get one more presurgery X-ray. And the mark had disappeared! *Amazing,* I thought. And we called Fermín to tell him the good news.

"It is the will of God," he said. "God is acting through him, to serve as a testimony to his family, so that you may spread that testimony to other people."

I still wasn't quite convinced, but after seeing what had happened with my brother, I gave Fermín the benefit of the doubt, and believed in him a little bit more. We started inviting him to our soccer games and began spending more time with him.

After all that, and the night he managed to calm me down and keep me from jumping out of that balcony, I didn't mind seeing Fermín around the house, and sometimes, I even sought out his company. When he would invite me to exercise with him, I slowly began opening up to him, and we started to get to know one another just a little bit better.

And that was how, little by little, I started to accept God into my life, to hear what He was saying, and to allow myself—through Fermín—to grow closer to Him.

But it would still be several more years before the word of God would be fully revealed to me. It happened during that difficult time in my life, when I had lost my job for the second time for being an undocumented immigrant, and I was forced to drive back to my parents' house, halfway across the state of California, in the middle of the night, because I was about to be deported.

God revealed himself to me on that long and stressful drive, when He gave me a sign of hope and a sense of understanding about everything that was happening around me. I didn't see it at the time because my relationship with God was not as close as it could have been. But now, looking over everything that has happened in my life, I realize that He was always there for me, walking alongside me with every step I took: when I first entered this country, and was almost discovered by border patrol agents; in people like Ramón Valerio and Sergio and Jeff Holden, who believed in me enough to ask me to work for them; in my family, who were always there to support me during the difficult times of my life; and in countless other people whom I've met throughout my life.

But the moment when I heard Him speak to me was shortly after I arrived at my parents' house in Mira Loma, having lost my job in Sacramento and being issued an order of deportation, and years after Fermín had spoken with me for the first time about gradually accepting God into the depths of my being.

It was on that sad day in Mira Loma when I picked up the phone and called Fermín to tell him what was happening.

"I can't take it anymore," I said, sobbing desperately. "I'm just . . . so angry . . . with God."

"Invite Him into your heart," he said. "But do it from your heart. He will do things you never thought possible, and He will put you in places you never thought you'd be."

And again, Fermín was right. I needed to put more trust in God, put myself in His hands, because He was the only one who can show me the way. I felt a great sense of relief, because that was the moment when I finally realized that it was He who guides my steps, and to whom I have entrusted my life. It is only with Him that I can move forward and find the peace and wisdom with which to face any kind of difficulty.

"You know what?" I replied. "I thought I'd already done that, but maybe I haven't. Maybe I was wrong. So right now, at this very moment, I am giving my life to Christ. I want to do it, and I want His will to be done. I'm sorry I got so angry, God. Please forgive me."

And we began to pray together. The two of us.

While writing this book, I was reading a Bible passage that reminded me of that time, which I'd like to share:

Jeremiah 29: 11–13

"For I know the plans I have for you," declares the Lord, "plans to prosper you and not to harm you, plans to give you hope and a future. Then you will call on me and come and pray to me, and I will listen to you. You will seek me and find me when you seek me with all your heart."

Fermín is an angel who never gave up on me, even when I rejected him. He put the seed of God's word in us. First my dad, then me, then my brothers, and finally my mom. But he wouldn't stop there, because he still had so much love and goodness to spread to many more people over time.

Once I decided to accept Jesus as my savior and began to establish a personal relationship with Him, I could see how my life was changing, how I was living life more fully. Every day I am made better thanks to Him, who treats me as His child, who cautions me when I do something I shouldn't, and then embraces me and continues to love me.

If it weren't for God, I would have lost my marriage. Life as a radio personality can be very demanding, because you're constantly out and about, working long and often unexpected hours. That can make it difficult to devote time to your family, but thankfully both my wife, María, and me, by seeking the Gospel, have been able to overcome even the biggest of life's challenges, and have been married for eighteen years now.

Suffice to say that if it were not for the word of God, many positive things in life never would have happened. There are many people out there who have amazing talents, but it is only through God that you can develop your potential. It is in Him that you can find the strength to persevere. And that would be everything when it came to the test I was about to face, just after accepting Him into my heart: my deportation.

CHAPTER 20

A RAY OF HOPE

Although Jeff and I had been working with the immigration attorney to find a solution, the day of my deportation hearing eventually came. I usually tend to forget about the bad things that have happened to me; I try to erase them from my memory and just retain what I've learned, the good things that I can draw on when I need them. The day of the hearing is blurry in my memory because of how stressful it was and the suffering I endured at the thought of being expelled from the country and leaving my family and the dreams I was working to build. I don't remember the exact date, but I know it was during the summer of 1995, just eight short months after I had begun working at La Super X.

That day, before appearing in court in San Francisco, I met with Jeff and the attorneys at their office. They explained what would most likely happen at the hearing: the judge would either confirm the deportation order, or he would allow me to apply for a work permit. They saw little chance of the latter happening, but they said they would do everything they could. Although I felt as if I were dying from fear of what awaited me in that courtroom, I can also say I felt a sense of calmness because I knew I was in the competent hands of a good team of lawyers.

We all left the office and walked to the courthouse, which was just a few blocks away. Outside, I met my parents and my brother Edgar, whom I'd decided to tell what was happening. We went through the metal detector and past the security guards, and once we were inside the building, we handed over our paperwork. I remember it being a very thick file packed with all the documents and briefs the attorneys had put together. Inside, the courthouse was crowded and the atmosphere was strange. There were mixed emotions being displayed from different people: some were very sad, while others were very happy. Others were standing in a line in front of a window, waiting their turn to either process their papers or receive an answer. It was a place where everyone was awaiting a decision, one that would determine the course of their future lives.

We entered the judge's antechamber and waited. By then, I was so nervous that I couldn't even think straight. When we were summoned, we entered. I took a deep breath and told myself that it was out of my hands now, and that all I could do was put my faith in God.

The courtroom was just like it is in the movies: a large room with a large platform at one end and two desks up front. Behind them were the benches for people attending hearings or trials to sit. The room was empty, and I don't know if it was my nerves or the air-conditioning, but despite the summer heat, I felt very cold.

Then the prosecutor and the judge entered the courtroom. I sat at the table with the lawyers, while Jeff sat on the bench behind us. Then the lawyers for the people began to present their case against me.

Jeff introduced himself to the judge and told him why was he there supporting me—how important my work was for the company and for the community.

Eventually it was my turn to address the judge. I told him my story: how I had come to the United States, and how I unsuccessfully tried to legalize my status as soon as I entered the country. I also talked about how—slowly, through hard work and the support of people who believed in me enough to offer me opportunities—I had gotten to a point where I was able to help out my family. By the time I had finished talking, I was unable to hold back my tears.

The judge told me that having Jeff with me there in the courtroom was notable, and that it spoke well of both him and me. But then he continued: "You have a very nice story, and I can see that you are emotional about it. But I'm not convinced."

When he finished speaking, he asked me if I had anything else to add. I said yes.

"I don't want my family to see me leaving here like a criminal. Because I'm not," I said, still in tears. "I know it was wrong to use false documents, but I never knew how bad it really was. I never thought it would come down to this. I thought I'd have to pay a fine, but being deported? Like a criminal? I don't want my parents to see this because the thought of it would kill them."

The judge said he still wasn't convinced by my explanation because what I had done was serious. My attorneys and the prosecutor continued presenting their respective cases, and I remember at one point the judge commented on what I'd been able to accomplish at a relatively young age—I was twenty-five at the time, and hosting a successful radio program—and on my involvement with the community, which made him think it might be worthwhile to give me a chance. He told me that if he did end up deciding to give me the opportunity, he would want me to tell my story to other people so they could learn from me and not do what I had done.

At that point, the prosecutor asked the judge if he could approach the bench, and I could tell they were arguing because they were raising their voices. I couldn't understand exactly what they were saying—I didn't know many legal terms, and my English still wasn't very good—but from what I could gather, the prosecutor was arguing that what I had done—using a fake green card and Social Security number—was a very serious offense.

Their discussion became even more heated, and I started to feel more nervous, because it seemed that the judge was agreeing with the prosecutor. I remember at one point I was asked to leave the courtroom, and the only ones who remained were the judge, the prosecutors, my attorneys, Jeff and my family. I thanked the judge for the opportunity to speak, and I thanked Jeff for being there. I gave him a grateful hug and left.

The expression on the judge's face when he asked me to leave gave me a bad feeling. I told myself that even if I were deported, I'd still find a way to keep moving forward, as I always have, and I'd find a way to take something positive from all of this. But nevertheless, it was deeply painful to think that I'd have to be so far away from my family.

Afterward, I came to know that the judge asked my father whether

I had relatives back in Mexico. He wanted to know if there was someone back there I could go to.

"Yes," my father answered. "But if he has to leave, that will be terrible for the family. His mother and I and his brothers are all here. That would separate us forever."

Jeff intervened and said he had collected many letters from people in the community and from clients of the company. They all testified I was a good person, and that I was important for the community as well. He handed them out to the judge.

"Thank you," replied the judge. "I will let you know about my decision soon."

And then he asked everybody to leave the room. Jeff, the lawyers, and my family came to join me.

While waiting to learn my fate, I was sitting on a bench in the hallway and crying like a baby. I prayed. I hoped and believed that the United States would in fact be the place I had imagined from a very young age—the place where my dreams would come true—and ever since my first day here, I'd worked very hard to reach those dreams. I also wanted it to be the place Fermín had told me about, where God would show me things I had never before imagined. But my hopes seemed to be dying quickly. The more I thought about my situation, the more I realized that what I'd done was very serious indeed, and despite all the good things I'd done in my life, the judge was holding my future in his hands.

Then a court officer walked up to me.

"Stand up," he said. "Go to that window over there. They're going to issue you a temporary work permit."

I couldn't believe what I was hearing. Was I understanding him correctly? I didn't want to ask, so I headed straight for that window. And I was even more surprised when I discovered that, yes, the judge had ruled that I was eligible to apply for a work permit. I'd been given a second chance! I didn't get the actual permit right there at the window, of course, just documented proof that the process was under way, and that it would be mailed to me when it was ready.

Then the people who were processing my paperwork said something that surprised me yet again:

"There aren't many work permits like the one we'll be giving you," they said. "There just aren't. It contains a special marking, even though you can't see it. If you get far from your home, your school, or your place of business within more than a sixty-mile radius, we will find you and deport you. You can't go anywhere else—do you understand?" This meant I couldn't even visit my parents! They continued. "Like I said, you can't see it on your permit, but we have all your details in our database, and we have access to that at all times. Don't even think about doing something without asking permission, because you can still be deported."

Now, thinking back on this, I wonder if they were just trying to scare me into behaving myself and obeying the laws. I don't know if they really could have "seen" this special marking on my work permit, or if they were able to track and monitor my movements. But regardless, I decided to comply with their instructions and would not leave the Sacramento area.

I never knew, nor did I ever ask, how the lawyers were able to convince the judge, or what their closing arguments were, but I will forever be grateful to them, to Jeff, and especially to God, for everything they did on my behalf.

Getting that permit solved almost all of my problems: I could stay in this country and keep my job, my source of income, my career.

Immediately, my family, my friends, and María—whom I met shortly after the hearing—and I started to request and gather testimonials from people asserting the fact that I was a good resident. We wanted to have as much evidence as possible to prove that I was an asset to the community, and that my absence would have a negative impact on it, thus securing my permanent residency.

A few days after that hearing, I went back to my job, after an absence of nearly three months. Right away, I met with my team, and we decided to run a campaign to announce my return to the airwaves. We also came up with a slogan to be used in promos broadcasted throughout the day: *Soon, the heart of the station returns*. In the background would be the sound of a beating heart.

During my first broadcast back on the air, I told my audience about what had happened to me, about why I had been gone for so long. I wanted to follow through with what the judge had asked of me, and let my listeners know that they should learn from my mistakes and not do what I had done. Then I added, "None of this is going to stop us from working hard and fighting for our dreams of moving forward."

The audience response was immediate. So many people could relate to what had happened to me, and they showed it: The phones were ringing off the hook with people who wanted to tell similar stories on the air, to let everyone know that they or someone they knew was going through the same ordeal, or had experienced a similar situation. Many told us of families being separated by deportations. All of these stories made me realize that I wasn't alone, and it only strengthened my belief that we must continue to strive to achieve our goals.

People also reacted favorably to the return of the program: In just a short time, we were once again the number one rated show.

I didn't think it was enough for my audience to hear my story and learn from my mistakes. It was very important for people to know about the serious risks involved in paying for forged papers, so I decided to add a new segment to the show where listeners could call in to ask an immigration attorney for advice. I made a list of all the lawyers I'd met while doing various events for the station, and invited them all to participate. Most of them agreed, and we began airing the segment regularly, so we could help address the concerns and questions of our listeners.

Inviting attorneys to appear on the air also gave me another idea: to add yet another segment, this time with doctors, so that members of the community who couldn't afford health care could ask questions free of charge. These were very successful as well, because even though we knew we couldn't address each and every caller directly on the air, there would still be thousands of people listening to the show who might be in a similar situation, or who knew of someone who was. It even helped me, because every day I would learn something new from these medical experts.

Meanwhile, I was still fighting my own battle to stay in this country permanently. My work permit was only a temporary solution, and the process of applying for residency was a long and slow one.

I remember a number of female work colleagues and family friends offering to marry me so that I could gain residence faster. Although I was very grateful, I always told them that I didn't want to encumber them or their families with that. It would also have been illegal, so that wasn't an option for me.

Being an immigrant in any country is always a challenge: You have to get used to new places and surroundings, to a completely different culture and lifestyle, and spend a lot of time learning a new language. You have to make new friends, find a new job, and start making your own way, among many other things. But undocumented immigrants face a much more difficult path, because in addition to all of the above, they have to live in constant fear of being discovered. They have fewer opportunities to develop and integrate themselves into a new society they want to be a part of and to which they already contribute with their work and their tax dollars.

For this, and for many other reasons, it is essential that we carry out a comprehensive reform of our immigration policies—one that recognizes that undocumented immigrants are not criminals, that the vast majority of them are good people seeking only a better future for themselves and their families, and that in doing so, they are contributing to the greatness of this nation of ours.

CHAPTER 21

MARÍA'S LOVE

When I came to the United States, my main focus was on getting ahead. But that didn't stop me from going out with friends and getting to know new people. I had a couple of girlfriends, young loves who lasted for only a short while. But near the end of high school, I was in a more serious relationship, and we continued dating even when I started working on the radio. As you know, I put in a lot of hours at work getting to know the business and earning a seat at the table. But she—I won't mention her name out of respect for her privacy—didn't like the fact that I was spending so much time there, or going out to nightclubs and parties where I could be an emcee, until one day she confronted me: "It's me or the radio."

And, well, we all know what my answer was.

After she broke up with me, she called my mom.

"Now that I broke up with your son, he's gonna lose himself in alcohol. Without me, he's nothing."

My mom was very concerned, and begged me not to start drinking. My parents were worried about this because even though I never drank before, they had seen how my brother succumbed to alcoholism. Of course, my mom soon realized that there was nothing to fear, because in the days following the breakup, not only did I not drink a single drop of alcohol. I didn't engage in any negative behavior at all. I can't deny that it hurt to learn she told my mom that without her I'd start drinking and lose my chance at becoming a successful broadcaster. But whenever someone tells me I can't do something, that just gives me more motivation to accomplish my goals. Putting that relationship behind me was a defining moment.

As I've mentioned before, my time in Sacramento was one of the most intense periods I've experienced. That city brought into my life so many things that I appreciate, and it helped me grow and find my own path in life. I'm not just talking about my career and the experiences and opportunities, like the highs of working for La Super X and the deep anguish of facing deportation and growing closer to God. I'm also talking about meeting my wife, my life partner, the mother of my children, who has stuck with me during the good times and the bad. I'm talking about María.

One day, at the La Super X studio in the fall of 1995, not long after returning to the show after my deportation hearing, I was told that a listener had left a letter for me. I opened the envelope to discover it was an invitation from a local priest to attend a fund-raiser to raise money to fix the roof of his church. Usually I get requests like this on air or over the phone, or when someone would come up to me on the streets and ask me to attend this or that event.

This priest was a faithful listener who thought the best way to reach out to me would be with a written letter, and one of his parishioners offered to drop it off at the studio. There was nothing inherently special about it: It was just an invitation to the fund-raiser, explaining what I was being asked to do and why the money was so important. He wrote a letter instead of making a phone call, as most people seemed to do. When I finished reading it, I decided that I should definitely participate in this event because I always loved supporting the community, especially when it came to raising money for a good cause. I picked up the phone and called the priest to confirm that I'd be going.

We also announced the event on the air, and some of my colleagues offered to join me. When we arrived, the priest said he wanted to introduce me to the woman who had dropped off his letter at the station. We spoke for a bit and then said good-bye. I didn't know that she was also from Ocotlán, but she knew that I had been born there, though she didn't mention any of that at the time.

Later I would come to find out that after we said good-bye, the woman called her daughter and asked her to come to the church. Her daughter said she couldn't because she had a lot of homework to do, but her mother insisted, saying she'd just met a nice guy who was also from Ocotlán.

"That's nice," she said. "But I'm still not going."

The mother wouldn't relent until her daughter agreed to come. When she finally got there, her mother introduced us, and told me her daughter's name was María.

This might sound like something straight out of a movie, but immediately I fell in love with her eyes. And she looked so beautiful in the green dress she was wearing and the way she had done up her hair in a bun. She wasn't wearing any makeup, which made me like her even more.

Although I can seem very outgoing on the radio, always cracking jokes and talking nonstop, in actuality, I'm pretty shy. And when you add that to the fact that I was standing in front of a girl I liked, well, I got so nervous that I could barely talk. For me, it was love at first sight. We exchanged a few words, though I couldn't stop stuttering. We talked randomly about the church, the repairs to the roof, and I said I thought this fund-raiser was a great thing to have organized. After that, we went our separate ways.

"There's something special about that guy," her mother said to her, when I was out of earshot.

"Oh really? What is it?" asked María.

"Just pay attention. Watch him for a while."

So she did, but after twenty minutes or so, María concluded that there wasn't anything special about me at all, and reported that back to her mom.

"You don't see it?" she asked.

"No."

"Look again."

"I already did," María said curtly.

"Well, notice how all the guys around him are smoking cigarettes or have drinks in their hands," she remarked. "He has a bottle of water, and hasn't had a drink of alcohol all night."

María looked at me again and noticed that it was true. She also noticed that when I finished one bottle of water, I'd ask for another one. And yes, I do drink a lot of water because for some reason my body works like a car radiator that constantly needs to be refilled all day long.

A few minutes later, we bumped into each other again. Neither of us can remember who made the first move, but we started dancing together. When the song was over, we exchanged phone numbers and pager numbers—you know, those devices that we used to send messages in the days before cell phones and texting. About two weeks later, after unsuccessfully trying to get in touch with her through her pager (she thought the messages were from somebody else), I finally called her on the phone and invited her to an event organized by the Consulate General of Mexico in Sacramento. For the occasion, María had carefully selected a long, gorgeous black dress. She looked amazing. And unlike the day we met, when I was wearing white pants with cowboy boots and a bright red shirt, this time, I was wearing a jacket and tie.

That night, some of the female coworkers at the station tried to make her feel jealous, trying to flirt with me or sit next to me, but they failed. María remained calm the entire time, laughing casually at my friends' antics, and I really liked that calmness and confidence about her. She behaved like that because not only is she not the jealous type, but she is also very confident in herself. It was also obvious to her that my friends were just playing around. They were curious because I had never taken a girl to a work event before. And, well, I'm sure they could tell how much I liked her. In the end, everyone had a good time that night, and María and I started going out more often.

For one of our first dates, I remember inviting her to a rodeo near Sacramento where I would be performing as the emcee. The organizers of the event were inviting people to participate in a bull riding contest. I wanted to participate, and I told María that I was going to put my name on the list. But she didn't agree; she said she'd rather we go skydiving than see me climb on top of that bull, which of course was very dangerous. But since I am very stubborn, I took advantage of a moment when we were apart and she wasn't watching to sign up for the event.

And of course, María was right, because I didn't last long. No sooner had I hopped on the bull's back than it bucked me off and I landed hard on the ground, and to add injury to insult, the bull managed to kick me in the back!

Man, how can anyone manage to keep from getting thrown off? I thought, lying there, dazed from the fall. I was so sore that I could hardly move, and María had to drive us back to Sacramento. The moral of the story: your partner is always right.

But I've always been pretty daring. Like the time, years later, when I got into a lion's cage. I'd been hired to emcee at Circo Hermanos Vázquez, and they also wanted me to appear in a performance with a group of clowns. And because I always say yes to everything, I did it.

Everything was going fine until I was asked to get into the cage with the lions. I was assured that it would be safe because the lion tamer would be inside with me. *Why not? It could be a great adventure,* I thought.

My mom was at the circus with me, and right before I entered the cage, I turned to look at her. Her face was completely pale and filled with fear, which was what got me a little scared. The last thing I heard was the trainer whispering softly: "Just don't show any fear."

But it was already too late: By that time, I had already shown fear—and much more—to the pride of lions. As I walked into the cage, I saw one of them looking at me as if to say, *Here comes a nice piece of meat.* I froze.

"Don't be afraid," the trainer repeated. "They can smell fear. They sense it. If they detect any, they'll charge at you."

I have no idea what happened next. I must have completely blocked it out of my memory. All I know is that I came out unscathed, because I'm still alive and I don't have any scars from that day. Later, I watched a video of myself, and I couldn't help but wonder, *What was I doing?* Moral of the story: Don't go into the lions' den.

But my circus adventure did not end there, because they also somehow managed to get me on the trapeze. How I didn't learn my lesson from my experience with the lions, I have no idea. Again, I said yes, and I joined the acrobats. While doing some of the moves they asked me to do—and mind you, I had never been on a trapeze before—something went wrong and I fell awkwardly. I had to grab hold of another acrobat in midair, which I was somehow able to do, but then he told me to let go, which I wasn't expecting. I fell down onto the net, which ended up being much more firm than I expected. When you go to a circus, you see acrobats bouncing off the net with such ease, as if nothing had happened, but it takes a lot of practice and training to be that graceful. In my case, however, I left frightened and in pain. Moral of the story: Ask about what you're getting into before you agree to do it.

After the rodeo where I got on—and got thrown off—the bull, María and I started getting together more often, and we always seemed to have a good time. We went to special events sponsored by the radio station, we talked a lot, and we were enjoying each other's company more and more. The same was true when we did simple things like go for a walk or even just for a bite to eat.

What I liked most about María and what I love about her till this day are two of her best qualities. The first is her emotional intelligence. She has the ability to peer deeply into someone, to understand them, and to know how to treat them. The other is her sense of family. In her, I saw someone with whom I could build a happy home, a future, and a family. The dream of having a family—which Fermín had planted in me the night he talked me down from jumping out of the window—had been growing over the past few years, and it was finally starting to take shape.

Ultimately I asked María to be my girlfriend one day when I just couldn't keep myself from telling her how much I was in love with her. We were in the car and I just asked her, quite directly, if she would be my girlfriend. I was so nervous that my stomach was in knots and my heart was pounding a mile a minute.

María said yes. I couldn't believe it. I was so happy that I didn't know what to say. It was then that I realized that I hadn't really prepared for the occasion, which I'd done on impulse. So I stopped at the first gas station I saw and bought her a rose. I picked out the prettiest one I could find, and I gave it to my new girlfriend.

• • •

No crean que estoy sonriendo a la cámara, ¡le tenía miedo al agua! ▮ Don't think that I'm smiling for the camera . . . I was afraid of water!

Con mi mamá en el campo, cerca de Ocotlán, comiéndome una galleta. ▮ With my mom in the country outside Ocotlán, eating a cookie.

¡Estate quieto, Jorge! ▮ Lie still, Jorge!

All photos courtesy of the author unless otherwise indicated.

Celebrando un cumpleaños con el saco y el moño de mi hermano Jorge. ▌ Celebrating a birthday in my brother Jorge's jacket and bow tie.

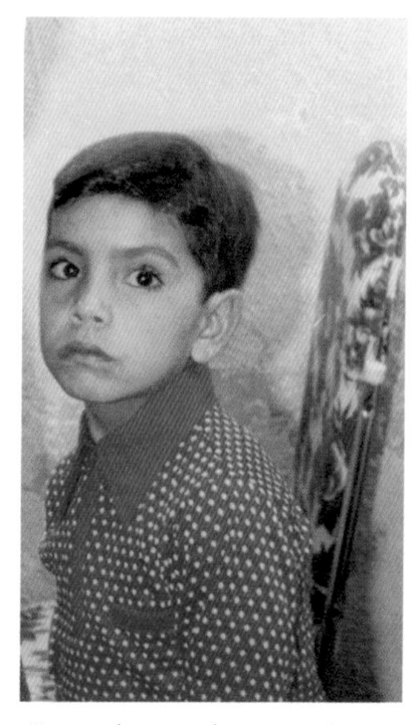

¿Por qué me están tomando una foto? ▌ Why are we taking this picture?

En el patio de la casa de mis papás. Esos son los zapatos gastados que le llaman la atención a mi hijo Daniel. ¡Pero qué feliz era! ▌ On the back patio at my parents' house. Those are the hand-me-down shoes that fascinated my son Daniel. But how happy I was!

El taller de bicicletas «Martín», en Ocotlán. ¡El original! ▌ Martín's bike shop in Ocotlán. The original!

La escuela pública en la que «estudiaba» y donde me comía unas deliciosas tostadas con chile. ▌ At the public school where I "studied" and ate a lot of delicious tostadas con chile.

Recién llegado a Estados Unidos, en Santa Ana, California. ▌ Newly arrived in America, in Santa Ana, California.

Con mi papá y con mi hermano Jorge al poco tiempo de que llegué a Estados Unidos. ▌ With my dad and my brother Jorge, shortly after I came to America.

El día de mi graduación de la preparatoria Saddleback. Me costó mucho trabajo, ¡pero lo logré! ▌ Graduation day at Saddleback High School. It was hard work, but I did it!

La foto típica que uno se toma y envía a la familia en México. ‖ The typical photo you take and send to family in Mexico.

Relajándome después de un duro día de trabajo. ‖ Chilling out after a hard day's work.

Me veo muy feliz en la cabina de Radio Éxitos. | Looking excited in the Radio Éxitos broadcasting booth.

Orange County Register/Cindy Yamanaka

Otro de los momentos más felices de mi vida: el día en que obtuve la ciudadanía estadounidense. ▌ Another one of the happiest moments in my life: the day I got my American citizenship.

Luz Gallegos, TODEC-Perris

Al final de la Caravana a Washington, escuchando al senador Robert «Bob» Menendez hablar a favor de la reforma migratoria. ▌ At the conclusion of the Caravan to Washington, listening to Senator Robert "Bob" Menendez speaking in support of comprehensive immigration reform.

¡A hacer lagartijas en público! ▌ Doing push-ups in public!

Con el noticierista José Armando Ronstadt, apoyando a la comunidad en el lavado de autos. ▌ With the news anchor José Armando Ronstadt, helping out the community at one of our car wash fund-raisers.

¡A darle bien, papuchón! Que quede muy limpio. ▌ Work that brush, Big Daddy! Get it nice and clean!

AP Photo / J. Scott Applewhite

En la Casa Blanca, hablando sobre inmigración. *De izquierda a derecha*: Emilio Estefan, yo, Lili Estefan y Don Francisco. ▌ At the White House, talking immigration (*from left to right*): Emilio Estefan, me, Lili Estefan, and Don Francisco.

AP Photo / Dennis Cook

Los senadores Edward Kennedy y Mel Martínez fueron algunos de los legisladores que nos recibieron en Washington al final de la Caravana. Antes de participar en una rueda de prensa sobre inmigración, el 14 de junio de 2007, platicamos amigablemente. ▌ Senators Edward Kennedy and Mel Martinez were among the legislators who welcomed us at the end of the Caravan. Before joining a news conference on immigration reform, on June 14, 2007, we had a friendly chat.

Official White House Photo

En la oficina Oval de la Casa Blanca, presentando una lista para conformar el equipo de trabajo en beneficio de una reforma migratoria. | In the Oval Office, presenting a list of team members ready to work toward comprehensive immigration reform.

Official White House Photo

Compadre, le traigo un balón de futbol. | Hey, *compadre,* I brought you a soccer ball.

Official White House Photo

Fue un honor haber sido recibido en la Casa Blanca por dos grandes anfitriones: el presidente Barack Obama y la primera dama, Michelle Obama... ¿Son muy altos o yo soy muy chaparro? ▌ It was an honor to be welcomed into the White House by two wonderful hosts: President Barack Obama and First Lady Michelle Obama. . . . Are they really that tall, or am I really a dwarf?

En 2010, después de nuestra entrevista en la Casa Blanca, el presidente Obama regresó a mi programa de radio. ▌ In 2010, after our meeting at the White House, President Obama returns to my radio show.

Letra D: Todas las anteriores. ‖ Letter D: All of the above.

La primer dama, Michelle Obama, en la cabina de radio cuando nos visitó y habló sobre nutrición infantil e inmigración. ‖ The First Lady, Michelle Obama, in the studio, where we talked about nutrition and immigration.

Official White House Photo/Lawrence Jackson

Listo para la entrevista con el expresidente de México, Vicente Fox, en la que hablamos sobre la importancia de escuchar las necesidades de nuestros paisanos. | Ready for the interview with former Mexico President Vicente Fox, during which we would talk about the importance of listening to the needs of our fellow countrymen.

Con Emilio y Gloria Estefan, grandes y sinceros amigos. | Emilio and Gloria Estefan, my dear friends.

En la cabina de radio, con mi amigo el periodista José Díaz-Balart, quien también formó parte del grupo de ciudadanos por la reforma migratoria. | In the studio with my friend, the journalist José Díaz-Balart, who was also part of the group of citizens supporting immigration reform.

Con la gran cantante Ana Gabriel. | With the great singer Ana Gabriel.

Angélica Vale y Angélica María, dos leyendas mexicanas del espectáculo. ❙ Angélica Vale and Angélica María, two legendary Mexican stars.

El día que ingresé al Salón de la Fama de la Radio, en noviembre de 2013. Junto a mí están el gran comunicador Larry King y mi amada esposa María. ❙ The day I was inducted into the National Radio Hall of Fame, in November 2013. With me is the great communicator Larry King and my loving wife, María.

Familia de turistas en Tierra Santa: queríamos recorrer los mismos caminos por los que anduvo Jesucristo. | A family of tourists in the Holy Land: We wanted to walk the same paths that Jesus had walked.

Edward y Daniel, mis dos grandes alegrías. | Edward and Daniel, my two greatest joys.

Shortly after we became boyfriend and girlfriend, we decided to introduce my parents to María's mother. María's parents had been divorced for a number of years, and ever since then, neither she nor her mother had had any sort of a relationship with her father.

We put in a lot of preparation, but I was still a bit nervous about it. When we introduced María's mother to my mom, they both just stood there silently, looking at each other. I had no idea whether that was a good or a bad sign until my future mother-in-law asked my mom if they had gone to the same school together, and it turned out they did: They had both been classmates together at the same school in Ocotlán. Suddenly I felt the tension slipping away, and I could breathe a sigh of relief. From that moment on, they got along just fine. It was also a good reminder of the many ways that María and I were connected. Even though she had been born here in California, she spent a lot of time in Ocotlán and Guadalajara as a child growing up. Her mother sent her back there every summer to visit family members and to learn Spanish, and she even hired a tutor for her so she could learn how to speak and write perfectly.

Our relationship was great, but like all relationships, it was not without an occasional problem. Ultimately, it's these bumps in the road that teach us the most, because they're opportunities to learn, both from our partners and from ourselves.

One of the fights we had, which was both tense and silly, was after a trip to an amusement park. My car was very old and not in very good condition. Instead of an antenna, it had a coat hanger, but at least it had custom rims, though I didn't have them installed! They came with the car when I bought it. On the way back home, we got a flat tire, and we asked María's sister, who was following in the car behind us, for help. The problem was that I had no idea how to change a tire, and neither did she. But María had a membership that allowed her to call for roadside towing service, so we called the number on the back of the card and waited for help to arrive.

"Where's the key to unlock the rims?" the tow truck driver asked, staring at the wheels.

"What key?" I asked.

It turned out that the custom rims needed a special key to release and remove them. I had no idea about this, and the person who sold me the car didn't mention anything about it. I do remember that when he handed me the set of keys, there was one that didn't seem to go with any particular lock, so I took it off the key chain so it wouldn't be so clunky. I stashed it somewhere in my apartment. Who knows where, though?

Yet we decided that our best option was to go back and find the key. All in all, it took us four hours to make the round trip to my apartment in Sacramento, find the key, head back to the car, change the tire, and finally drive back to my apartment a second time. Of course, María was very angry at me, not to mention exhausted. I was too. And we argued a lot. Moral of the story: If you're out with your girlfriend, make sure you know your rims!

The good news is that this one bad experience didn't stop us from using the car to go out on other fun excursions. And on one of those occasions, our families came with us to an amusement park: María's mom and siblings, and my parents and my brothers. My mom has always been concerned about my health, especially since I had a heart murmur when I was born. Of course, it disappeared as I grew, and I used to go hiking with my grandfather when I was a kid, and I never had any problems. But my mom thinks differently, and would rather take all possible precautions. Just in case.

This particular time, we were standing in line for one of the attractions that descends twenty-two stories in less than four seconds. My mom pulled me out of the line, and the rest of the group asked her why she was doing that.

"Because of the heart murmur," she said.

"The murmur is closed," María replied. "He's a grown man. Let him get on the ride."

María was right. The heart murmur didn't bother me one bit. But I agreed to do as my mom asked, saying that I didn't want her to worry. Yet, in fact, I was actually scared. I figured, why not use the heart murmur as an excuse?

• • •

After María and I started dating, I used to go to to her house every Friday for dinner and then I'd go to church. But I didn't tell her about that last part: I just said good night and left. Soon she became suspicious. Why hadn't I told her about my spiritual beliefs? I guess I just saw them as something very private. Besides, we had never really talked about my faith, so I hadn't had an opportunity to bring it up.

"This guy is really nice," María once told her sister, "but I think he has another girlfriend."

"Why do you think that?"

"Look, every Friday, he leaves right around six o'clock," she explained. "He thinks he's smarter than me, but he'll see. Next Friday, I'm going to take away his phone and pager, and if he doesn't take me to wherever it is that he's going, I'm not giving them back."

Back then, in 1996, cell phones were becoming more and more common, and I always carried mine around with me, just in case something came up and I needed to get in touch with my coworkers or my family.

And the following Friday, when we finished dinner, María did exactly what she told her sister she was going to do. She asked if she could borrow my cell phone and pager, which was a bit of a strange request, but I gave them to her anyway. When I did, she stuck them in her purse. *Uh-oh,* I thought.

"What's going on?" she asked in a very serious tone. "Wherever you're going right now, you're taking me with you."

I started to laugh, and asked why she wanted to go where I was going.

"Because you've been doing this same thing for a while now," she replied. "Every Friday you leave here right after dinner. I know you're hanging out with some other girl, and you're going to take me to her right now."

"No, I'm not taking you."

"Look, either you take me with you, or we're done. Don't lie to me."

I could see that she was very angry. I walked up to the car and said, "I just don't know if you'll like the place where I'm going. It might be too different for you."

"Why?" she demanded angrily.

"Well, it's kind of a meeting."

"I knew it. You're in a cult."

"No, it's not a cult."

"Well, you're involved in something, because you're telling me it's a different sort of meeting and that I might not like it."

It was then that I explained that I'd been attending Bible classes. Until then, I'd never mentioned that I was a Christian. But I invited her to join me, and she hopped in the car without so much as a moment's hesitation.

That day, the preacher, whose name was Gamaliel, was talking about the time in his life when his parents were separated and about the impact that had had on him. He didn't succumb to alcoholism, like so many other children do when they don't know how to express the pain of feeling isolated from their parents. Instead, he used shopping as a way of coping with it.

María felt herself identifying with his story, because she had suffered a similar experience. Her parents had separated when she was only seven years old. Her father had really distanced himself from the rest of the family. Her mother told her about the eventual divorce, but after that, the subject was never brought up again. Even further, her mother decided for herself that she would never love another man or even bring one into their home, because she did not want to expose her daughters to another bad relationship or any type of potential danger. Instead, she devoted herself solely to taking care of her family.

María would later tell me that whenever she would start feeling angry about her parents' divorce, she'd just go shopping with her friends. It never rose to the level of an addiction, but neither did it alleviate the deep sense of pain that she was feeling. So on that evening, there in the church, listening to Gamaliel telling his story, María felt that she had been called there by God, and decided to accept Jesus into her heart.

María knew that her mother would not be happy about her decision and decided it would be best to keep it under wraps for a while. Her mother was a very devout Catholic; she did a lot of work in her parish, and it was she who brought the invitation to the fund-raising event for her church to my office. But María did invite her sister to attend church with us, and soon enough she also felt the call of God.

The two of them decided to keep the secret for about four more months, before finally telling their mother, who, as predicted, reacted quite angrily. She told them they had been brainwashed, and she asked them how they could betray the memory of their grandparents, among other things. But they were calm and patiently explained the reasons they had made their decision to accept Jesus Christ as their Savior.

Her anger lasted for nearly a month, until the sisters were finally able to persuade her to accompany them to church. But their mother was only there for a couple of minutes before she decided to stay outside the rest of the service. It would be many more months before she made peace with her daughters, before she was able to convince herself of the positive changes it had brought about in them. With time, after witnessing the deep sense of devotion and faith exhibited by the other members of the church, she ended up converting as well. Eventually, other family members converted as well.

After spending nearly a year getting to know one another, María and I decided to get married. For the proposal, I wrote a poem that took a long time to complete. It read:

María "Gordis" soon to be Sotelo, I ask you to be my wife, and I hope it's not too late!
(If this is your wish too, and you feel it from the heart, write "yes" ________)
Today, the 20th of December, 1996,
Is marked in my heart as
The most special day of my life.
For today you will know that I love you truly,
And that I will for all of eternity.
My love, you came by
The grace of "God,"
To give strength to my life,
And that is what I asked "Him" for,
Both day and night.

I thank "God" because "He" put me
In your path to a better destiny.
Our love was the perfect union
Of the greatness that may start
When "God" is the guest
Of honor in our hearts.
I remember I did not want to fall in love,
But it happened suddenly,
I touched your red lips, and you kissed me,
And that was when I felt the need to call you "Love."
Now, my Gordis, "God" has placed you
Like a seal upon my heart,
And you are the finest sign of my love.
I invite you to walk with me
Through life together, that I may be
A part of yours, linked together
By the hand of "God."
I know that "God" always favors perfection
And now "He" has given it to me
In the greatest way of all, that is your heart.
Forever your Gordo, "Eddie Sotelo," thank you my "love"!

María was very surprised to receive this, because I had never made these types of gestures before. She read it in silence while my heart was pounding away. By then, I was completely certain that María was the one with whom I wanted to start a family and spend the rest of my life. After she read it, her eyes were filled with tears. And she said yes. She accepted.

I couldn't have been happier, and neither could she. We hugged. I felt like the happiest, luckiest man in the world. Now we could begin to build our own family, and I was very nervous but also very happy to know that we were starting a new stage in our lives, and that we were doing it together. Finally I was going to be able to share all the dreams I'd been building up for so many years with the woman I loved. It was, as they say, the first day of the rest of my life.

María and I got married early one afternoon in Sacramento, in December of 1996. By then, the radio show was well-known throughout the city, and I was on my way to solving my residency status since the process was going fairly well. The wedding wasn't an extravagant one, but still there were about two hundred guests.

María and I decided that we wouldn't see each other that day until the moment she walked down the aisle. I was nervous all morning yet very happy, thinking about everything that had brought me to that point: the difficult start in this country, the beginnings of my career, the pain and stress caused by my undocumented status, growing closer to God, the day I met María, the way we fell in love, and the moments that brought us together and allowed us to truly know one another.

Despite my nerves, I spent that morning attending to details—helping set the table arrangements and such—until finally the moment came, and there, in the church, I finally saw María walking down the aisle toward the altar where I was standing. She wore a simple, traditional, long white dress. She chose it because it was perfect for her. As I watched her walk, I was sweating profusely, both from nervousness and the excitement of knowing that my dream of starting a family with a woman whom I loved and who loved me was finally coming true. I was beginning a new stage of my life, and in my hands I held a new responsibility. When she stood by my side and took my hand, she realized just how nervous I was, but her presence helped calm my nerves.

The moment when we both said *I do* was one of the most emotional times of my life. I felt an enormous sense of joy welling up throughout my body.

My parents never stopped crying during the entire ceremony. Their son was getting married, and he would be leaving the house now for good, to go out and start a family of his own. It made them happy to see the two of us so happy together, knowing that I had found someone who complemented and appreciated me. But they were also very sad to see me leave the nest. I guess I'll have those same mixed feelings when my own children get married, but I hope there are still many years ahead before that happens.

Meanwhile, our family, friends and listeners who were in attendance gave us so many wonderful things: We received more than two hundred gifts, and we will always be grateful for their generosity.

There was no honeymoon, because we decided we'd rather spend the money we had on a party so we could share our joy with everyone, but also because I had just started working at a new radio station in San Jose—the KLOK—so I couldn't ask for any vacation time just yet. María agreed that it was more important that I focus on my new job and getting the program up and running.

We also made another decision about our future finances. Our housing options were basically reduced to two: Either we rent an apartment in the Bay Area, or we make some sacrifices and buy a small house outside the city in Salida, near Modesto. María was leaning toward renting an apartment; she was worried it would be too exhausting to drive that far to work every day, but I thought it would be better to invest in our future and buy a house. Even with all the sacrifices we would be making, once it was paid off, it would be ours. If we rented a house or an apartment, all the money from those payments would just be going into another person's pocket. So we finally decided that the best option would be for us to buy a house.

The one we decided to buy was a one-story, all-wood, cream-colored house with a small backyard. It cost $92,000, which was a fantastic deal at the time. The price had dropped a number of times before we had a chance to see it, because the other interested parties simply weren't able to pay what the owners were asking for. Once we saw the property, we really liked it, and we thought the asking price was fair, so we decided to make an offer. They wanted $500 to close the deal, and we agreed. It was our first home. It was true I'd have to drive two hours each way to get to and from work every day, but I was sure that it would allow us to set a good bit of money aside to save for the future.

Also, I saw the commute as something positive, as it gave me time to think about ways to improve things, both in my family life and at work. I also used the time to communicate with God. Sometimes, these periods of loneliness and boredom are the ones that help us to become better people. Instead of getting angry because we still have a long way to go before we get home, traffic isn't moving and the person a few cars ahead is distracted and making the traffic worse, it's better to focus on our spirituality and reflect on that day, what we did well and the ways we need to improve. That's what I did and still do, and that's why I never complain about the traffic: I always look at it as an opportunity.

The decision to move and buy that house in Salida reminds me of a story a preacher at the church once told. It goes like this:

> *A successful building contractor called one of his employees, a skilled carpenter, and told him that he would be in charge of constructing a house that the company was funding. He instructed the carpenter to order all the necessary materials and to oversee the entire process from the beginning.*
>
> *The carpenter eagerly accepted this mission. It was his first opportunity to supervise an entire construction project, so he studied his blueprints and double-checked each and every measurement.*
>
> *Then he thought to himself, "Since I'm in charge, why not cut some costs, use less expensive material, and pocket the extra money? Who would ever know?"*
>
> *Once the home was painted, nobody would be able to tell the difference, and so the carpenter put his plan into motion. He bought secondhand wood, and ordered inexpensive concrete to use for the foundation. He used the cheapest wiring he could find, cutting every expense, while still maintaining that he was using the finest building materials available. When the house was ready, his boss took one look at it and said, "This is amazing. You did a fantastic job. You have been as good and faithful a worker as any. You have always been honest with me throughout the years, and I want to show you my gratitude by giving you this house."*
>
> *We reap what we sow. We cannot plant weeds and harvest flowers, nor can we sin and expect justice. Our actions have consequences, so bear this in mind: every day we plant seeds, either for the Spirit or the flesh.*
>
> *What kind of seeds will you be planting today?*

We wanted to plant seeds that would produce lasting fruit, so even though it represented a huge up-front sacrifice—because for a long time, most of our money would be going toward making the house payments—it allowed us to begin forming a strong foundation for our future.

The first few months were difficult, because we had no furniture. We had enough money to buy the house, and literally nothing else. Also, the floors were covered with a very light-colored carpet. María and I weren't in the habit of taking off our shoes inside the house, so the carpet quickly got dirty. Since we couldn't afford to have it professionally cleaned, I decided to shampoo the carpet myself. I rented a cleaning machine and brought it back to the house.

To make a long story short, I caused a flood.

I hooked up the hose incorrectly, and water gushed everywhere. I didn't understand what exactly happened to cause the flooding; in fact, at first, I thought that was part of the normal cleaning process. When I finally realized the mistake, the floors were already completely soaked, just like the old house in Ocotlán when it rained.

María tried to tell me that I was doing something wrong, but I thought it was she who didn't know what she was doing, that the next step—the vacuuming—would come later, and that first the carpet had to be thoroughly soaked so it could get a good, deep cleaning. What a mess! What should have taken me only an hour or so ended up lasting the entire day, and María was super angry with me. Moral of the story: Again, your partner is always right.

Something similar happened with the grass in the front yard. Since we couldn't afford to hire a landscaper to come and take care of it from time to time, I went and bought the simplest lawn mower I could find.

"Are you sure you know how to use that thing?" María asked.

"Yes, of course," I said, but honestly I didn't have a clue.

I set the blade level way too low, and ended up cutting into the ground and leaving ditches all over the yard! It was kicking up little stones and shooting them at the side of the house, too, but once again I figured that was normal. María was inside fixing something to eat, and when she came outside and saw all the holes in the yard, she started cracking up.

"You know what, Eddie? You'd better stick to your radio job," she said, laughing. "From now on, I'll be the one mowing the lawn."

And that's how it was. There were no more ditches dug in the frontyard. Moral of the story: If you see rocks flying all over the place, something is wrong!

There was another time when María mentioned she wanted the garage to be a different color, so I decided to surprise her by doing the paint job myself. Hadn't I learned by then that home-improvement jobs just weren't for me? To top it all off, one of my uncles wanted to help do something for us, so he offered to give me a hand. I thought a little extra help would make the job even easier, so I accepted. What I should have done was tell María about my plan in the first place and have her weigh in on the project. She was the real expert when it came to painting. She had painted the walls of her room in the house she used to share with her mom and sister. But I didn't, and instead my uncle and I went ahead with the plan. It turned out to be a complete disaster! The floor was left splashed with paint because we didn't use a drop cloth, nor did we tape up the edges.

"Dear, you'd better stick with to the radio business," she said once again.

And of course she was right. You're better off sticking to what you know how to do. But at the end of the day, we always supported each other, whether at home or at work.

Of course, not having furniture meant we had to sit on the floor. And that's what we did for a while, until we were able to buy our first couch and set of tables. One of the reasons why it took so long before we could buy any furniture is because nobody would give me a line of credit. I had just gotten my residency and had no credit history, so applying for a credit card was difficult. After two months of living together, we had to borrow María's mother's credit card so we could buy a washer and a dryer. Before that, María was going to her brother's house in nearby Modesto to do the laundry. We had decided that María would not work, and instead would be in charge of everything around the house, except for the times I intervened, which, as I said, always ended in disaster. She also helped me become better at my job by connecting more with the community, as she was always attentive to their needs, and passed them along to me. She kept me informed about important news and events that I would have missed out on while working in the studio.

It was also around this time when, one day in early 1997, not long after getting married and moving in together, I got some more great news: My residency application, which had been submitted months before we even got married, had finally been approved. I remember that I was on my way home when María called to tell me that the envelope containing my green card had arrived in the mail. Tears of joy started streaming down my face. I felt a great weight being lifted from my shoulders, and I thanked God for all of His goodness, and for guiding me through all of the trials which I had encountered along the way.

Married life is full of moments of discovery in each other, in terms of both profound and superficial things that help us to grow and understand ourselves better. I remember one moment in particular, after we had just moved in together: I had come home early, and María had fixed shrimp soup, which smelled delicious. We sat on the rug, as usual, but when I took my first sip, I had to force myself to choke it down. As it turned out, María prepared the soup by simply putting the shrimp in a pot of water and adding a can of tomatoes. That was it.

"What's the matter?" she asked me.

"You know what?" I said. "Let's fix something else. I don't really feel like shrimp tonight."

I had no clue that María didn't know how to cook. Back when we used to have dinner at her house every Friday, everything on the plate was delicious. And when we moved in together after the wedding, she would give me a cup of homemade hot chocolate every morning. But one day, she didn't.

"Well, that's over now," she calmly said.

"Come on, why can't you fix me one?" I protested.

"Me? I don't know how to make those."

"Huh?"

"My mom is the one who comes over and makes the hot chocolate," she said, as if it were the most natural thing in the world.

I didn't know what to say, because I had always assumed that she was the one who made them. That same day, when I got home from work later that evening, María had another surprise waiting for me: tongue tacos. She made them herself, just like she did with the shrimp soup. I could tell that she'd really tried, and plus, tongue was one of her favorite things to eat. Yet it wasn't one of mine; in fact, I don't like it. But I didn't have the heart to tell her this, so I gave them a try. Suffice to say, I finished the rice, and, with my fork, just pushed the leftover tongue around on my plate.

"What's the matter?" she asked, looking worried.

"It's just that . . . I don't like tongue."

"What!?" she exclaimed, and laughed.

"Do you think you could fix something else?"

"See, I'm not a very good cook," she calmly explained.

I fell silent, not knowing whether to believe her or not, because that was the first time she had ever told me that. I had always thought that it was she who had fixed those Friday dinners at her mother's house. I should have put two and two together, and realized that the shrimp soup and hot chocolate were not just coincidences.

"But . . . all those times I went to your house . . ."

"Yeah, that was my mom," she said bluntly.

But María was determined to learn to cook, so she asked her mom to come stay with us for a couple of weeks so she could teach her all her recipes and methods. And to my great fortune, the plan worked perfectly!

About a year later, on March 29, 1998, I received another one of the greatest joys in life: the birth of my first child, Edward. We had been waiting for months, ever since the day we'd found out that we were going to be parents, and were filled with excitement, making plans to prepare for his arrival.

If you are a parent, you already know all the things involved in preparing for your first child—all the hustle and bustle mixed with waiting on pins and needles—and how those first few days are so busy that there just doesn't seem to be enough time for it all.

As I mentioned before, I never like missing work, and when María gave birth to our son, I decided that I would take my cell phone with me and do the show right there in the hospital, even if that meant using the bathroom in the maternity ward!

The nurses were all very confused when they heard noises coming from the bathroom and didn't know if there were several people inside or what, because I was using the sink and other different parts of the bathroom for sound effects to try to convince our listeners that I was actually at the Acapulco Festival. Eventually, María explained what was going on, and they couldn't stop laughing. The show that day was a huge success.

Besides the immense joy, Edward's birth brought a new dimension into our lives, one filled with many new responsibilities. We had to care for him, educate him, and raise him with good values. I often heard my parents and aunts and uncles say things like, *When you have kids of your own, you'll understand,* and I always ignored them. But when Edward was born, I quickly realized what they were talking about.

Having a child not only taught me how to be a dad, but also how to be a better person in general. It forced me to sit down and think about what kind of a man I wanted my son to grow up to be, how to guide him down the best path, instill him with a sense of discipline, and give him the tools he needs to make the important decisions in life.

It also gave me the strength to strive for a better life and to achieve even more at work, because I wanted to give my son not only a good life, but also a good example to follow. To put it another way, it was one more push to make me even more responsible.

Meanwhile, the show continued to be a success, and even surpassed other morning shows in terms of ratings, which prompted the company to shake up the schedule.

This new version of *Piolín por la Mañana (Piolín in the Morning)* quickly became number one among the target audience. And we kept on taking to the streets to help out the community, delivering food and water wherever it was needed the most.

I knew that the broadcasting company who owned the station, Excell, also had a station on FM as well. In addition, I knew that another company, HBC, wanted to start an FM morning show in Spanish for the Bay Area market, in addition to the one they already had. Knowing these two things got me thinking: *If I'm doing so well with a morning show on AM radio, with more listeners than the competition, then we could be even more successful if we started broadcasting on both frequencies, AM and FM, and that would be better for everybody.*

So I approached the owners and floated the idea that we also start broadcasting on FM radio. At first they refused; I was told that the entire format of the station and its audience was very different from my program: While my show was based on regional Mexican music, across the airwaves they were transmitting romantic music. Adding my show to the FM morning schedule could cause confusion and, ultimately, damage ratings.

"Just give me a chance," I insisted. "I'll do whatever you want. And you know what? You can fire me if it doesn't work out."

While they considered, I kept arguing that it would be a good idea. In the end, they took my advice. They scheduled my show to be broadcast on both frequencies on the same day that our competition would start broadcasting on HBC's massively powerful signal.

Bam! It wasn't even a competition, because the other program just never took off. The ratings were low and gradually faded away.

I decided to take advantage of the momentum behind *Piolín in the Morning*, and once again I invited artists to get involved and work to help out people in need. As with previous programs, and from what I've always learned from my family, I knew that helping others and sharing what you have is an important thing to do that ultimately benefits us all.

So this time, with this program, I would invite artists to help out sick people who couldn't afford to pay for their medications, or ask them to accompany me as I took donations to food banks, or to come play with my listeners and me in the soccer tournaments that we organized.

As I mentioned, one of the things I missed most when I came to the United States was the family gatherings we would have in Ocotlán, when my grandfather would invite everyone to come play together on Sundays. Gradually, I started to bring that tradition back, right here in America. It started with bringing food to the agricultural workers around Sacramento. Those meals gradually became events that people started looking forward to, and which I also enjoyed myself, since it gave me an opportunity to share, to get to know new people, and generally to have a good time. Then I started organizing soccer games.

Organizing the soccer games was rather simple: All I did was invite listeners to come and be a part of the Piolín Team or the Artists Team. That was all there was to it. During the games, we'd collect funds for nonprofit organizations that, in turn, would help out families in need, especially those who couldn't afford their medications. The very sad reality is that many people in our community lack basic medical insurance and the money to visit a doctor.

Among the many artists who participated in these tournaments were groups like Los Tigres del Norte, Los Elegidos, La Banda El Recodo, Los Huracanes del Norte (who were drenched in sweat halfway through the game because they were so out of shape), Los Rieleros del Norte, and singers like José Manuel Figueroa and Pablo Montero.

By the way, the time we played Los Tigres del Norte, they beat us on penalty kicks. But the next day, when I got on the air to talk about the game, I said that we had beaten them. Within minutes, I had a call on the line from the band members, saying, *Hey, it's not true! We won!*

Moral of the story: You have to learn how to lose gracefully.

Everything looked bright in my life. The values my family had instilled in me were helping me to make my program stronger, and I was building my own family, which was the most important thing for me.

CHAPTER 22

THAT'S THE FEELING OF MEXICO

Once I crossed the border, I understood that I could never go back to Mexico, at least not until my legal status was in order. If I had gone back to Mexico, I wouldn't have been able to return to the United States unless I crossed the border the same way I had the first time, and that was an experience I definitely didn't want to relive.

I really missed Mexico. I missed the people whom I'd left on the other side of the border—my family, neighbors, and friends; the land itself; and the food back in Ocotlán, where to this day, every time I go back for a visit, I make sure to have some torta sandwiches, birria, tacos, and some delicious seafood.

I'm very proud of everything I've been able to accomplish here in the United States, but Mexico is the land where I was born, and I'm thankful to God for having allowed me to see light for the first time there. Every time I'm in Mexico, I feel very proud of its culture, its traditions, and its cheerful, warm, and friendly people. Every time I stop in Guadalajara on my way to Ocotlán, I'm always struck by its beauty.

Mexico is where I learned the value of work, and also where I learned that hard work is the best thing you can do if you want to get ahead in life. That's why I'll always love the country where I came from, because it planted in me the seeds of wisdom that would allow me to grow into the person who I am today.

The first time I was able to return to Mexico since the day I got on that bus in Ocotlán was in late December of 2000. Even though I had hoped to make my return sooner rather than later, this first visit back didn't happen until a few years after I got my green card, when I was finally able to visit with María and our son Edward (Daniel had not been born yet). It took me a while because I've always believed in saving money and only spending it when you have enough to do so. I always tell people that, and I try to teach my kids to be careful with the money they have. For a long time, my financial situation was such that I couldn't make the trip without going into debt, so I chose instead to start saving up for it. When we had enough money, María and I looked at each other and said, "Well, it's time to put the green card to the test."

So we packed up our suitcases and prepared ourselves to finally return to Mexico. María, Edward, and I drove down to Tijuana, where we boarded a flight to Cancún via Mexico City. There, we spent a couple of days at the Xcaret archaeological site. Before returning to Ocotlán, I wanted to have some quiet time to spend with my family as I slowly prepared myself for the rush of emotions that would wash over me when I would finally be reunited with my extended family and birthplace.

It would be my first time visiting Cancún, and when we landed and headed for the hotel, I was amazed to see with my own eyes the stunning colors of the Caribbean, the jungle vegetation, and the warm, comfortable atmosphere all around us. On our first night there, we attended a fabulous show that's often performed at Xcaret, showing the essence of Mexico through traditional clothing, food, music, dancing, fireworks, and much more. It lasted for an hour and a half, and each state was represented. It was an intense visionary journey through our culture, our traditions, and our values, everything I try to remind people of back in the United States.

I was really enjoying the show when a song that I had never heard before began to play. *"México en la piel"* ("Mexico Under Your Skin") is the title. I got goose bumps, and felt a rush of emotions: a mix of joy, relief, and sadness for all the years I had been away. In many ways, I think that what I was feeling, after having spent so much time focused on the future, on achieving my dreams and building a solid foundation for my family, actually made sense. I was profoundly in tune with what I was and where I was, the land that had given birth to me and watched me as I grew.

When the mariachi band playing the song reached the verse that says, *That's how Mexico feels. . . . That's how Mexico feels. . . .* I couldn't help it anymore. I started crying. I thought that since it was night and everything was covered in darkness, nobody would see the tears, but all that was happening to me must have been pretty obvious, because a woman asked me in English if I was okay. I told her yes, and not to worry.

I immediately decided I needed to find that song so I could play it over and over, so when I saw the album was for sale as I was leaving the show, I bought it without so much as a second thought. When I returned to the United States, I played the song during my show, and I told my listeners about how I came across it. I liked it so much that when Vicente Fernández visited the show for the first time, I gave him a copy of the CD and told him that not only did he have to listen to it but he also had to sing the song.

Sometimes people will ask me where I found this song, because it's not an easy one to find, at least not in its original version. I always tell them that I bought it during my first trip back to Mexico, when the mariachis from Xcaret Fundadores performed it. Even today, I will often close the show with that song.

When I play it on the air, or anywhere else for that matter, I usually encourage people to keep the faith, that one day they will be able to return to their country of origin and feel the same things that I felt when I went back to Mexico. I really hope and believe in that. I know it's possible, and because of that we must fight to achieve our dreams, on each and every day, in each and every moment.

After spending a few unforgettable days in Xcaret, we flew to Guadalajara. As we made our descent, I watched the scene unfolding outside the window. I saw the hills in Jalisco and thought back over my childhood, about the times I went out to play in the fields and collect firewood. When I stepped off the plane, I was hit by the smells of Guadalajara, the surrounding lands of the state of Jalisco, and all the memories that were connected to them.

Then, as I stepped down from the plane, I saw my uncle Juan. I walked straight to him and gave him a big, strong hug. We stood there, locked in that embrace, filled with joy and happiness. Then I introduced him to my wife and my son Edward, and then everyone hugged and began to cry. Seeing him again was so intense because I felt as if I'd received an enormous gift—being able to see my family again and being able to set foot in my homeland. My heart was pounding.

There were times when I thought I'd never be back in Mexico again, and yet here I was, reunited with family members I'd left behind. I'm sure that all immigrants who have had the opportunity to return to their homelands have experienced moments similar to this one—the joy and excitement of seeing their families again—all the while reminiscing over everything that has happened during the years in which they were away, struggling to get by.

After we hugged, I told my uncle Juan, who always liked to exercise and keep himself fit: "It's incredible. You look just the same as I remember you."

My uncle wanted to take us out to a nice restaurant that evening, but we refused. I explained that what I wanted the most were some local tacos and tortas that I'd loved so much as a kid and yet so often couldn't afford. So he took us to a little restaurant that's famous for their steamed tortas. Just thinking about how they are made will make anyone's mouth water. The tortas consist of a local style of bread called a birote, which is a little chewy and very tasty. It is steamed and stuffed with chicken and a special sauce. When we arrived, I asked for the owner, and I was told he had passed away. To remember the old times and the memory of his father, I ordered one of those specialty tortas. It was just as delicious as I had remembered.

Afterward, we went to another restaurant that also served tortas with pork known as "El Rabano," which I also thoroughly enjoyed.

After we finished eating, we went to see the rest of the family. It was a huge surprise for them, because I'd decided not to tell anybody I was coming. I wanted to see the surprised reactions on their faces.

The first person I saw was my uncle Pepe, who was already in the United States when I crossed the border. I introduced him to my wife and son. Then we went around, visiting all the other family members, and when relatives would ask me what I had missed the most and what I wanted to do, I asked them to take me to play soccer, just like my grandfather did when he used to get the whole family together on the weekends. So that's what we did. We all piled into a couple of trucks and headed for a local soccer field. I wish that my grandpa Bartolo had still been alive; it would have put a smile on his face to see us all together again. We missed him dearly on that day.

Our visit happened to coincide with the First Communion of two of my little cousins. I remember they brought birria and refried beans, tortilla chips, flautas, and many other delicacies to the celebration.

The day after the First Communion, we went to the home of my uncle Chuy, may he rest in peace, and his wife, my aunt Socorro, and their children. They live in a tiny house that surprisingly has space for all of the essentials—a living room, a kitchenette, a single bathroom, and even two bedrooms. When I see it from the outside, I can scarcely believe that so much stuff can fit inside.

"Mom, I'm craving some of those tacos we had yesterday," my son Edward suddenly said. Apparently he was still thinking about the ones we'd eaten the day before at the First Communion party. Quickly, my aunts and uncles and nieces and nephews began warming up the leftovers. As we ate them, we appreciated the food on our plates more than we would have dining on the most expensive dish in a fancy restaurant.

I find the kindness of my people to be such a wonderful thing. It can be hard to find anywhere else, and it has always inspired me to help others and to do better myself. Treating people well and sharing however much or little you may have doesn't impoverish us; in fact, it enriches us all. It makes us better and happier people.

We never stopped eating during that trip. We stopped at every taco stand and ate tortas and sweets whenever we craved them. Of course, I couldn't miss the chance to eat at all the places I loved so much, like the one that serves fish tacos topped with roe, and María could never skip her favorite: pork dish and sweet potatoes.

María loves Mexican food just as passionately as someone who was born and raised there. In a way, Mexico is just as much her homeland as it is mine, since starting at a very young age, she would spend long periods of time with family in Mexico. One time, when María and my children were in Ocotlán to attend my uncle's funeral, one of my uncles asked them if they were hungry. María said yes.

"Where would you like to go?"

"They sell picadillo tacos by the train station," María suggested.

"How nice is it that Eddie married a girl from Ocotlán," he replied. "Sometimes, my nephews come by with these uptight girls who don't even want to try anything new, and yet you come here and already know where the good stuff is!"

But María wasn't the only one who appreciated the food in Ocotlán. My kids have also become big fans of some of the delicious dishes of my homeland. My second son, Daniel—born in 2006, in the midst of organizing the marches and the Caravan to Washington—loves churros, and just the other day, he asked his mom when we'd be going back to Ocotlán, because there is a particular one there that's stuffed with caramel.

"Daniel, do you remember where we can find them?" asked María.

"Yes, Mom. They're by the church."

Ever since they first visited Ocotlán, my two children—Edward during that first trip back to Mexico, and Daniel a few years after he was born—fell in love with my country. They both love eating the food (Daniel never forgets those caramel-stuffed churros and the steamed tacos), playing with their cousins, and walking through the town and the countryside. They enjoy the sense of freedom, because rules tend to be more relaxed there.

It's a blessing to be able to take these trips with my family, visiting the people we love so much. That's why I think it's essential that we are a voice for all of those who have crossed the border in search of a better future, so that they may have the same opportunity to reconnect with their loved ones and get in touch with their roots. We cannot give in. We must succeed.

CHAPTER 23

LOS ANGELES COMES KNOCKING

Getting a green card was a huge relief, but it also became a reminder to never let my guard down and instead to work even harder. Sometimes, when we achieve our goals, we fall into a rut and lose sight of the fact that the key to moving forward is to keep giving it your best, day in and day out.

As time went by, La Super X became so successful that it started attracting the attention of larger companies who watched us with interest and sometimes with concern, because we were leading in almost every ratings category.

The station's success had grown to such a point that the owners decided to accept an offer and sell La Super X to Excell Communications.

Jeff was tasked with breaking the news to me and explaining what it meant for the program.

"The company that bought us out wants you to stay on with them," he said. "They want to bring me on board too, so we can continue to work together. So nothing is going to change on that side of things. However, the company is based in San Jose, which means you'll have to move."

That was not the only change I was facing, and not the only factor in the decision I would soon be making. The other was that the show would have to be moved to the afternoon, because the company already had a very successful morning show.

María and I gave it a lot of thought, and in the end we decided to make the move. And while I would no longer have the coveted morning hours, one of the main reasons we accepted the new conditions was the fact that the Latino market is much larger in San Jose than it is in Sacramento. Plus, the signal on which the new station ran—KLOK, broadcasting at 1170 AM—reached as far as San Francisco.

In San Jose, the program ran in the afternoon and evening hours, and we got off to a decent start. I reworked my list of contributors for the different segments of the show and invited new artists. We booked our first interview with a big-name performer: Lupillo Rivera. He was one of the first to really believe in what we were doing. Until that day, no other top-tier artist had agreed to be interviewed on my show, because I just wasn't well-known enough at the time. Yes, my show had been number one in Sacramento, but as I had mentioned, the Latino market in Sacramento was much smaller than it was in San Jose.

Lupillo put his trust in me and agreed to appear in person on the show. That was when he was at the height of his career, and his appearance gave us a huge boost in ratings and inspired the whole team to get better each and every day. When the interview first began, I was pretty anxious, but my nerves calmed down fairly quickly once we all started talking and laughing about things like his family, how he'd come to the United States, and how he had managed to achieve so much success. I always try to bring out the human side of the famous personalities I interview, so we can all learn more about them and about how they've managed to get to where they are today.

And not only did Lupillo agree to be on our show; he also accepted our invitation to participate in one of the charity soccer games I often organize with my listeners. I'll always be grateful to him for that.

The program and the events that I was organizing were such a success that the show was rebroadcasted—or syndicated, as they say in the industry—to other parts of California, and even to other states. In about two years, we became the most listened-to show on the air. And after our third year, the competition, HBC, took note of us in another way: In virtually every city in which we were being retransmitted—Denver, Phoenix, Reno, Dallas, and El Paso—we were outperforming all of their programming. Also, their FM program that was being broadcasted out of San Jose and which went on the air the same day as my show went on FM as well was facing stagnating ratings. But their biggest fear was that my program would start being broadcasted in Los Angeles and that we would take away a big part of their audience.

So they decided to reach out to me. Gary Stone, who worked for HBC in Los Angeles, was the one who called. And as it turned out, they caught me at a very opportune time, because my contract with KLOK was finishing up in November of 2002.

"We're interested in talking with you," he said.

"I'm quite comfortable here," I replied. We didn't have a lot of money, but we lived a comfortable life, our older son was attending a good school, and María's family was close by, so we were able to visit them often.

I was also concerned that this was just a dirty play to get me out of the game. As I mentioned earlier, there can be a good deal of jealousy in the communications industry, and I wanted to proceed very cautiously, especially since I'd already endured hardships due to the envy of others. It wasn't just the issue with the immigration authorities; there were also the occasional comments in the hallway like, *Why does he have this or that?* or *How did he get to be the emcee at that event?* or *How is he appearing on that TV show?* I know that comments like that reflect more on the person making them than the person they're directed at, but still, I had to be careful.

I decided to mention it to María. Although I really was quite comfortable working at KLOK, I wasn't exactly thrilled that nobody had bothered to talk to me about renewing my contract. This was rare; usually a contract extension is sent out a couple of months before the previous one expires, but this time I hadn't received any updates, despite the fact that I was showing up at the station each and every day, even after my contract had expired.

Gary was back in touch with me barely a week after that first call. He and the program director, Eleazar, had come to San Jose and taken me out to lunch at an Outback Steakhouse to try to convince me. I was told I would have the morning show time slot and they made me a very tempting financial offer, but nothing was set in stone. I told them again that I didn't have any real reason to leave, since they had always treated me well and I was grateful for that. Plus, I didn't think much of the idea of moving.

"Just say yes," Gary said.

"I just can't do that right now," I replied. "Look, you wouldn't like it if the roles were reversed. At least let me speak with them first, in case I do decide to go ahead and accept your offer."

So I worked up the courage to talk to the general manager. I still hadn't made up my mind as to what I was going to do, but I wanted to make sure everything was clear and on the table, so that I could consider all of my options. He always kept an open-door policy, and when I walked in, he greeted me immediately.

"I'd like to know what my situation is with the station," I said. "I don't have a contract right now, but I still keep coming to work every day."

"And?"

"Well, I need to know what's going on. I have a family and I have to be thinking about my career. What's the next step? What are my opportunities to grow? Are there any plans to broadcast in Los Angeles?"

"Why are you asking about Los Angeles?" he replied, suddenly interested.

"Well, I know you bought a small station there, and I'm just curious about what's going on with that," I explained.

His response amazed me. "Well, think about it over the Thanksgiving weekend. If you want to go, think it over, and it'll give me some time to think as well," he suggested.

"Okay, that sounds good," I said, and left the office, puzzled.

Honestly, I froze. The station manager's response truly surprised me, and I hadn't mentioned specifically that I wanted to leave. I just wanted to know what my future was at KLOK. I'd been working for them for five years, generating excellent ratings, the show was a huge success, and yet none of that seemed to matter. Or if it did matter to him, he wasn't showing it.

That weekend, we went to Fermín's house, since we had planned on spending a couple of days after Thanksgiving with him and his family. Of course, I decided to tell him about what was going on at the station, because I wanted his advice. I told him that María and I would be praying for help in finding an answer. I had doubts about my future with the company because the general manager's attitude seemed very strange. But on the other hand, María was in favor of staying, because things were going well in San Jose and her family was nearby. Also, she didn't know Los Angeles at all. A move meant adapting to a new city, making new friends, and much more.

Fermín invited me to go for a walk by the hill near his house, so that we could speak more calmly.

"So tell me, what's going on?" he asked.

I summarized the previous couple of weeks, and told him that I didn't want to act on my own behalf, but instead to let God's will be done.

"And yes, I am curious about the possibility of moving to Los Angeles," I added.

Fermín then asked what my wife thought about it. I told him that she had a number of doubts, so he suggested that we continue to pray in hopes of finding an answer.

Our uncertainty continued throughout the weekend. There were even some tense moments between María and me, and because of that, we prayed even more. And as if that weren't enough, I got a call from Gary asking me if I'd come to a decision. I told him no and that I would need a couple more days to make up my mind.

"You know, it doesn't matter that this is Thanksgiving weekend," he said. "We can come to you. We can talk with your wife to help convince her. This is serious."

Finally, Monday came, and the general manager in San Jose and I had arranged a meeting. María and I prayed again, asking God to send us a sign, because we wanted to do His will, not ours. We asked Him to open whichever door He wanted us to go through, and to close the door to the place we didn't belong.

When the show ended, around ten in the morning, I sat there waiting to hear from the general manager, who had said he would call me when it was time to meet. But an hour went by, and I still hadn't heard anything from him. I called María, told her what was going on, and continued to wait.

Since I hadn't slept in days due to the stress, I wasn't feeling well. I was exhausted and anxious. I'd even developed a nervous tic in my left eye, which was twitching away nonstop.

What should I do? I wondered as the waiting continued. I decided that since he hadn't called me, I would go and track him down, so around noon, after waiting for two hours, I went to his office and knocked on his door.

"I don't have time to talk with you right now," was all he said.

Nothing like that had ever happened to me before. Especially not with him, who had always kept an open-door policy. I was completely taken aback, and I started to shake. A lot. A wave of feelings were rushing through my body: anger, frustration, confusion. I just couldn't believe that, despite all the success the program was having, the director just didn't seem to care.

"Hey, we had an appointment, and now I'm about to leave for another appointment," I said. "I need to know what's going on."

"Just give me a sec," was all that he said.

I called María again and told her what had happened. I said I didn't know what to do.

"You know what?" she said. "I don't want to go, but this is the sign we've been waiting for. This has never happened to you before." And she was right; usually, whenever I went to the general manager's office, he'd set aside whatever he was doing and invite me in. "Call Gary and tell him we're in," she concluded.

"Are you sure, my love?" I asked, not wanting to make a decision if she wasn't completely on board. I know that if you're happy with your family and your family is happy with you, you're happier and more successful at what you do. So I said, "I just want us to be happy and content, wherever we are."

"Yes, I'm sure," she answered.

But before I called Gary, I decided to try one more time to speak with the general manager, to let him know what was going on and to give him the opportunity to make an informed decision. I went back to his office and went inside, this time without knocking.

"Look, I've been asked to go to Los Angeles," I said. "I hope you don't take advantage of this, but I really don't want to leave. I want to be completely honest with you, as I always have been. I've lost sleep over this. I don't know what to do. I'm really happy here, but my wife and I have been asking God to give us a sign."

"Well, go ahead and do whatever you like." That was his answer.

"Are you sure?"

"Yes."

I can only assume that the general manager had never expected this to happen—that I'd leave the station—because I'd been there for so long by that point. Maybe he thought I was making a scene or some sort of ill-conceived play to gain an advantage. He knew I was happy and settled in with my job and my life; he knew I was loyal to the show and the station, and perhaps he just didn't give it the serious consideration the situation deserved.

I left the office shaking uncontrollably. I called up a friend of mine who went by the nickname of "Sawtooth" because he wore braces at the time (his real name was Eduardo, the same as me) and who also had a young son. I asked him if he could pick me up because I was in no condition to drive and I had been driving a company car, and I had just walked out on my boss.

Even though Gary had never made me a concrete offer—we had only talked about the program schedule and some hypothetical monetary figures—I decided to call him back and give him my decision: I was leaving the station to accept his job offer. The deal was done.

As soon as I finished talking with Gary, the general manager at KLOK called me.

"Come back! Where did you go?" he said.

Huh? Hadn't he just said I could leave if I wanted to?

"I told you I had an appointment," I replied.

"Come back to the office. We need to talk."

"No. I already made my decision, and this is just getting way too exhausting for me."

"Just come back. Or tell me where I can meet you. I can go to your house," he said with a worried tone in his voice.

"No. Don't come. Please." And with that, I hung up the phone.

After that, my phone was ringing off the hook. He had called my wife and tried to convince her to change her mind. María called me right away and asked me what to do, and I told her it wasn't worth calling him back because I had already told Gary that we were going ahead and moving to Los Angeles. We had made a decision, and I had given him my word. María agreed.

After those tense few calls, I felt a little bit more calm, and called Gary again to set up the details of the new job. Eventually we agreed to terms. He asked me if I would go ahead and sign the contract before he took us to Los Angeles to get situated.

I agreed.

And then off we went to Los Angeles.

CHAPTER 24

"TO SUCCEED!"

There's an old saying that goes, *Things happen for a reason,* and I've always found that to be true. I was sorry that my departure from KLOK happened the way that it did, but there was a reason behind it: God was trying to tell me something. As it so happened, the move to Los Angeles proved to be a turning point in my career that I never expected and took me to places that I never before imagined.

Before making the official move, we visited L.A. in early December of 2002 to find a house and get to know the city. Gary and his wife, Claudia, picked us up at the airport. They welcomed us warmly; they showed us around town and helped us with our home search, so from that first trip alone, we were able to find our footing and begin to take root. We were honest and up front with them, saying that we were here because God had opened the door for us. We never thought we'd be making such a move away from where we were, but we had received a clear sign.

Our permanent move took place less than a month after the first arrival at the airport that began this new phase of our life. Before hitting the road south to Los Angeles, María turned to me and said, "Well, here comes the next challenge."

Moving to Los Angeles was a big change for everyone, not just for me. María wasn't convinced at first that we should leave the Bay Area for Southern California because she didn't know anybody in the area, she'd miss her family, and it would be hard for Edward to adapt to a new school. But after accepting the decision that God had helped us to make, things got a little easier. In fact, ever since we first arrived in L.A., María and I had been praying constantly and asking God for enlightenment. *Your will was done, and that is why we are here now, living in the City of Angels,* we repeated.

Although we didn't have any friends in the city, María soon got to know the area and started meeting people. Good food and good weather made things easier for her. Soon enough, she started to feel more and more at home, and now she's fascinated with Southern California, and says she doesn't ever want to leave.

The change wasn't too difficult for Edward, who was five years old at the time, either. He quickly made friends at his new school and his teacher was great. He connected well with the kids, and María got involved with helping other teachers and parents to organize events at the school.

For me, adapting wasn't much of a challenge, since I knew the area fairly well from my early years in America, living in Santa Ana. Another thing that made the transition easier was the fact that my life, like that of many people, has been a constant series of changes and challenges. Some of them were unexpected and appeared right out of the blue, like this move to Los Angeles. I had never even thought about coming to this city, but when God granted us this opportunity, we decided to grab it by the horns. You do the best you can and live life as it comes, and make the most of it, regardless of any surprises that pop up along the way. This opportunity presented itself just when I was starting to feel settled in the Bay Area with a radio show that broadcasted in seven or eight cities across a number of states, and confident that the opportunity for growth would sprout from there. But clearly, life had something else in store for me.

At the press conference where I was introduced and my new morning radio show was announced, I showed up wearing diapers. No shirt, no pants, no shoes or socks. It was completely my idea: a way to present myself as having been reborn in Los Angeles. Nobody knew me here, my show had never been broadcast in this city, and so—in more ways that one—I wanted to start from scratch.

On the other hand, being a talk show host in L.A. meant a lot more competition and many more responsibilities, so I thought I'd start out with something strong, something that would remain etched into everyone's mind. And that's exactly how it played out, because when I showed up, everyone fell silent and I could see a collective look of surprise and amusement on everyone's face, including the station manager, who had no idea about what I had planned on doing.

His wife called María to tell her what was going on at the press conference, and to see if she knew anything about what I was doing. And María was just as surprised as she was, because I hadn't told her about it either. It was an idea I'd come up with on my own, at the very last minute, and it turned out to be a hit because it was all over the media, drawing attention to the new program.

There were many things about the show that were going to be new and different. When I got to L.A., I was told that the program would be airing from four until eleven in the morning—seven straight hours of broadcasting! The show would retain the same name as the previous one—*Piolín in the Morning*—and the schedule meant that I'd have to wake up at two a.m., which in turn meant that I'd have to be in bed, with my eyes shut and drifting off to sleep, by seven thirty at the latest. Of course, I wasn't always able to do that, especially when there was an event I had organized or I went to assist a family member that needed some help. But going to bed early wasn't anything new, since I had had to do it for my previous morning shows, yet this was at least a full hour earlier than what I'd been used to.

So in the evenings, whenever eight came around, I'd head to the bedroom while María and Edward would stay up late watching movies in another room. Edward has always liked going to sleep late. But I am amazed by his sense of discipline, because if he has to get up early the next day, he is always able to do it without any problems whatsoever.

The sale of HBC brought to the table that, during the broadcast, it would link to TV programs in New York and Los Angeles during the commercial breaks. This meant we had to prepare additional material to use with these interactions. We had to think of ideas for what we were going to say, make sure that everything went well during the commercial breaks, that the team transmitted flawlessly, and that we returned to our regularly scheduled broadcast on time. All of this meant a new workload that I wasn't accustomed to during my previous shows.

In a nutshell, not only had my workload tripled, but my responsibilities had grown as well, which meant more time spent away from home. Occasionally, I slept at the station, simply because there weren't enough hours during the workday to do everything that needed to be done. But what else can you do other than put in all of your efforts to make sure that everything turns out the best way possible? While this extra workload was tough, it was also an opportunity to achieve my dream, to bring the show to more cities throughout the United States, and to give those communities the chance to enjoy and benefit from the various programs of the show—listen to what their favorite artists have to say, learn about their rights as immigrants, get information on their health, and improve one another's lives.

Upon waking up the morning of the very first broadcast, I asked God to take away my anxiousness, but I knew it wasn't going to be that easy. So right from the outset, I expressed how I felt, I talked about my nerves, and I got a lot of calls from listeners offering support. Not many people know this because they're only familiar with Piolín the joker or Piolín the activist, but there is another side to me: the person who exists away from the microphone and does regular, day-to-day things with his family. And while I really do enjoy what I do on the radio and promoting events or participating in marches, I have always been shy and reserved. When people get to know me personally after having listened to my persona on the show, they always tell me that they never imagined that I could be so introverted and quiet.

Also during that first show, I sent a *Piolimobil* with flowers to my aunt Nena, who first welcomed us upon our arrival in the United States, and I said on the air, *This is the result of that opportunity which you gave me when I showed up at your door after arriving here in this country. Thank you, Aunt Nena.*

And thus, the segment of the show in which I give thanks to my listeners and their friends and family was born.

The show started off well, and gradually it became quite successful. We got a lot of calls, and the ratings showed we were connecting with listeners in a positive way. On the other hand, we didn't want the new program to be the same as the old one at KLOK, so we worked hard to add new content, especially the segment where immigration attorneys answered questions from listeners. I also added a new segment with a sexologist; I invited more doctors with different specializations; and we brought in family and marriage counselors. My inspiration for doing all this came mainly from my experience as an undocumented immigrant, but I also wanted to address a need I saw among many people who, despite having lived in this country for years, still didn't have sufficient living conditions to enable them to break through.

The program showed that it still had a lot to offer. It continued to grow, reaching a much greater scale. In just a short while, it was being broadcast in several states by about sixty stations, impacting more and more people all across the country.

For example, one day I got a call from the family of a boy named Brian. They were trying to raise enough money for their son to have a heart transplant, and they didn't have the necessary means to pay for all the expenses. Brian was about seven years old, with a great sense of charisma and love about him. I remember talking with him on the air, and his first words to me were: "Piolín, my mom told me that you're gonna get me the heart I need to live."

Of course, I felt a huge sense of responsibility after hearing that from a child. I paused and thought to myself, *How do you respond to a seven-year-old boy who needs a new heart?*

"Yes, *m'ijo*," I said. "Let's ask God for your heart."

And we began to pray. Immediately, people started chipping in any way—from washing cars to holding bake sales—they could to raise funds for Brian's operation.

The family did some research and realized that it would be cheaper to have the operation done in Mexico, so they decided to go there once we had raised enough money to pay for the surgery. Time was quickly running out, but we were able to collect enough to cover the costs. Sadly, the family couldn't find a donor in time and Brian died before he could have the operation. I felt an intense pain when his bereaved parents called me with the news. It was with profound sadness that we thanked everyone for helping Brian, and we explained what had happened in the end. It hurt us all deeply to know that our efforts had been in vain and that we weren't able to save the life of a child as beloved as Brian. I'm still in touch with his family to this day.

But the world is not lacking in coincidences. Two or three years later, I came across a similar case: a child who desperately needed a heart transplant and whose family couldn't afford the operation. And what's more, the child's name was Brian, and he was just a couple years older than the other Brian had been when we met. I couldn't believe it.

Brian was in a hospital in New York, though his family was originally from the state of Puebla in Mexico, and they had immigrated to the United States a few years earlier. Again, we immediately started asking for help. Fortunately, this child had more life left to live than the other Brian had been granted, and therefore we had a larger window of time to work with. I decided to go to New York to visit him in the hospital, and I remember joking around with the nurse, then I turned to Brian and said, "Hey, what a good-looking nurse! I think I'll stick around for a while."

"Yeah," he replied. "She's pretty, right, Piolín?"

We brought him a laptop so he could listen to the show right there in the hospital. Then I prayed with his family for his continued health, and I said good-bye. It was December 30, and the next day I had been invited to make an appearance by Otto Padrón, who gave me an opportunity to participate on a New Year's TV event hosted by Raúl de Molina. Right when the show was about to begin, I got a call from Brian's dad.

"A miracle has happened," he said. "Our prayers were answered: They found a donor. It's a young child who sadly passed away, but his heart will live on in Brian."

The surgery was a success, and Brian is still alive to this day. I'm deeply grateful to God and to the all the people who helped to make this happen.

But despite the show's success and the joy I received from knowing that we were able to help more people than ever, not everything was coming up roses. At this point, we were starting to run into some instances of envy, which, as I mentioned many times before, is pretty common in the industry. There were even some people who told María and me not to buy a house in L.A. because we wouldn't last more than a couple of months there.

I also used to get a lot of discouraging messages from peers and colleagues who clearly didn't believe I deserved to be where I was. For example, when I mentioned I wanted to give out "Piolistickers" for fans of the show to put on the bumpers of their cars—a promotional technique I had used to great effect when I was in Sacramento—people would say things like: "Don't forget that you're basically a country boy, Piolín. San Jose is nothing compared to Los Angeles."

"What does that have to do with anything?" I replied.

"Well, this is a much bigger city. You can't just go around slapping bumper stickers on cars. It's ridiculous," they insisted.

I can't say that comments like that didn't hurt, but the worst thing you can do to yourself when someone tries to put you down is to believe them. When you're convinced of what you want to do, the best thing is to stay focused and move forward. And, as you know, when someone tells me something can't be done, it just motivates me even more to stand up for myself and my ideas.

"Well, I'm going forward with the Piolistickers anyway," I said.

And I did with full determination. I convinced the bosses and we got them printed up—each one with the name of the show and the station identification—and I hit the streets to distribute them. And they really worked! Even after all these years, there are still a few of them floating around in the city. Even people who don't speak Spanish can identify me from the bumper stickers. I've seen them on cars in Mexico, and soldiers serving overseas have sent in pictures of them adorning tanks. I've even seen pictures of soldiers wearing the T-shirts we made up, emblazoned with the show's slogan, *"¿A qué venimos?" "A triunfar!"* ("Why do we come? To succeed!")

The new show gave the chance to fulfill another dream, this one for my parents: I could finally buy them a new car to replace their old one, which was starting to break down. And I still couldn't get the image out of my mind of the burns on my dad's back from overheating in that car, so I wanted to get him a new one as soon as I could.

I wanted it to be a surprise, so I took my parents, along with María and my kids, to a car dealership without telling them anything. All I said was that we were getting some maintenance work done. When we pulled in to the dealership, my dad started to protest, saying that the repairs would be more expensive there. What they didn't see was that one of the cars on the lot had a huge bow on top. We told them it was for them and said it was a gift from our kids—which obviously wasn't true, but I knew that by saying that, they couldn't refuse the gift. That was the first time my parents had a brand-new car. It made me very happy to see my dad's face filled with joy.

"Oh, son . . . you're gonna give me a heart attack!" he said.

I was able to give my parents something to help them get around more easily, and thus show my gratitude for everything they've given me, and I couldn't help but feel complete. In the end, the most important thing in your life, after God, is your family. And the best thing about having a family is knowing that you can rely on this group of people who take care of one another, look after one another, and always stick together.

In 2006, I got a call from a listener who told me that Congress was debating a bill that would make it illegal for people to aid undocumented immigrants, even if it were unintentional.

The proposed legislation was known as the Sensenbrenner Bill, H.R. 4437, and it stated that if you stopped to help an injured person on the street, you had to ask if he or she was in the country legally before you could offer any assistance. The most shocking part of the bill was that if the person said no and you still helped them, you could be held criminally liable. It was unbelievable! How could it be possible—if this bill were to become law—to say to someone who was about to die, *Hey, I'd love to help you, but first I need to know if your paperwork is in order. . . . Oh, you don't have any documentation? Sorry. I can't help you. . . .*

I asked the attorneys who were on my program to explain this to the listeners, and we discussed the issue further. Immediately after the show, we were contacted by a number of nonprofit organizations dedicated to supporting immigrants. So I asked the lawyers what we could do, and they gave us several options, one of which was to stage a march. They said it was a peaceful way to protest.

"I want it to be peaceful," I agreed with them. "If we're going to march alongside these organizations, it has to be a peaceful one. We need to send the message that we are not violent people, that we came to this country to build, not to destroy, and that we are willing to fight for our dreams."

The political climate at that time—in the middle of the previous decade—had become extremely polarized on the issue of immigration. On the one hand, the undocumented immigrant community was growing, and there were no solutions to remedy the situation. On the flip side, the voices asking the government to crack down on immigration were growing more and more insistent.

It was important that we did something to show the nation how we contribute to this country, how committed we are to it, and how we deserve to be recognized for it. So we reached out to NGOs and other broadcasters in both Spanish and English and invited them all to meet with us and organize a march.

Besides all the people I met and all the attention we brought to the issue of immigration, organizing this march brought about issues that helped me get to know myself better. I learned from them; I grew stronger and became even more convinced that what we were doing was to benefit all. Although the march was composed of a large number of individuals and organizations, for some reason my show was the one that drew the most attention from the media. Some people complained that I was invited to speak at certain events while others were not. I guess these types of comments come with the territory, so I tried to stay focused on what was most important—that we all came together to show a united front and to demonstrate that we are a community that can rally thousands of people around the same idea and beliefs.

Leading up to the march, I suggested to my listeners that they all wear white T-shirts, bring a bag to collect the trash as we walked through the streets, and carry American flags. I was speaking from the heart, because I believe that when you're in this country, you must represent and respect the national symbols. Plus, it would send a powerful message to those who oppose giving documents to undocumented immigrants: we are good people, peaceful and hardworking, who love this country and are ready and willing to commit to it.

Some people didn't like my suggestion, and said that we should be carrying the Mexican flag instead, or the flag of whatever country you happen to come from. I countered by saying that the American flag would be seen as a positive statement, but that the participants themselves could decide whether to bring a flag or not.

Ultimately, most of the people who participated in the march followed my suggestions. And it wasn't just people from Los Angeles who were getting involved. People came from all over the country, because they listened to the show and felt that it was important to join in, to represent our people, and to demonstrate our commitment to this country.

On the big day—Saturday, March 26, 2006—I arrived very early, around six in the morning, to broadcast a special edition of the show from an improvised studio right there on the street. The march was set to begin at ten o'clock, but even as I got there four hours early, people were already starting to gather. And then the artists who were going to be interviewed on the show started arriving: people like Kate del Castillo, Jessica Maldonado, the members of Los Elegidos, and Gerardo Fernández, among others.

When we signed off to join the march, I was surprised by the sheer number of people, almost all of whom were wearing white T-shirts, waving American flags, and carrying trash bags. We picked up all the garbage we could find in the streets, though we could barely move because of the huge crowd of participants. *What a great turnout,* I thought. So many emotions were running through my body: the joy of seeing so many people united around a common cause, pride in my community for the exemplary behavior that was on display, and excitement for what this all meant: the ability to raise our voices high and strong. But above all, I felt a great sense of responsibility to push onward, never back, and to make sure that our needs were addressed.

We were on the way to the Getty house—the L.A. mayor's home, and the place we had chosen to end the march—and I was trying to see just how far this sea of people stretched, but since I'm so short, I could barely see past the backs of the people in front of me. And thanks to the massive size of the march, it took me longer than I expected to reach the mayor's house, where a stage had been set up for the organizers and leaders of the various organizations to speak. I remember helicopters flying overhead, and at one point a flock of white doves was released.

When it was my turn, I went up to the podium and told the crowd of marchers that we had to stand firm, and that we had to do so with a steadfast devotion. That we should ask God to touch the hearts of the politicians in Washington, so that they might stop tearing apart families by deporting people and that He also help them to understand that we all came here to help build this great nation and we consider the opportunity to contribute to be a blessing.

I ended my speech by asking, "Why do we come here?" And the response was immediate and unanimous: "To succeed!"

Afterward, when I saw pictures of the march, I was still in disbelief. Some media reports estimated that there were five hundred thousand people in attendance, while others reported that the total was, in fact, more than a million. Whatever the actual figure was, the most exciting and gratifying thing for me was that originally we only expected a few thousand to show up. Instead, it turned out to be massive and unprecedented.

Nor could I have imagined what the march would mean for my career, in every conceivable way. Some years later, a Twitter follower left me a message saying there are pictures of me during the march in a university textbook titled *Media Essentials* by Richard Campbell, Christopher R. Martin, and Bettina Fabos. And *The Los Angeles Times* included me on a list of the one hundred most influential people in Southern California. But most important, the march had a positive impact on ordinary people who—like you, me, and other immigrants—have been coming to this country for hundreds of years to achieve their dreams. These are the things that make me proud, especially since the march was a collaborative effort that many people took part in.

With all of this as a backdrop, shortly after the march, on April 4, 2006, my second son, Daniel, was born. It was another of the greatest joys of my life. That day, when the contractions started, I wasn't at home, and my mother-in-law, who was staying with us to help prepare for the new baby, took her to the hospital. It was a twenty-minute drive from the house. As soon as she was admitted, they took María into the delivery room, because Daniel seemed to be in a big hurry to make his entrance. When I was finally able to see him, the instant pride of being a father once again filled me with more hope and joy.

According to the lawyers and policy experts who were advising us, the next step in the process was to gather letters from citizens, so that the political representatives in Washington who received these letters would know that they represented real votes.

Initially, the goal was to push back against the bill, but we were also facing the need for comprehensive immigration reform. The proposed HR 4437 had support in the House of Representatives, but after the march it ended up languishing in the Senate and was never passed. True immigration reform, though, has also failed to make any headway, and although it's been nearly ten years since the first of those marches, the system in this country is sadly stuck in a rut, despite the fact that the issue is constantly being brought up by the media, and political leaders on both sides of the parties say it needs to be dealt with. The current immigration system makes it all but impossible for someone who is not a highly qualified and specialized worker to legally find a job. But these are precisely the sort of workers that this country needs, as evidenced by the number of undocumented workers who cross the border every year to work in the fields, in the service industry, in factories, and in so many other places that need decent, hardworking, committed people . . . people like those in my own community.

After the march in Los Angeles, we decided to set up a caravan to Washington so we could speak directly with senators and representatives and explain our needs face-to-face. I invited all of the people who had sent in letters addressed to their congressmen, and many of them accepted. That was when a number of organizations began asking me to make a public statement about which presidential candidate I would support. This was in 2007, with the elections coming up the following year.

"My flag is not a party," was my reply. "My flag signifies the people's need for meaningful immigration reform, and both parties are responsible for carrying it out."

I also added that the microphone in my broadcast booth was open to any candidate who wanted to be interviewed, and that they could use my show as a way to express their views to the people, who could then decide. Ultimately, it wasn't my job to tell the listeners whom to vote for.

All I wanted was for innocent, hardworking, honest people trying to carve out a better life for themselves and their families to have the same opportunities that I had.

And that's why it's so important that we take action. If the rights of undocumented immigrants aren't being respected, if nonsensical immigration laws are being passed, then no matter where we come from, no matter how long we've been in this country, it is our right and our duty to raise our voices in protest, and to do whatever we can to make the future brighter for our children and the next generation.

CHAPTER 25

A TOUR BUS FOR IMMIGRANT RIGHTS

In 2006, the same year we organized the first march, we also started a campaign to convince permanent residents who hadn't yet applied for citizenship to start the process of becoming American citizens. It was important that we let our voices be heard through our votes, so our politicians would clearly understand our needs and concerns and our problems and the solutions we want for them. As more Hispanic immigrants become citizens, the more of a voice we will have, the more influence we can exert when it comes to what laws get passed, and the more demands we can make in terms of politicians meeting our needs and respecting our rights. To set an example, I decided to apply for my own citizenship to support the campaign to get more Latino voters registered.

I had been a legal permanent resident for several years, but I had never given too much thought to becoming a citizen. When I got my green card, I was just filled with happiness and relief and focused on continuing to work hard. I remember at some point I considered starting the application process, but I kept it on the back burner, simply because my job and my family were absorbing all of my time.

But a number of things happened that made me start to change my mind. The first was the proposed bill HR 4437, which inspired our first march and would have made criminals out of anybody who provided aid to an undocumented immigrant. What I learned from that scare was that the law can be changed at any time, and so I thought to myself, *Wow, what if I won't have a chance to become a citizen later on?* Then I wouldn't be able to voice my opinions at the voting booth. And speaking about changing laws, I learned that Mexico no longer required its people to renounce their citizenship in order to take on another. I was worried that exchanging my Mexican passport for an American passport was somehow a betrayal of my heritage. But that just wasn't true at all; in fact, I've since met many people who have become U.S. citizens, and doing so doesn't make them any less Mexican. Actually, there's an enormous sense of pride in being able to represent both nations. When you get right down to it, we were all born on this earth, and no matter what part of the world you come from, we are all the same. There is only mankind, only one human race.

Another factor that convinced me to get my American citizenship was the many advantages that come with it, including the ability to get documentation for family members. But even more important is the opportunity to vote in the country in which you live, to choose the people who represent you, and to have an impact on the laws that are passed.

And, well, as I mentioned, I wanted to set an example for the listeners who were embarking on this campaign with us, because by that point, I was fully aware of just how important it is for us to put weight behind our words. So in the summer of 2006, I formally applied for my naturalization. I mentioned it during the show whenever I could, and the campaign grew so intense that we even had staffers driving out to potential citizens' homes to deliver the necessary forms, study guides, relevant information, and other documentation.

Studying for the test was not easy for me. It was partly due to the fact that I was never very good at school, but it was also because I was still struggling with my English. But that wouldn't stop me from fulfilling the promise I'd made, and so I listened to the study guide on my way to work every morning. Then, when I got home later that evening, María would ask me sample questions to make sure I was retaining what I had learned. She had always been a very good student herself, and she was a big help to me. But even then, when I was taking the actual test itself, there were some questions that left me thinking, *You gotta be kidding me—where did they get that one from?* I couldn't remember all of them, of course, and I was especially bad at remembering dates. Numbers weren't my strong suit. There were just some questions I couldn't answer, and no way did I even think about taking a cheat sheet into that exam room! But in the end I think I only missed two questions, and so I passed my exam. Now all I had left to do was take the oath of allegiance.

When the time came to pledge allegiance to this great nation, on May 23, 2008, about two months after I'd passed the test and almost two years since I'd started the application process, my experiences from the day I came to this country flashed like a movie before my eyes. I saw myself crossing the border, I saw my uncle's house, I remembered all my early jobs, the drive back to L.A. after being served with my deportation order, the words of the Lord promising to put me in places where I had never been, and everything that came after that: my achievements, the new challenges and difficulties, and love and sincere friendships. At that same ceremony, I saw many of my people also taking the oath, as were so many immigrants from other parts of the globe. We were all filled with joy and embraced one another happily. I couldn't hold back the tears, and began to cry from all the excitement. Finally, all of the sacrifices had paid off, which showed me once again that when you're fighting for something and you refuse to give in even when circumstances are tough, you can succeed.

Each of us has a story to tell, and each story is equally valuable. As I reflected on that notion, I could feel the spirit of those who came to this blessed country before us, the people who fought for the opportunities we now enjoy, so that we might become citizens ourselves. I also thought about all the effort put in by my father and mother. This was a huge reward which I was receiving, and now I had two nationalities, two countries instead of just one.

Thanks to my own citizenship, my mother also applied to get hers. My mom took a little bit longer, because she requested that she take the test in Spanish, and because there are fewer locations that provide that, she had to wait until 2013 to take the oath of allegiance.

The Caravan to Washington in support of immigrant rights was of huge importance to me. It was a significant moment in my life because it was a unique opportunity to contribute to the community and to my people by helping them to improve their situation in this country.

Who would have thought that two decades ago, when I arrived here with no money and no papers, that now, as a United States citizen, I had the chance to summon a movement calling for the American dream—the dream we all have when we come here—to finally become a reality for so many people?

Honestly, I'm not trying to—and I don't want to—portray myself as some sort of hero. That's not me, and I don't think that I am. I'm just one more person helping to build a safe path toward comprehensive immigration reform, where the laws will allow all immigrants to live and work in peace in this country. I'm not the first person to fight for this, and I won't be the last, because before any of us got to this point, people have been fighting the good fight, and until the status of those people who come here to work hard and contribute to the greatness of this nation has been resolved, people will continue to fight so that our aspirations and contributions are recognized. We all contribute in our own ways to making this dream a reality, and nobody is going to snatch it away from us.

The Caravan to Washington was organized in conjunction with many other organizations, including the nonprofit group TODEC (Training Occupational Development Educating Communities) Legal Center, which was the first one to approach us when we put out the call, several representatives from churches, and some members of the media, such as the journalist José Ronstadt, who was with us for the duration of the trip, and many others who helped spread the word about what we were planning to do. The idea was to travel the country, gathering up letters from American citizens and delivering them to their respective senators and representatives to pass an immigration reform bill and put an end to the long years during which the legislature ignored and avoided this issue. The response from the public was huge: in just a short amount of time, we had managed to collect one million letters.

The caravan started as a group of about fifty cars (more would be joining us along the way) setting out from Olvera Street in Los Angeles on June 10, 2007. Before we rolled out, I made a call on the air: "Let's see if any artists will loan us their tour bus!"

I said it just for effect, but somehow I was hoping it could actually happen. And it did! Marco Antonio Solís and the Horóscopos de Durango offered us their bus, and immediately we accepted. My team and I, along with some reporters, all piled in. José Ronstadt and the immigration attorney Enrique Arévalo also joined us.

Along the route, many more people and organizations joined the caravan, including members of Conjunto Primavera and Tony Meléndez, in addition to members of TODEC, who had been with us since the beginning. Just like that, the movement gradually began gathering more and more people, including families traveling in their own cars. I also remember someone on a motorcycle who stuck very close to us the entire way.

The rider was a man named Victor, and I'd met him a few days before the caravan set off. He worked at one of the stations that rebroadcasts our show, and he told me that he wanted to join in and ride the entire way with us on his bike. But it wasn't an easy ride to make because of the terrain, which I would tell him.

"Please, Victor, just hitch your bike to the Piolimobil and ride with us. It's just too dangerous."

But he was adamant about riding his motorcycle all the way to Washington. There was a scary moment when he fell, and we didn't know whether he would be able to make it. Worried, we pulled over and went back to see what had happened, but luckily he was uninjured and able to make the rest of the trip safely.

And of course, I didn't want to stop broadcasting the show, but there were a number of logistical challenges that we had to overcome if we were going to be able to stay on the air. One of the solutions we found was to broadcast the show via the different company stations along the way. That made things a little easier, but many of the stations were spread too far apart from one another, so we had to solve some of the technical issues in order to be able to transmit while on the road through a mobile computer that we installed in the tour bus.

The most surprising thing was not only the sheer number of people who wrote letters asking Congress to take up the issue of comprehensive immigration reform, but also the people themselves who came out to support us at every step along the way: people waving signs that reflected hope and that showed their love and support. Many of them worked in construction jobs or in the fields, and some even leaned forward as we drove past, as if praying for a reform to take place. And in every town we drove through, people brought out food: sandwiches, tacos, tamales, and much more to sustain us on the road. It was times like these that I realized that the need for comprehensive immigration reform was even greater than I had ever thought.

I remember talking about everything that was going on one day with Ronstadt and Arévalo, and they asked me what I felt about everything I'd seen.

"A greater responsibility," I replied.

When we got to stations in cities like Albuquerque, Dallas, or Chicago—where we could transmit our signal—seeing people gathered outside, waiting for us, praying and holding images of Jesus Christ, made a huge impression on me. These experiences made me feel a sense of pride and kept my sense of commitment strong. I will never forget the looks of hope that I saw on people's faces, on the entire extended families that were there. And most important, it wasn't just Latinos, but immigrant families from all over the world, and even White Americans who knew and understood the reasons why we had come to the United States. It's a huge calling, because it touches a sensitive nerve that runs to the heart of this great country: the United States is a nation of immigrants. Its greatness is due—it always has been, and always will be—to them.

The journey was demanding for a number of reasons. First, we didn't have much time to rest, and it's hard to get a good night's sleep on the road when you do. And then there were the calls from opponents saying that we'd never accomplish our goals or that they would be waiting for us further down the road, ready to block our path (something which never actually happened). Sometimes I look at pictures taken of that trip and I realize just how tired and pale I look. But when I think about it, I realize that none of that mattered, because knowing what the trip meant to so many people gave me the energy to keep on going.

When we arrived in Washington on June 14, 2007, four days after leaving Los Angeles, we were greeted by several members of Congress, including the late Ted Kennedy and Bob Menéndez, who, like others with whom we had the opportunity to speak, treated us very well. We were invited into their offices and they listened to what we had to say. They seemed open-minded, they spoke honestly and directly, and they told us they were proud of what we were doing and trying to accomplish.

"When you go back," I remember Ted Kennedy telling me, "please, tell the people that even if we fail to grant them residency, we will keep on fighting to at least get them work permits and Social Security numbers, so they won't continue to be hassled and they can be allowed to work in peace. It would be a small step, but a safe one."

Senator Kennedy's words gave me a lot of confidence, and his intentions seemed sincere to me.

"Senator," I replied, "when I was undocumented, all I wanted was at least to have a work permit."

"I'm very glad to hear that, because there are many people and organizations out there who disagree and would simply put a stop to the discussion right there."

"I'll talk with the people," I promised. "I know it's problematic, because there are those who believe in an 'all or nothing' strategy. But I believe in compromising. I think having a work permit and a Social Security card is an important step. A first step, but still an important one."

Shortly after that meeting, I received a call from Univision anchor Jorge Ramos. I had met him years before, and he is someone whom I have admired ever since I first read an interview with him in which he described how he was able to break through in America. I felt I could identify with his story, and I decided to reach out to him. I told him my own story, and I asked if we could keep in touch to discuss immigration issues. He agreed immediately, and eventually a friendship started. During the days of the Caravan to Washington, we had been in constant contact because of everything surrounding the issue of comprehensive immigration reform.

"Piolín, congratulations!" he said. "The possibility is there for talks to move forward in Congress. And that's thanks to the work you've done."

Up until that time, a conversation about immigration reform was unlikely to happen, and I was thrilled to know that our caravan had served for something good, that at the very least it had opened up the possibility of new discussions regarding immigrant rights. There was, finally, a glimmer of hope.

When I returned to Los Angeles, I decided to fulfill my promise to Senator Kennedy, so I gathered together NGOs and fans of the show to offer their opinions about the possibility of getting a work permit instead of permanent residency. There were those who disagreed, telling me that I was settling for a piece of the pie when what we wanted was the whole thing. But the majority of the people who responded said that a work permit and Social Security card were all they really needed. *We are listening to the voices of our people,* I thought to myself. *The voices of our undocumented brothers and sisters.*

"Many of us have our papers," I said on the show, "but there are those who have nothing, and we have to put ourselves in their shoes."

Later, Ted Kennedy himself called in to the show to do an interview, and I could hear the emotion in his voice when he sang, *"Ay, Jalisco, Jalisco, Jalisco . . .* you have a girlfriend, whose name is Guadalajara!" From what I knew of him, Senator Kennedy was someone who was very supportive of our community and who truly did believe in comprehensive immigration reform.

The debate over the specifics of that reform continued to roll along between members of the immigrant community and members of Congress. Things seemed to be progressing. But in late June of that year, the Senate ended up voting against an immigration reform bill that was on the table and that would have legalized the status of millions of undocumented immigrants. I remember following the vote live, and I was so frustrated at seeing the results that I couldn't hold back my tears. I called Jorge Ramos again to talk about what was going on.

"Don't get discouraged, Piolín," he said. "We have to continue the fight."

And I completely agreed, because we have to keep on moving forward, even when things don't seem to be going our way. We have to keep the struggle alive so that one day we can achieve our dreams.

I continued to stay focused when I was criticized for my stance on immigration reform. Of course I think that the best possible solution for the millions of undocumented immigrants in this country would be a law that grants them a pathway to citizenship. But if that presents too much of an obstacle and prevents us from negotiating a successful resolution to the status of undocumented immigrants, then accepting a work permit would be a good first step. That, at least, would allow them to work in peace, to move about freely, to feel safe and protected by the authorities, to know that the taxes they are paying are being reinvested back into their communities, and much more. When I first came to this country, I would have given anything for the opportunity to have a work permit!

I know that feeling was shared by many immigrants who were in the same situation I had been in, and when I expressed my opinions on the details of immigration reform, I was also looking to express the needs of this community. I never wanted to delve into political debates or anything like that. So I decided the best way to handle the criticism was to be respectful of both the arguments and the people who made them, because one of the things I've learned is that even if I disagree with someone's views, I can still respect the person. That's the only real way to live and grow as a person. And by listening to other points of view, especially those you don't necessarily agree with, you always end up learning something new.

The impact of my public participation in support of immigration reform also brought about something that now makes me laugh because of how ridiculous it was. It happened at the Los Angeles airport, just a few years after I participated in the march and in the Caravan to Washington. I was catching a flight to attend an event being staged by the radio station. When I got to the security checkpoint, I realized that I'd forgotten my driver's license, and therefore had no way of proving my identity. And there was no time to go back to the house because the flight would be boarding very soon.

"I forgot my ID. . . . Does that happen often?" I asked the TSA agent. "What do you do when that happens?"

"Yes, of course it happens," she answered kindly. "I don't think it will be a problem. I just need to talk with my supervisor."

She asked me a few routine questions about my personal information and then called for her supervisor, who arrived just a few moments later. Watching her as she approached us, I could tell that something wasn't quite right.

"Are you the guy who helps out immigrants?" she asked in an odd sort of way.

"Well, I'm in favor of anyone who conducts themselves well," I said. "People who pay their taxes, who learn English, who work hard, who have a clean record, who help grow the economy and who contribute to this great country of ours. Living in the United States is a blessing."

"Ah, that's too bad, because you won't be traveling today," she said.

"I gave you all the information you asked for, and I answered all of your questions. What's the problem?" I protested.

A few days earlier, I had interviewed President Obama in the studio, and I showed her a picture of me with him so she could see for herself that I wasn't pretending to be somebody I'm not.

"Look, I'm not trying to brag or anything," I said, "but I just interviewed the president on my show a few days ago. The Secret Service checked out everything about me, what kind of person I am, everything. They even looked in my shoes! I'm really not trying to pressure or manipulate you in any way, but I was just told that this sort of thing happens all the time, and in the end people are still allowed to travel."

"I'm sorry, but you won't be traveling anywhere today," she insisted dryly.

"Okay, then, thank you," I said, and then left the line and headed for the exit. But then I noticed that the first TSA officer I had spoken to—the one who had told me that my situation was a common one—was following me.

"I'm so sorry," she said when she caught up with me. "She should have let you through. I feel bad for having called her."

"Don't worry. You were just doing your job," I replied. "In fact, I should be thanking you for making sure that flying is safe for all of us when we have to travel."

"Yes, but I couldn't help but overhear how she spoke to you."

"It's okay. Really. But thank you for what you said."

And that was it: I wouldn't be flying that day. But I learned a valuable lesson: Next time, I'd better not forget my driver's license!

Eventually we decided to organize another march in Los Angeles, this time in May of 2010. And again it would be focused on immigration reform, on the importance that migrant workers have for the economy, and to protest a controversial law that had just been passed in Arizona, SB 1070, which, among other things, allows the police to stop anyone purely based on the speculation that he or she might be an undocumented immigrant. Once again, we wanted our voices to be heard, so that Washington wouldn't forget that this issue still needed to be resolved. And just like the previous march, we were joined by a number of artists, including Gloria and Emilio Estefan, Kate del Castillo, Jessica Maldonado, Demián Bichir, and many others.

I called a lot of them myself, to personally invite them. I believed it was very important that we show a united front, and let people know that we were concerned about the status of all immigrants. And the response I received was overwhelmingly positive. I remember, for example, that Emilio and Gloria Estefan had a commitment in Las Vegas the same day on which we were planning on holding the march. I only learned that they would be in Vegas the day before, and even though they had the previous commitment, I thought it would be worthwhile to call them. And in the end, they were able to reorganize their calendar and attend the march.

Just like 2006, I broadcasted the show from the starting point of the march, several blocks from the mayor's house. We walked peacefully and in tight formation, and did exactly what we wanted to do: Remind everyone about the importance of the immigrant community, and that the contributions that immigrants make to this great land of ours need to be recognized. When we reached the mayor's home, I took Emilio and Gloria straight to the airport so they could fly to Las Vegas and fulfill their obligations there.

• • •

I had met Gloria and Emilio some years before that march, during an event that was part of my radio show. I knew I liked them as soon as we shook hands, and we stayed in touch after that. Gradually, our friendship grew from sharing ideas and values, as did my admiration for them as people. They're both so humble and down to earth, and treat everyone equally, whether you're famous or not. They encourage ambition in others and like to see people get ahead.

Plus, Emilio has an uncanny ability to turn negative situations into positive ones, and always have a good time in the end. For example, in 2008, he invited me to participate in a program he produced every holiday season called Nuestra Navidad. We would be doing a segment in Mexico City, showing how we celebrate Christmas in Mexico. I'd also be visiting with children and asking them to send greetings to young cancer patients at St. Jude Children's Research Hospital in Tennessee, which was supported by the Ronald McDonald House charities.

A portion of the event would be recorded at the National Auditorium, right in the center of the city. But in the end, due to technical difficulties, we weren't able to record inside the auditorium, so our only other option was to record outside the building. I was a little worried because we didn't have the proper equipment for recording outdoors, but Emilio wasn't concerned. Immediately, he started chatting with people there on the street, and before long we had solved our problems and would be able to record there after all. I was in awe. Watching him work inspires me to do better myself and to not worry so much about the small stuff, because any problem can be solved with determination, imagination, and a little bit of good humor.

When we started rolling, I was touched by something that happened, something that taught me a great lesson about the generosity we, as people, are capable of. I knelt down on the sidewalk to interview a child who had a soccer ball with him and was doing his homework while his father was working as a street vendor. I told him about the other children at St. Jude, and asked him to send them a message. Instead, the young boy handed me his ball. He said it was the only ball he owned, but he wanted me to give it to the children in the hospital. I couldn't accept it.

"But they need it more," he said.

Seeing such generosity from a child left me speechless, and of course we donated a new ball to the Ronald McDonald House so they could pass it on to the young cancer patients in Tennessee. I don't think that any other gift could have been more significant than that one.

CHAPTER 26

STAY STRONG

I think many Americans aren't fully aware of the strong sense of solidarity that our community feels toward this country and the ones we love, or how grateful we are to be here. So I think it's incredibly important that we show non-Latinos who we truly are. When a non-Latino hears about why we cross the border, when they learn about the needs back in our homeland and about our desire to provide more opportunities for our families, then most will understand our motives.

Jeff Holden, who hired me in Sacramento and did so much on my behalf, is a clear example. He not only helped me to legalize my status, but he has become something of an angel to many other Latinos who have just arrived here, who have already been here for some time, or who were even born here and yet still lack the basic means to be successful in life. Jeff helps them apply for scholarships so they can further their studies, and he does this based on what he's learned from reaching out to the Latino community. When I talk with him, he often tells me how well-prepared our people are, and what a shame it is that oftentimes they don't have the money or the opportunities—or the documents—to fully develop. And although his work doesn't just focus on the Spanish-speaking community, it's clear just how much Jeff is doing to help it. It's times like these, when I'm talking with him or remembering everything that he has done, that I believe there's a reason why God led our paths to cross. I'm just filled with pride every time he sends me pictures of people whom he's helped with a scholarship.

• • •

One of the things we wanted to achieve with the marches and the caravan was for average Americans to understand our reality, for them to learn who we are and to see what we, as a community, are doing for the country. And the fact that so many people had attended the marches and participated in the caravan had caught the attention of a new and different audience that until then had remained on the outskirts of the issue: politicians. That's why we were received by Senators Menéndez and Kennedy and Congressmen Lincoln Díaz-Balart, Mario Díaz-Balart, Joe Baca, Hilda Solís, and Grace Napolitano when we got to Washington. After that, two presidential candidates—Hillary Clinton and Barack Obama—realized just how strong the show's draw was, so they reached out to us and asked to be interviewed. Of course I agreed, because it would give my listeners a chance to hear the plans and proposals directly from the candidates' mouths, and the listeners could also ask questions and express concerns.

That was how Hillary Clinton's team—when she was still one of the Democratic Party candidates—contacted me to set up a telephone interview, which we aired live on *Piolín in the Morning.* She was the first of the candidates to do so, and shortly after her interview, Obama would visit the studio in person. In fact, I was the first Spanish-language radio host to interview him, and the same thing would happen four years later, when our studio would be the first one he visited as President of the United States.

I especially remember his interview while still a candidate because of something that happened at the very end.

"There's something important that you should know," I said on the air, "something that all the candidates should know, and that is you can count on my support whenever you might need it, whether it's a disaster like Hurricane Katrina, or anything else."

And that gave me a reason to tell a few stories about how our people have chipped in and helped out this country. I told him that our community doesn't care whether their donations go to help other Latinos; just that there is a need at any given time, and that there might be a way for them to help. In fact, to this day, I can't remember anyone ever asking me whether our disaster relief collections—canned food and other staples—were going only to Latino victims. That's one of our greatest strengths: We're involved in this country's needs, and we care about the well-being of all Americans, not just those in our immediate community.

"Since you're campaigning online and on television urging people to vote for you," I continued, "I'd appreciate it if your campaign would acknowledge what our people are doing, so that others can see how we are contributing to this country, so that they can see how the vast majority of us came here to build a better future for our families, just like all the other citizens of this great nation. If people begin to see that, then public opinion could swing in favor of immigration reform that helps these families gain more opportunities. Besides, my listeners don't just help people who live in this country, but also their own families when they wire money abroad. Just imagine the quality of the people we have here, the generous hearts that they have." At this point of the interview, I brought up a recent example of my community's solidarity with all Americans, when we had gone to Houston to collect food and other donations for those affected by Hurricane Ike. "Look, I'm proud because I have listeners who might have had just a gallon of water for their own family, and yet they decided that the hurricane victims needed it more than they did. Some even carried it to them in person."

Obama listened with great interest to what I had to say about the need to raise awareness of the important role our community plays in building up the greatness of this country.

"Very well," he replied. "It's clear that you want comprehensive immigration reform to pass. Why don't you ask your listeners to vote for me? Tell them that. You know I'm the person who can get that done."

His question was a double-edged sword, and I couldn't fully commit to it because I wanted to get this message out to the entire country, not just one party.

"With all due respect, I cannot do that, and I'll tell you why," I replied. "First, I have to interview the other candidates so they can express their own proposals to the listeners, who can decide for themselves whom to vote for. I don't want them to do something just because Piolín said so. Also, the needs of the Latino community here in Los Angeles are different from those in Chicago, New York, Texas, Colorado, Nevada, Oregon, Florida, and so on. So I'm afraid I can't do that." Here we both started to laugh, because we were both feeling a bit nervous and we had to release some of the tension. Then I continued. "What you're suggesting is very interesting, very interesting indeed. And again, you can count on me and my listeners if you need anything, not just on the immigration front, but also when it comes to disaster relief or issues concerning health, education, whatever. And I'll say the same thing to the other candidates as well."

My answer annoyed some of my colleagues, who wanted me to endorse one party or one candidate. They argued that if I did that, it would create a better platform and gain more exposure.

"But that's not my intent," I'd say. "If it were, I would have said what he wanted me to say."

Maybe they had wanted me to do that because it would be good for the show or perhaps even for my career in general. But I stood my ground because I was convinced that what I had done was for the best: the most important thing was that the listeners make their own decisions based on the arguments put forth by every candidate I interviewed, not just because of my opinion.

Interviews with the primary candidates were a sure sign that the program was growing in size and scope. Since coming to Los Angeles, I had been syndicated in so many more cities than the ones in which the original broadcasts were being aired. Even though ratings were already quite high in cities where *Piolín in the Morning* was being broadcasted—Los Angeles, Phoenix, Dallas, El Paso, San Francisco, and San Jose, among others—there were other major cities with large Latino populations that were still missing from that list. That was when I started to make a strong push to get a presence in cities like New York and Chicago. New York presented an especially tough challenge, because nobody wanted to give us a chance.

"The problem is that your show is specifically directed toward Mexicans," I was told, as if this were an excuse not to add the show to their regularly scheduled programming.

Unlike California, New Mexico, Texas, and other states and cities where most of the immigrants are from Mexico, New York has huge

Puerto Rican, Cuban, and Dominican communities, and while there are Mexican immigrants who live there, they don't represent the majority of the Latino population in that city.

"No, my program is not just for Mexicans. It's for immigrant families from anywhere." That was my answer.

After many months of struggling, we were offered a slot on a New York station, but it had a very weak signal. Fortunately, they had a great team, and before long, the show took off and got really good ratings. We were able to show those who didn't believe in the program's potential in New York that even though the listeners' backgrounds were different, they could all still identify with the issues we were discussing. The same thing would happen in Chicago as well.

This is something I've always said, something I've always insisted on: no matter what your nationality may be, there are things that unite us beyond our language. A good joke can make everyone laugh. The same holds true for positive messages, as it does for the question with which I identify—*¿A qué venimos?* (Why do we come?)—and for the response: *¡A triunfar!* (To succeed).

The success we garnered in New York and Chicago opened many people's eyes and brought us many new opportunities. The show was being broadcast in more cities than ever, and we had a presence on over sixty radio stations. But unfortunately, with prosperity came staff turnover in the New York and Chicago offices. After that, the attention and promotion given to the show was never the same, and that had an effect on us.

Meanwhile, back in Los Angeles, I continued to organize soccer games with listeners and get professional artists and athletes involved as well. On one occasion, we organized a game to help raise funds for the family of a Salvadoran soldier who was killed in action in 2004 while on a mission in support of American troops during Operation Iraqi Freedom.

I first learned of this story one day while watching the news. They showed how his mother and sister lived in a run-down home. He had been sending them money and had broken ground on a new home for them so they could live better lives. But without his help, they now found themselves in a very sad and very difficult situation. I was so moved by the story that I decided to share it with my listeners. I also managed to get in touch with his mother and sister in El Salvador and I told them that we were going to help raise enough money to finish the house that their young soldier had begun.

I invited Mauricio Cienfuegos, a Salvadoran player who had played both for his national team and with the L.A. Galaxy club team, to attend the fund-raiser, and he eagerly agreed. As has always been the case, a nonprofit organization was responsible for collecting the funds—for ethical reasons, I never, for any reason, manage or otherwise handle the money collected at these charity events—and we finally collected enough donations to finish constructing the house.

The show was also beginning to reach across national boundaries, as was evidenced by this case with the Salvadoran family, along with a couple of trips abroad I made with my listeners, because our community is not just limited to those living inside the United States.

One of my dreams was to see live one of the classic rivalries of Mexican soccer: Chivas vs. América. When I got my green card, I realized that I could finally fulfill that dream, as I could go to Mexico to watch the game and come back to the United States without any problems. When you don't have papers, you can't leave the country, because you probably won't be able to get back in. I decided to invite a few of my listeners who had never been able to attend the classic matchup either. That's something I always like to do whenever I'm about to experience something new and exciting: share it with my audience and give more people the opportunity to do the same. So I organized a competition to select those who would be attending the game with me, we bought the tickets and everything, and we headed to Guadalajara to watch the game. I can't remember exactly how it happened, though I expect it was all because of the tight budget we were working with, but we ended up all crammed into one little car, piled on top of each other. It was a bit uncomfortable, but once we finally got to the stadium, nothing could take away from the enjoyment of the game!

On another occasion, at a listener's request, we crossed the border and went to a drug and alcohol rehab center in Tijuana to bring some food to the inpatients there. We left Los Angeles with several cars packed with everything we had collected.

The staff of the rehab clinic warned us that we would be seeing some pretty shocking things there, and they weren't exaggerating. I remember one scene in particular that stunned me: a room filled with people walking around in circles, nonstop. The skin on their arms and legs was covered in sores and filled with holes, and they seemed at once frenzied and hopeless. The sadness I felt watching and listening to them was crushing.

Before leaving Los Angeles, I noticed that one of the people accompanying us, a man, had brought his twelve-year-old son.

"Paisano, why did you bring your son?" I asked. "This type of clinic is not a place for children."

"I want him to see what drugs can do to a person," he replied. "I already told him about the dangers of using drugs, but I want him to see with his own eyes what happens to people who use them."

Unbelievable! I thought to myself.

"Well, if you think it's okay," I said. "He's your son."

After we left the clinic, I asked the boy how he felt, and I could tell that the images had shocked him. It is incredibly sad to see what happens to people who let alcohol and other drugs take over their lives. I know from firsthand experience that seeing the effects of substance abuse up close and personal leaves a much bigger impression on you than just being told about it.

On yet another occasion, a man named Fernando called us from a pay phone. He was practically begging for our help, as his family was about to leave him because he was an alcoholic. He had already tried to stop drinking several times, none of which was successful. After spending a few anguishing minutes on the phone with him, he finally agreed to go to a treatment center, and now he's doing fine. He's very grateful to God for giving him the opportunity to recover. I'm still in touch with him to this very day; he attends almost every event we organize, and always offers to volunteer his help. But what gives me the greatest joy of all is knowing that those of us here at the program were able to help him.

Another one of the miracles I've experienced is something that happened to another listener, this one much smaller than the other. It was in December of 2012, and on one of those rare occasions when I took some time off for the holidays. I was relaxing at home when I received an e-mail from someone asking me to make a surprise visit to a twelve-year-old boy who was in a children's hospital suffering from leukemia.

Since I hadn't been in the office, nobody else knew about this, and I went to visit the child on my own, which was rare, because I would usually bring a whole group of people with me on visits like this. Usually it's because we're collecting toys for a child or hosting marathon fund-raising events on the radio to raise money to cover medical costs, but obviously, this time, I couldn't do all that by myself. But so many people love bringing help and happiness to others, and my colleagues and listeners often ask me if they can come along.

I asked what the boy liked and was told that anything that had to do with the Lakers, like a T-shirt or a hat, would be perfect. There's a shop next to the hospital, and for some reason I thought I could pick up a present there. But it turned out that I was wrong, and they didn't have any Lakers memorabilia. So I called a friend who knew the area and asked him where I could find what I needed.

"Well, there aren't really any sporting goods shops nearby," he said. "You'll have to go back to Burbank or Hollywood."

And that was really far away. Just then the store manager came up and greeted me. I told him what I was looking for, and he also said that he didn't know of any nearby places to get a Lakers T-shirt or hat. But then I saw a soda truck driver stocking the shelves, and I thought to myself, *This guy must surely know the neighborhood, since he probably makes deliveries all around here.*

"Hello there. How are you?" I asked.

He turned around and recognized me.

"Hey, what's up, Piolín?" he said.

"Listen, brother. Sorry to bother you, but I'm looking for a sporting goods shop. I want to pick up a Lakers cap."

"Hmmm . . . that's a tough one. There isn't much around here. You're better off going to Hollywood or Burbank."

"That's so far away, and I came here just to visit a sick boy in the hospital who is a big Lakers fan."

"Let me see, I might have something," he said. "Let's check my truck."

At first I was excited at the possibility of having found a gift, but then I started worrying about other concerns: What's if it's a used hat? What should I do? The boy's immune system would be weakened, so I couldn't give him something old that might put him at further risk, and how would it look to the family if I brought a secondhand gift?

When we got to the truck, he opened up the back and pulled out a small box containing a bunch of new hats. We started to look through them, but none of them had a Lakers logo on it! When we were about to give up, I happened to see one that we hadn't noticed before, with the colors gray, gold, and purple.

"Hey, brother, pull that one out," I asked. At least it had the Lakers colors on it, which was a good sign. And my hunch was right. Not only was it exactly what I was looking for—it also had the NBA logo on it, which meant it was authentic! It's crazy to see how God can work in such mysterious ways.

"Are you okay, Piolín?" he asked, since I looked so shocked.

"Yeah, bro . . . it's a blessing from heaven!" I said.

What followed was a bit of a difficult negotiation, because he didn't want to accept payment for the hat, but in the end I was able to convince him to take something in return. I said good-bye, thanking him profusely, and headed for the hospital. I asked a nurse about this young patient I was looking for, and she showed me to his room. I poked my head inside and could see that he and his dad were both fast asleep. I tried not to wake them, but the father slowly opened one eye.

"Piolín!" he exclaimed. It was a total surprise, because nobody knew that I was coming.

"Yes, it's me," I answered, whispering so I wouldn't wake up his son. "I came to visit your son, after getting an e-mail about him from one of my listeners. Here, I'll leave the Lakers hat with you. I don't want to wake him."

But no sooner had I said that than the boy woke up, and the first thing he saw when he opened his eyes was the hat in my hands.

"Hey, that's the one I always wanted!" he cried out.

No, this is too much to be a coincidence, I thought to myself.

"Someone get me a stretcher, because I'm about to faint," I said. Then I told the boy the story about how I came to find that hat. He listened to every word, and when the nurse came to check in, she could see that we all had tears in our eyes.

"Look at my new hat!" the boy told her. "How cool is this!"

The nurse smiled when she realized what was happening. Then she approached me and told me about another family who had just come in to admit their daughter, who also had leukemia, into the cancer ward. They had heard that I was there in the hospital, and asked if I would come and meet them.

"Yes, of course," I replied. "As soon as I'm done here, I'll go visit with them."

After saying good-bye to the young Lakers fan, I walked up to the nurses' station and asked about the other family. The nurse took me to their room, where I introduced myself. They told me they were from Zacatecas, Mexico.

"Ask Piolín to help us," the girl's mother said to the father, seconds after everyone had introduced themselves.

"No, are you kidding me?" he replied. "Everyone who needs help calls Piolín. He already did us the favor of coming to visit us here. We shouldn't bother him anymore."

"It's okay. What's the problem, paisano?" I asked.

He didn't have a chance to answer, because right at that moment the nurse entered the room and began to explain how all the equipment they would be using worked. Since they didn't speak English and the nurse didn't speak much Spanish, I—after struggling with the language myself for so many years before finally being able to speak and understand it fairly well—offered to serve as interpreter. That took us some time, but once the nurse left the room, I pressed the father again to tell me what was going on. Finally, he agreed to speak.

"What happened is that they pulled me over for driving without a license. I got a ticket, and now I could be deported at any moment."

"Just tell me the truth, please," I asked. In the past, I've had people try to hide the fact that they have something bad on their record from me, and, well, that just doesn't do anybody any good. "Is there anything else other than the fine? Are you in any other sort of trouble with the authorities? Were you driving drunk or anything?"

"No, just without a license."

I ended up calling Enrique Arévalo, the immigration attorney, and told him about this family's situation. I asked if he would be willing to help them out, and he agreed. Thankfully, everything worked out well for them, as they now have legal residency in this country.

Stories like these are why I don't believe in coincidences. There's always a reason for why things happen, and God never ceases to amaze me with His miracles. I told this story on the air one day, and said that it was not only a miracle for this family, but for me as well. It's important for our people to keep their faith strong when faced by the many challenges life throws at us, and this case is a clear example of that. This man, like me, was in danger of being deported, and now he is a legal resident.

As I've mentioned before, there are so many times when people have told me that I won't be able to achieve what I've set out to do, that my ideas are impossible to achieve because I simply won't be able to do it on my own or find support. But comments like these just give me more of a reason to keep trying and accomplish my goals. And that's exactly what happened when I suggested that we invite Paulina Rubio to deliver a donation of tacos to the warehouses and factories where so many of our people work: I was told she would never agree to do it.

"Well, at least let me talk to her," I said.

So I did, and she agreed. She and I both went out and delivered the food; she talked with the people, she learned that many of them were big fans of hers, and all in all, she was delighted with the experience. She told me to call on her whenever I needed her help, and I did.

That wasn't the first time I invited an artist to help deliver food to our people. That was something I'd started back in San Jose, and it was a success, though I guess it didn't hurt that the first artist who agreed to participate was José José, who is a popular singer.

Over time, I began inviting other artists to participate, often in the same capacity. Almost all of them were happy to accept, and they really seemed to enjoy the experience. Though I think that the ones who enjoyed it the most were the people for whom we brought the food, the people who got the chance to meet some of their favorite performers and talk with them up close and personal, including the members of Maná, Lupillo Rivera, Jenni Rivera, José Manuel Figueroa, Cristian Castro, Enrique Iglesias, Banda El Recodo, La Arrolladora Banda El Limón, Los Tigres del Norte, Aracely Arámbula, Pablo Montero, Valentín Elizalde, Espinoza Paz, Alejandro Sanz, Ninel Conde, Los Huracanes del Norte, the comedian El Costeño, and many more. This also gave the artists a new and unique way of interacting with their fans.

The generosity of so many of these artists never ceases to amaze me. For example, when Vicente Fernández was on the show, he gave us one of his suits so we could auction it off as part of a fund-raiser for a children's hospital. Jennifer Lopez gave us a very elegant hat, Pepe Aguilar gave us a bracelet he was wearing, Angélica María and Angélica Vale left us the scarves they were wearing and Pitbull donated a designer watch. These are just a few examples of the many people who made such contributions. In fact, it's become something of a tradition now, where the artists who visit us in the studio leave some item or article of clothing that we can raffle off, and we then donate the proceeds to a children's hospital.

And speaking of Vicente Fernández, one of the times he stopped by the studio in Los Angeles, we wanted to thank him for all the generosity he's always shown us, for believing in our program and for supporting us with his presence. I'd been thinking for quite some time about what we could give to a man who already has it all. Finally, an idea came to mind: a trowel! Before becoming the famous singer he is today, Vicente Fernández worked as a bricklayer in Tijuana. We thought it would be a good idea to give him something that would be a tribute to his origins and the long road he had to travel to stardom, because that is something that I always admired about him. We decided to have it engraved with a Bible verse. I was a little nervous when it came time to give him the gift, because I wasn't quite sure how he would react, but he really seemed to like it and he thanked us from the bottom of his heart.

Once the show had started to grow and attract a wider audience, it became more common for artists and celebrities to visit with us in the studio. I usually never get nervous interviewing any of them because, while I admire them deeply, I always feel at ease in their presence and I always try to remain calm and confident. But when Aracely Arámbula visited the show, even I got my tongue tied up in knots. She showed up wearing no makeup but was still as beautiful as ever. I was speechless, and since I couldn't stop making mistakes, I tried to play it off as if I were feeling a little sick.

"My brother's a doctor," she said. "If you like, I can have him give you a shot."

If I'd had a mentor like Grandpa Bartolo when I first got here, perhaps the story would have been a little different, at least when it comes to my ability to deal with certain situations. As I've mentioned, early on in my career as a radio talk show host, I encountered a lot of jealous and envious people. And the frequency and intensity of these encounters only increased when I arrived in Los Angeles.

I know situations like this come up in any job, not just in the communications industry, and people with malicious intentions are everywhere, but there did come a time when the accusations and nasty comments started to hurt so much that I just didn't know how to react.

Several times, I would call Emilio Estefan, with whom I had already formed a close friendship. I cried on the phone, sitting there in the radio station's parking lot. He talked with me about the issues I was encountering frequently, and the people who were spreading lies about me, trying to bring me down. Some calls were longer than others, but on one occasion I spent hours sobbing in the darkness, feeling completely alone, with only Emilio on the other end of the line, listening patiently and offering his advice. It was nine o'clock at night in Los Angeles, which meant it was midnight in Miami, where he was.

"Be strong," Emilio would say. "Calm down and take a deep breath."

But I kept crying like a child.

Meanwhile, Emilio took the time to stay on the line and reassure me that things would be okay. He said that I had to stand firm, and that he'd been through many similar situations when he first arrived here from Cuba.

"These are the challenges that we face in life, and you have to stay strong," he repeated.

Then he asked me to call him the next day and tell him how I was feeling. I was doing a little bit better by the time I reported back to him. But I also thought to myself, *What must they think of me now? I'm a grown man with a family, and yet I was blubbering like a child!*

In this industry, sometimes it can seem like you have no friends, or, at least, you're not quite sure who your real friends are. And that feels awful. But Emilio and Gloria have been tried-and-true friends throughout the years that I've known them.

I remember not wanting to go home on nights like that, because I didn't want María and my kids to see me crying, as if I'd been defeated.

I guess there are lots of folks out there rooting for people to fail, who don't like to accept the reality of your success, especially when you're a person with not much of a higher education, like me. I suppose some people might think to themselves, *I'm smarter than him, but I've never gotten what he has,* and that must be a painful thought. But there are ways of dealing with that kind of frustration without the need to harm others. It's a shame that more people don't realize that. But it's also important that you learn how to deal with those people who let frustration take over their lives; you have to bear in mind that these people will do more harm to themselves than to anybody else. Talking with Emilio really helped me come to terms with this and be able to overcome these challenges, to realize that I shouldn't let others bring me down, to put myself in God's hands and keep moving forward believing in myself to get even stronger and achieve even more.

I've never spoken about these late-night calls with María or with anyone else. The pressure felt so intense that I didn't want to bring anxiety and worry into my family. Emilio was the only person I felt I could trust at that point in time: a very important figure in my life who has always given me his trust and his sincere friendship without expecting anything in return.

After those calls, I'd always tell Gloria and Emilio just how grateful I am to them for the time they've given me, for Emilio's words of wisdom that helped me to see things more clearly and allowed me to set the pain aside and never give up.

CHAPTER 27

OPTION D: ALL OF THE ABOVE

One of the promises that President Obama made to me the first time that he came on my show—back in 2008 when he was still just a candidate—was that he would make a return visit after he had been elected. And he delivered on that promise, but not before Michelle came by the studio with their two daughters.

The interview with President Obama took place in 2010. Before that, I spoke with him on the phone, and told him that I wanted to form a group of people who weren't looking for political positions, but who wanted to support the push for immigration reform and address any other needs facing the American people as a whole, not just the Latino community. He thought that was a very good idea, and I promised to give him a list of names later on. We agreed to keep in touch.

The opportunity to start building that list of people—a group of independent citizens—first presented itself shortly after that phone call, when I was invited to the White House to record an interview with the President. I wanted to bring him something, a small gift to commemorate that meeting and to thank him for symbolically opening the White House doors to my listeners. I remember hearing that other people had brought him basketballs and footballs, so I decided it was time that someone gave him a soccer ball.

Once I entered the Oval Office, we took a picture together, and looking at the photo, you can see that I have one leg raised up. The reason I always lift my leg up is because it's my signature pose for pictures. Many people criticized me for raising my leg in a photo with the President, but honestly, I don't even realize it when it's happening!

After we took the picture, I gave him the soccer ball and we conducted the interview just as we planned. I also gave him the list of names I had promised him, which included Emilio Estefan, Don Francisco, and an immigration attorney by the name of Jessica Dominguez. He had a few names of his own to add to the list, and that's how we started working to form this group.

Years later, when the midterm elections of 2010 were getting near, a representative from the White House reached out to me to see if we could set up an interview with the President on *Piolín in the Morning*. We agreed on a date, and had the Secret Service come by right away to check out the studio. It was just like in the movies, and you can even search the Internet for a video of the Secret Service at our station. They inspected everything very thoroughly, showed me what movements I could make, and where I would have to sit. Since the studio has a window that looks out over other buildings, soldiers and other Secret Service agents were placed at different strategic locations all around. It was crazy.

I had no idea that the President's visit would be preceded by such a thorough investigation! There were just so many restrictions the Secret Service gave us about what we could and could not do, the ways we could and could not move, and when I was actually interviewing Obama . . . *ay carambolas!* I barely moved at all because I didn't know whether I should or not.

But I was also nervous about the questions I would be asking him.

During the inspection, something funny happened when one of the Secret Service agents was asking me questions. He mentioned that his mom listened to the show all the time, and she admired the work I was doing on behalf of immigration reform.

"If you like, I can give her a call and say hello," I offered.

"Thanks! Yes, she would really appreciate that," he replied. "But now I have to ask you another favor: Please don't tell her where I work. She doesn't know."

And that's exactly what I did. I called her up and told her that I had met her son, and I could tell that he was a great person. She was so excited to have gotten that call, and seemed really appreciative.

When it was finally time to interview President Obama, we were all set. He entered the studio; we shook hands and spoke briefly, which was when I told him I would be asking him questions that had been sent in by our listeners. And with that, we went live.

As with previous interviews I've done on my show, I had asked listeners to submit questions for me to ask on the air, and I used those questions to guide the flow of the interview, because I wanted to address the issues that were most important to our audience. I don't remember each and every word we exchanged that day, but for the most part, the interview went like this:

"Do you remember when I promised you that I could come back and make an appearance on your show after I was elected President?" he asked on the air.

"Of course," I replied. "And with that, let's get this interview started. Mr. President, I'd like to give you the option of selecting the first topic of our discussion."

"Whatever you'd like to talk about, Piolín, we'll talk about."

"I'll just give you a few choices. Are you ready?"

"I am."

"Option A: immigration reform. Option B: immigration reform. Option C: immigration reform. Or option D: all of the above."

We started to chuckle.

"I think I'll choose option D," he replied. "All of the above. Of course."

The first question I asked him had to do with the disappointment felt by many in the Latino community regarding immigration reform. It had been one of Obama's campaign promises, yet so far we had not seen any significant progress in this regard. I told him that many people thought he didn't put as much effort into immigration reform as he put into health care reform.

"Piolín, I know I'm in your house here," he answered, sounding a bit annoyed, "but I have to say I disagree with what you just said. I am not a king, I'm a president, and I can't just say something and have it be done."

I said that I agreed with that, but back when he appeared on my show as a candidate, he had talked about pushing it through Congress. I told him I held him in the highest respect, but that I was just passing along the concerns of my people, and that I was sure I wasn't the first person to have brought up that issue.

I don't think very many people, if any, thought I would be posing these sorts of questions to the President. Most assumed that I wouldn't bring up the issues they wanted answers to. But I did, even if it made my guest a bit uncomfortable.

President Obama responded by saying that he was indeed fighting on behalf of reform, but it was the Republicans who were staunchly opposed to it.

"Mr. President, it's both parties," I protested. At that time, early in his presidency, the Democrats were the majority party in both the House and the Senate, and not all of them had voted in favor of immigration reform, though they had when it came to health care reform. "Tell us how we can help and we will gladly do so. Remember when I gave you that list of people who are willing to do whatever is needed? Please, tell me what we need to do."

When I finished with the questions, I insisted again that we must continue to support and stand firm for immigration reform. The President agreed.

After that, in 2011, when the President and his team had finally finished putting together the list of individuals who would be campaigning in support of comprehensive immigration reform—though not seeking public office—we all agreed to gather together for a meeting at the White House. The group was comprised of a number of different figures from the entertainment, media, and public advocacy arenas. The President attended the meeting, along with people like Emilio Estefan, Don Francisco, Eva Longoria, América Ferrera, José Díaz-Balart, María Elena Salinas, among others. The group stressed the need for immigration reform that would solve the difficult situation faced by millions of undocumented immigrants currently living in the country. I also talked about how disappointed people were about the lack of progress being made on this issue, and everyone seemed a bit surprised that I had mentioned that. For his part, Obama insisted that he was still trying to convince the Republicans. Although the issue has yet to be resolved, the President, close to the end of his mandate, is trying to help improve the situation of millions of immigrants by delivering an Executive Order.

Obama was not the first President I had interviewed. Years before, when I was still working in San Jose, I went to Mexico, where I met with President Vicente Fox. I had been in touch with his staff to propose a meeting with him, and they agreed. I flew to Mexico City and met with him at Los Pinos, the official presidential home. My purpose was to tell him about the needs of our people living here, in the United States, and about developing more ways to support them through the consulates. I felt that the Mexican consulates in the United States could be taking a more active role, and that's exactly what I told him. I also asked him if we could speak on the phone from time to time so that I could pass along sentiments of our people. He agreed, and we were in touch several times throughout his presidency. Overall, President Fox was very relaxed throughout the entire interview.

When I returned to San Jose, I broadcasted the audio portion of that interview on the air, along with another one I did with some children from the streets. I remember that the latter interview attracted a lot of attention because of one child in particular, a charming little twelve-year-old filled with great charisma and energy.

"Hey, why are you out here sniffing cement?" I asked. "Why do you live on the streets?"

"Because there are no jobs," he told me.

It was incredibly sad to see a child as bright as him with such a bleak future. Not to mention the fact that he was worried about finding work at such a young age. I find these sorts of things, which happen all the time and all over the world, really tragic. After the interview, I took him out to lunch at a pizzeria near the Zócalo plaza, where we continued to talk. I gave him some advice and a bit of financial aid, and to a certain extent, we became friends.

I don't know if that interview with President Fox resulted in any official changes in the way the Mexican government treats our compatriots who live on this side of the border, but we did start to notice that the Mexican consuls began opening up to our program and would often lend a helping hand toward our listeners.

For example, if someone needed assistance sending the body of a deceased family member back to Mexico, and we announced it on the show, they moved quickly to help. If someone got lost trying to cross the border, they quickly called the INS to investigate, and because of that, many people were rescued. I remember that the Mexican consul in Santa Ana at the time came on the show to answer questions for my listeners, and before we ended the interview, he gave out his cell phone number on the air so that those who needed his help could reach him directly. I was very surprised by his gesture, and I'm truly grateful that he did so, especially because many people would later tell me that they did, in fact, reach out to him, and he did come through with the help that they needed. Later, the consuls in Los Angeles also reached out to people through my program. After seeing the positive impact that their support had in our community, I hope that other consulates across the country get more involved with their local communities and develop closer relationships with them.

For all the Latinos in this country, having a close and effective relationship with their consulates is an important thing.

And now that I'm on the topic, I'm reminded of a story involving a consul that truly impressed me and which I remember fondly. When I was working in San Jose, back in 2001, there was a devastating earthquake in El Salvador, and we at the show decided to organize a car wash fund-raiser to generate some money to help the affected families. We invited the El Salvador consul to attend the event, and he came all the way from San Francisco to participate.

"The consul has arrived," I was told, right when the car wash was in full swing.

"Ah, yes," I said. "His presence here means a lot. I'm glad that he came. Maybe it would be best if he joined in with the Red Cross to collect donations."

I thought they'd take him off to some place where he could be highly visible by everyone there, and yet comfortable at the same time. But apparently he wasn't there for photo opportunities, because right away he rolled up his sleeves and started washing cars. I was shocked; I'd never seen anything quite like it. After we finished, I had a chance to speak with him, and he turned out to be a really good guy, which didn't really surprise me.

I had the opportunity to meet other consuls from other parts of Latin America. They represented all sorts of people, and I was amazed by how committed many of these consuls were to their respective communities.

I've been told so many times that my show is only for a Mexican audience because I'm Mexican myself. And many times I've been able to prove that the people who insist on this are wrong—the proof being the success the program has enjoyed throughout its existence, even in the cities where the majority of the Latino population is not of Mexican descent.

This fills me with a lot of pride, because it proves that all the programs I've done over the years have served as a bridge to unite different nationalities. And despite whatever differences we may have, we Latino people will always find ways to help each other and find new ways to get ahead.

CHAPTER 28

JUST TWO MILES LEFT TO GO

I believe that the greatest success you can achieve in life doesn't come from the outside, but from within your own family.

That's why my faith in God is my highest priority following my wife and children. It is because of my family that I wake up every morning and give everything I have. I know that not everything is perfect, but I believe that everything I do and everything I have is thanks to God and to my family, who molded me, to María, my constant companion, and to my children.

I'd like to share with you something that I heard the other day in church, and I think it's especially important to everyone with a family of their own. It's a verse from the Gospel of Matthew, followed by a very brief reflection.

> ***Matthew 6:33***
>
> *But seek ye first the kingdom of God, and his righteousness; and all these things shall be added unto you.*
>
> *This is the order of things:*
>
> *1. God*
>
> *2. Marriage*
>
> *3. Children*
>
> *Before making any decision in life, you have to ask yourself how it will affect your relationship with and your commitment to God, to your spouse, and your children.*

That's why, whenever María and I have to make a tough decision that affects our family, we give ourselves over to God and ask Him for the wisdom to choose the right path.

Building a family can be a challenge, and the path to happiness together can be filled with tests. I can't say that my own marriage has been without challenges, but in addition to our faith in God, there is something else that has helped us out from the very beginning: the affinity between María's family and my own was such that, from the moment they met, the two families often appear to be one. It has been a tremendous blessing.

When our two families get together—parents, grandparents, cousins, nephews, and anyone else you can think of—we always have a good time, playing soccer or volleyball, or simply cooking, just having fun as if we were all kids again. These gatherings remind me a lot of the ones my grandfather Bartolo used to organize on Sundays, and we always tried to involve everyone in everything that we do. We also try to celebrate all the holidays by gathering both families together, and at least once a month we try to organize some sort of a get-together. Some bring food, others play the hosts, someone brings the karaoke, and we always have a great time.

But it's one thing to get along with your spouse or with your spouse's family. It's something else entirely when you have children, when you're trying to educate them and make sure they have the best opportunities available.

The first thing I felt when María told me she was pregnant with our first child was a big sense of responsibility. It was a responsibility I wanted to take on, of course, one that I'd been dreaming about for a long time. Now I had finally been given the chance to start building a family of my own. I would not only be looking out for María and myself, but also for our child, and any of our future children.

Thanks to the closeness that I seek to have with God, and thanks to the example set by many people who started out from the bottom and achieved success—people like Don Francisco, Humberto Luna, Jorge Ramos, Oscar de la Hoya, Emilio and Gloria Estefan, and others—I've learned valuable lessons that I can apply to my own life. As soon as I found out I was going to become a father, I knew I would have to make sure that my children got a better education than the one I had. I think that instinct comes naturally to any parent: you always want your son or daughter to have a better life than you did.

That's why I had been saving money all those years, the reason I sacrificed the comfort of sleeping in a bed or renting an apartment closer to work or buying new furniture or taking expensive vacations. That's why I always ignored those people who told me I needed to buy a luxury car, to move into a bigger place, or to buy so many things that I simply didn't need. That wasn't my goal; I wasn't looking for ease and luxury. My goal was to build a family and be in a position to provide a better education for my future children. I also knew that I had to provide a good and stable home, one in which they could grow to their fullest potential.

María and I prepared for the birth of our first child because we wanted him or her to have a home built on a strong Godly foundation, love and safety that would enable him or her to grow up to be a responsible person.

That's why I prefer to be consistent with the children. María and I are always looking for new ways to teach them so that they can learn to be disciplined in all aspects of life, whether it's their faith in God, in school, or in exercising. I focus on fitness with the kids, and María handles their studies. We both work together to strengthen the spiritual part. That way, we try to balance our roles, and between the two of us, we try to provide Edward and Daniel as much guidance as possible.

The first strategy for teaching discipline is to do so by example, so I try to make sure that my kids see me as being constant, careful, and focused on what I'm doing, particularly when it comes to fitness. When you say that something's good for them, the best way to prove that is by doing it. So, no matter how tired I might be when I get home from work, I always find time to exercise.

I always tell my kids that, in addition to getting a good education, they should find a sport to focus on, because athletics teach you how to compete, which is a perfect preparation for daily life.

Whenever I'm traveling and I see other parents playing games with their children, going for a run, or doing any sort of physical activity, I really miss my own kids and the time we spend exercising together. So no matter what, I make the extra effort to do physical activities with them, or go to their basketball games or karate lessons. I love seeing them play; it fills me with excitement, and it's a very important part of my life.

One of the physical activities I enjoy sharing with my kids is going for a bike ride. One time, I told Edward the story about my first bike, about how I had dreamed of it and worked hard until I had collected all the parts and was ready to put them all together and assemble it. I also told him that I never even got to ride it once. But that was a different story; the important thing, I said, was that I earned it. And best of all, the guy who made it all possible, the bike shop owner, now lived in Los Angeles, still selling and repairing bicycles. We both thought it would be a great idea to buy our family bikes from his shop.

And so one day we went there to the shop. I happily greeted my old boss Martín, and bought my kids their first bikes. And that was how our family tradition of riding bikes together was born. We always had a good time exploring new places, whether out in the countryside or in our own neighborhood.

But one time it didn't go quite so well. It was the day we decided to ride to my sister-in-law's house, who lived about eighteen miles away from us. We were enjoying the ride, having fun and exercising at the same time, but with only two miles left to go, I had to stop and call María because we had encountered a small problem: all of our tires were flat. How could something like this have happened?

The first bike to go flat was the one Daniel, my younger son, was riding.

"Daddy, I can't keep going," he started to say.

"Why?" I asked, turning around so I could see him. And that's when I noticed that neither of his tires had any air in them. So I got off my own bike so I could tug his along with me while we walked. By that time it was already seven o'clock in the evening; it was starting to get dark, and Daniel was getting really tired. I was too, but I wasn't going to just leave the bikes behind. That didn't make any sense. But not long after that, Edward said he was having problems with his bike too.

Hmmm, I thought. *I'm gonna have to call María to come and pick us up.* But when I checked my cell phone, I realized that I wasn't getting a signal, so we had no choice but to keep trudging along until we got to a place where I had reception. I was dragging my bike as well as Daniel's, and Edward was pulling his. Finally we got to a place where my phone could pick up a signal, but the problem now was that I really had no idea where I was! It had been a while since we were on main roads, and by then everything was dark, so I could only give a vague description of where she should come and look for us. We were exhausted and more than a little nervous, but all we could do was wait and hope that she found us.

But how did the tires go flat? Well, I had planned for our route to circulate along certain streets, a decision I later regretted when I realized how dangerous it would be: Cars would be passing us at high speed, and any sort of distraction could potentially be fatal, especially for my younger son. So I decided it would be better to get off the main streets and cut through some vacant lots. But I never thought about the fact that those places are often overgrown with dry weeds and shrubs that are covered in thorns, and we had them to thank for all the punctures we had in our tires.

"I can't believe it!" Daniel said, disappointedly, when María finally arrived to pick us up. "We only had two miles left to go."

I was impressed with how committed he was to the plan. Eighteen miles is no small undertaking for a seven-year-old and a fifteen-year-old.

When it comes to educating our children, another important aspect is learning to be careful with money. María and I give them each a weekly allowance that's enough for their school lunches and nothing more.

They each have different personalities and needs, and therefore each has a different way of managing his money: Daniel usually spends his allowance on whatever happens to catch his eye, whereas Edward saves everything and often asks us to take him to the bank so he can deposit it into his account. But in either case, we always remind them of the importance of making good decisions with their finances. And finally, we're teaching them to fulfill their obligations as members of the church, and to pay their tithes out of the money they earn.

I want to pass on what I learned from my own family about being responsible with money and the problems that come from wasting it. In my home, I saw examples of each. I always told my older brother that I couldn't believe how easily he spent his hard-earned money on alcohol.

I think it's important for kids to start thinking and learning, at an early age, about what they want to be when they grow up. They can discover what they like and don't like, and in addition to what they learn from school, they'll have some knowledge and experience that they can draw from as they move ahead toward college. That's why I suggest they look for work experience in the profession that interest them. For example, Edward, who is now seventeen, wants to be a lawyer, so we encouraged him to look for a part-time job or even an unpaid internship at a law firm, which will allow him to be in close contact with people actually practicing law, and to learn a few things from the inside that can help him decide whether or not this is really the career for him.

Another thing we want our children to learn about is our own roots: the culture from which their parents come. That's why I speak Spanish with them, why we take them to visit Mexico whenever possible, and why we tell them stories about the country where I was born. Both Edward and Daniel are very proud of their Mexican heritage. Daniel, for example, even refers to himself as being Mexican. Sometimes, his classmates try to correct him and tell him that he's an American. So he doesn't get confused, María tells him that he can always say he's Mexican American. We've talked to them both about my life, about how I got here and how I got ahead, how I organized the marches to address the problems facing other immigrants. We show them why it's so important to support all members of the community, not only your own family members, and how vital it is that we all remain united.

Both Edward and Daniel are proud of their dad's success, and that's something that makes me very happy, but it also fills me with a sense of responsibility, because I always have to set a good example for them. Sometimes, when I'm walking down the street and somebody asks if they can take a picture with me, Daniel will jump in and say, "I'll take it!" And sometimes, I hear Edward saying he wants to be like me or even better than me, and while that may be a bit of a concern for him, since he sees it as a challenge, we always encourage him to pursue his dreams—his dreams, not anybody else's—and that whether or not he becomes as well-known as his dad, the most important thing is to be a good person, to fight for what you want, and to always give your best.

I'll never get tired of repeating how important it is for parents to spend quality time with their children and with each other. Not too long ago, my team at the station took some uniforms to a school in South Central Los Angeles thanks to an invitation from the coach. When I got there, I saw that a number of parents—who were probably just busy with their work schedules—would simply drop off their kids and then leave.

"You know, Piolín," the coach said to me, "it doesn't bother me that they just drop their kids off, but sometimes it's important for the parents to be here to watch them play, to motivate them and that sort of thing. Sometimes it seems like they just bring their kids here as if it's a day care service."

There was another occasion where I was asked to be a guest speaker at a school and tell the students what it is that I do and how I came to be here in the United States. They also wanted me to explain the phrase that I always use on the show: *"¿A qué venimos?" "A triunfar!"* ("Why do we come? To succeed!"). When I finished with the talk, a student whose father was a construction worker came up to me.

"I'm happy, but I'm also sad," he said.

"Why is that?" I asked.

"My dad is a construction worker and he loves listening to your show," he explained. "So today I told him, 'Dad, since you like the show so much, you have to come to school with me today.' But he didn't. He stayed home watching TV."

I could tell this was really bothering him.

"But you know what?" I said. "Your dad works really hard. Remember, being a construction worker is really tiring."

Deep down, I was truly touched by his wish that his father had been there with him that day. Now, more than ever, I realize that maybe they both would have enjoyed spending some quality time together, but I can't be judgmental in situations like this. So I asked him if he would give me his dad's phone number. He did, and I called to say hello. I also told him that he had a very smart young son, and to take good care of him.

When you're a parent, it can be easy to let yourself get carried away by your job obligations—the desire to provide for your family so they can have everything they need—and put aside what's really important: spending time together. Something similar happened to me back in 2002, when, because of my job, I couldn't give my son Edward (Daniel hadn't been born yet) as much of my time as I would have liked. The discussion I had with that young boy made me think a lot about that time, and it prompted me to devote more time to my children. You never know where your next life lesson may come from.

Spending some quality time with my kids is always fun, and it also allows me to get to know them better. I learn a lot from them, from the questions they ask and the answers they give me to topics they talk with me about. And also from things that happen spontaneously.

Sometimes, children have a tough time separating reality from fantasy, and never was this more true than when my younger son, Daniel, saw the movie *The Muppets,* where I play the role of a TV executive. My family couldn't come with me to the movie premiere, so we decided I would watch it again later, with them, at home. I remember we were all piled in the master bedroom.

One of the scenes in which my character appears had just been shown, when Kermit the Frog asks if he got the job. It's a funny scene because I answer in Spanish and that leads to some confusion because Kermit thinks my answer is the exact opposite of what it really is. Suddenly, we heard somebody start to cry, and María and I turned to see Daniel in tears.

"What's the matter, Daniel?" we asked him. But he wouldn't answer; he just sat there looking disconsolate. We started to wonder whether one of us had unintentionally done something to upset him. "Why are you crying?" we kept asking him, time and time again.

"My daddy didn't give Kermit the job," he said, bawling.

It took everything we had to contain our laughter.

The innocence of a child can teach us a thing or two about the way we see the world. And sometimes, it does so in humorous ways. When Edward was about six years old, he was asked once in school about what made him proud of his father. It was a question they were asking all of the students as part of an activity. Everyone brought up their parents' jobs and what they did. When it was Edward's turn, he stood up in front of the whole class, bubbling over with pride.

"I'm proud of my dad because he crossed the border in a trunk and nobody saw him!" he said.

The teacher didn't seem to take that very well, and asked him to think of something else that made him feel proud of his dad. But Edward was adamant and stuck with that story.

Well, that was during the time when immigration reform was all over the media, and was quite a controversial issue. I remember going to the school after that incident, and having some of the other parents looking at me skeptically. Luckily, I already had all my documents in order by then.

Each of my children has a very unique style, a different talent and personality. Edward is calm and quiet; he likes to observe and doesn't talk very much. Daniel is restless, wants everything to happen quickly, and always speaks his mind.

Daniel also has a bit of a spark inside of him, and while Edward can be somewhat reserved, Daniel is more outgoing. This proved true on the last day of first grade, when María went up to Daniel's teacher to thank her for her work with the students.

"Well, Mrs. Sotelo, I have to say it was an incredible year," the teacher said. "Daniel has a special sort of energy. In fact, just today he said something to the class that I think I should tell you so you can tell this story as well."

"Ah, okay, then. What is it?" María asked.

"At the end of class today, I said, 'Bravo, children. You are all moving on to second grade. Now, tell me, what do you want to be when you grow up?' They all took turns answering me. One wants to be a police officer, another one wants to sell houses, and so on. When it was Daniel's turn, he said, 'I want to be a rapper.' 'A rapper?' I said. 'You mean you want to be rich, right?' But he said, 'No, teacher, money is not important. I want to be a rapper so I can have all that bling-bling! The big watch and the big chains!' "

"My goodness," María replied, laughing. "Well, I'm glad he said that, because I would have been more worried if he said he wanted to be a rapper so he could walk around with a pretty girl on each arm!"

Whatever their personalities might be, and whatever path through life they may choose, I love them both and I love them equally . . . and I love their hugs! And I'm proud when they help one another out. Like when Edward gives Daniel advice on how to be a better basketball player.

Sometimes they fight, as all brothers will do. But I always tell Edward, "Son, as the big brother, it's your job to help Daniel. He listens to you and pays attention when you talk to him."

Edward always listens to me and tries to get along better with his little brother, to be a role model and to support him. And when they work together, they often do things that are surprisingly touching.

One day, I came home particularly tired and hungry after a long day's work. I opened the refrigerator door and saw a box inside with a label that read *For My Dad*. I opened it to find it filled with strawberries and chocolate. They both know that I love strawberries and chocolate; it's something that María has been giving me ever since we started dating. Now, every year on Valentine's Day, I know what I'll be getting, and sometimes I'm not the only one who gets to eat them, since everyone else seems to enjoy them too. But this time they decided that this batch should be just for me, and they put them in my own special box. It was such a lovely thought, and when I saw it, my exhaustion disappeared instantly.

These are the kinds of family moments that give me the strength to keep on going, and that make the stress and the problems of daily life vanish into thin air.

• • •

When it comes to a relationship with God, María and I insist that our children maintain an active spiritual life, and that they study The Word each and every day, because it will help them whenever they encounter difficult moments in life. I tell them time and again that, when I think back over all the challenges I've faced, I know I would have failed many of them if I hadn't held true to the word of God.

Proverbs 22:6

Train up a child in the way he should go: and when he is old, he will not depart from it.

"Now I know why so many people go into depression when they hear that they or a family member has become sick," I tell them. "And I understand why they may seek refuge in alcohol. They are lacking the word of God, and believe instead that alcohol is going to help them, that it will relieve their pain. Kneel down and ask God to give you strength. Let us read His word, because His promise is that He will help us through any challenge. And when an obstacle presents itself, there is always a reason behind it. In that sense, we are like water: we must never stagnate; we must always be on the move. We have to keep moving forward and learn more each and every day from the word of God."

I hope that María and I have planted seeds in them, seeds that will grow over time and help them both to find their paths in life, to become good people and find true happiness.

CHAPTER 29

NEVER STOP LEARNING

Learning from successful people is a valuable resource. Right when I arrived in the United States, while scanning the classified ads for job openings, I would also look for articles about people who came to the United States and started out on the bottom rung, washing dishes or doing landscaping work or selling tacos out of their homes, and now own their own restaurants or other businesses and who have become important leaders in their community.

I like to read these types of stories and think to myself, *If this guy could do it, why can't I?* It was through these real-life success stories that I found the motivation to become better myself.

One of my very first sources of inspiration was Humberto Luna, one of the most famous Spanish-language radio broadcasters in the nation. Like me, Humberto was born in Mexico and came here to live in the United States. I liked to listen to his program—where I could get the latest news and listen to artists talking about their music, and, most of all, I liked to laugh at all his jokes. Through Humberto, I learned that I too could achieve my dreams, that it didn't matter that I'd come from Mexico with little in the way of either preparation or money, because working hard and refusing to quit can take you far. And besides, listening to his show gradually got me to fall in love with the radio.

I will always be grateful to Humberto Luna not only because he's been a great source of inspiration but also because he's always been kind to me whenever our paths cross. And last, but not least: Humberto opened the door for all of us who would come after him.

Besides his show, I loved watching *Sábado Gigante* with Don Francisco, because he's someone with whom I've always been able to identify. Watching his show was one of my favorite pastimes during those first few years of living here in the United States. When you first come here and don't have much in the way of family, *Sábado Gigante* offers a way of connecting with the part of yourself that you feel you left back in your home country; it made me feel like I belonged to a much larger community of people with whom I had many things in common.

I learned a lot from Don Francisco, and it was on his show that I first introduced myself publically as Piolín. It was back in 1998, and I remember it well because my son Edward was barely a month old at the time. I was on a panel of judges for a competition. He had invited me and I accepted, but I also wanted to bring a few of my listeners along with me, so that they could share in the experience of being at Don Francisco's show. That was when I was working on the radio station in San Jose, and we were operating on a very limited budget, so paying the travel expenses of a few fans wasn't really feasible.

So I called up *Sábado Gigante* and was able to speak with one of the producers. I explained the situation; I said I knew they were having some contestants on the show, and that I'd love to have a few of my listeners come along and participate. And of course, I couldn't help but mention how much I admired Don Francisco and how much the show meant to me during my first few years here in the United States. The producer told me she would check with her boss and that she'd get back to me with any news either way.

A short while later, she called me back to say that Don Francisco had agreed to my request. And that's how I happened to appear on *Sábado Gigante,* along with several of my fans, which made me quite happy indeed.

When I moved to Los Angeles, my friendship with the producers of the show and with Don Francisco himself continued to grow. I learned many things from him, one of which is the discipline that it takes to run a show like his, and another is the fact that you always have to invest a lot of time in preparation.

Now, every time I see the show, I'm reminded of how important it is to be aware of everything that's going on around you. It's the first thing I noticed on his set, where it was obvious that he was keeping an eye on everything, from the production to the costumes to where the cameras were set up. I remember saying to myself, *How cool is that!* It's simply amazing to watch him work, and that work ethic is why he is where he is today and why he's achieved so much success.

It was largely because of this experience that I knew I should follow my own intuitions when I first started working on the radio. Back in those early days, I knew that I couldn't simply be content with just being behind the microphone. I wanted to learn about all areas of the industry, and so I started to gain knowledge and experience wherever I could—producing, adding sound effects, writing, promoting, reading the news, pretty much every little facet of radio broadcasting. Not only has this given me insight into all aspects of my show, but it has also given me the opportunity to continue learning new things.

I was also incredibly struck by how Don Francisco was always able to give you a few minutes of his time, no matter how busy he was. One time, just a few seconds before he had to go on the air, he, looking very calm and collected, asked me how I was doing and how I felt. All of his attention was focused on me. And not only that, but every time I've seen him, he's offered me some very positive tips and suggestions that have really helped me to improve as a host myself.

One of the most important pieces of advice he gave me was when he said: "Don't ever let yourself think that you've made it. Don't ever believe that. Keep on doing what you had to do to get to where you are. Keep on working hard." Ever since then, whenever someone asks me how I feel about the success I've managed to achieve, I have to stop and think for a moment before I realize that I don't really look at success the same way that they do. I don't because, to me, success is something that can change in an instant. It can come quickly, and vanish just as fast.

On one occasion, Don Francisco invited me out to dinner in Los Angeles, and I told him that I never forgot his advice and that I repeat it to myself all the time. I'm not sure if he realizes just how much I admire him, though occasionally I drop a discreet hint, or how important his friendship has been to my own career.

Another person from whom I learned quite a bit is Oscar de la

Hoya. I've always been inspired by stories of people who work their way out of the neighborhood by struggling to grow and make something of themselves. Reading his memoir was what gave me the final push I needed to write my own memoir, so that others might end up seeing themselves reflected in me, learning that anything is possible, finding the right path that takes you where you want to go, learning as much from your victories and achievements as you do from your failures and mistakes. I've known Oscar for some time now, and we've formed a friendship for which I'm very grateful.

I place a great deal of importance in gratitude. And when someone is confident enough in you to let you be around them and learn from them, make sure to show your appreciation whenever you get the chance. Yes, you can say, "Thank you," but it's also important to do things that show how truly grateful you are to that person for the opportunity that he or she gave you. When someone puts their trust in you, they're giving you a gift that can't be bought. It's something you earn, and when someone trusts you enough to become close with them—allowing you to see the world as they do, to learn from them—then you should recognize that you're being given something incredibly valuable, something that you should treat with great care.

That is why, whenever I'm speaking about a particular person, I'm speaking about what I, myself, personally know about them, not about whatever gossip or rumors might be floating around. And if I'm asked about a specific person in an interview, I always make sure to be clear and tell them that I will talk about only the things I know to be true. This is something that I've discussed with many people, both in public and in private, with television celebrities and members of the media. And I always try to respect people's privacy.

Opportunities to learn can be found in all areas of life, from the most simple to the most complex. You can learn from anybody, not just the experts or the celebrities. I'm convinced we must seek out experts in our fields to see what we can learn from them, and that's something I also try to apply in my personal life. But it's not just what they say that can be valuable; it's also what they do, which is why I'll often simply ask these people if they would let me sit back and watch them as they work. That's why, for example, I'll occasionally ask comedians like Javier Carranza El Costeño if I can sit in and watch them prepare their routines, because I'm inspired by the discipline with which they work.

You can also learn new things in the most unexpected of ways. The important thing is to always reflect upon what you've learned, and to be able to change or improve whatever is needed to make yourself better. One of the first lessons I learned when I started out in radio was from a broadcaster on Radio México, who once invited me to emcee an event at a nightclub in Riverside.

"Ah, but I didn't bring a change of clothes," I said.

"That's too bad. I guess you can't come, then," he replied. Then he said, "You'd better learn from this. You always have to have a change of clothes, because you just missed out on a great opportunity by not having them."

And he was right: I would have been up onstage in front of a huge crowd of people, which is something I had never done before. If I wanted to break into the business, I had to be prepared for whatever might come up. And ever since then, I always bring a change of clothes with me everywhere I go: clothes for going out, clothes for the gym, whatever the occasion may be.

Finally, I think that learning is something that you don't only get through interacting with other people; it also has to do with the strength and determination that we each carry inside of us. For example, learning English has always been a challenge for me. When I first came to America, I did many different things and worked a number of different jobs, so I guess my brain was overloaded. But I've never given up, and although it's been a long time coming—after having built a career in Spanish and having done fairly well in this country—I keep on trying to learn the language better. I even recently bought the American English Rosetta Stone course so I could study the language at home, and with discipline, I'm putting my skills to practice. One reason that motivates me is that I don't want to ever again lose out on a role because of my accent, which has happened to me on more than one occasion. But I also think it's important to learn the language spoken by the majority of the people in this country. Sometimes I'm amazed by the fact that I've been able to find a career that uses almost no English, and that's not so much a matter of pride but rather an opportunity to work harder, get better each and every day, and learn proper English. And it seems that my efforts are starting to pay off, because people tell me I've improved a lot, and that makes me happy.

Having achieved a certain amount of success doesn't guarantee me anything, and so every day I push hard not only to maintain the level that I have, but also to increase it. And never was that more clear than when I started auditioning for parts in Hollywood, where—regardless of my career or my résumé—I was always treated like just another guy.

Appearing in movies is something that caught my attention ever since I first arrived in the United States. I searched the classified ads for jobs in the film industry, and I loved signing on as an extra. Whenever I was able to participate in the making of a film, I was filled with so much excitement and enthusiasm that, although I knew it meant I'd have to spend an entire day there on the set, I would still have enough energy left over to go back to work cleaning apartments or whatever I might have been doing at the time.

The more involved I got in the radio business, the less time I had to pursue movies. But the desire to participate and appear on-screen never really waned, and so whenever I have the opportunity to go to a casting call for a movie or TV series, I take it. Sometimes I get chosen, and sometimes I don't. But in the end, whatever the result may be, I always try to engage my listeners, because I owe them so much for who I am and where I've come to be.

When I got the chance to work on the movie *Beverly Hills Chihuahua*, I decided to approach the director, Raja Gosnell, with a special request.

"I'd like to invite a few of my listeners to attend the premiere," I said, "so they can walk down the red carpet and see how it all feels."

Raja agreed, and decided we should select people from different cities around the country, like New York, Chicago, Los Angeles, Bakersfield, Fresno, San Jose, San Francisco, Las Vegas, or various locations in Texas.

On opening night, we picked them up in a limo. Some of the listeners who got invitations started to become emotional, even crying. "What's wrong?" I asked. "Are you feeling sick? What's the matter?"

Then they would tell me that they just never thought they would ever have such an experience. I could really identify with that sentiment, because the same thing has happened to me on a number of occasions. But that's what life is about, isn't it? To explore and experience things you never thought you could.

When we arrived at the premiere, they all walked down the red carpet, in front of all the cameras and reporters, just like the Hollywood stars did. Inside the theater they met and mingled with celebrities like Andy García, George López, Paul Rodríguez, Edward James Olmos, Cheech Marín, among many others.

Once the premiere was over, there was an after-party at the Kodak Theater that we all attended. We celebrated with artists and filmmakers alike, and it was great.

After the movie's release, I was given five actual dogs from listeners who had apparently dropped by the station and left them there as gifts. And all of them looked like Rafa, the character whom I voiced. It was such a thoughtful gesture and I was truly appreciative, so my first inclination was to keep all five dogs. Why not? They were gifts, right? So I took them all home with me, but we quickly realized that we couldn't take care of so many dogs, because each one deserved love and care. We decided to find the best possible homes for them, and gave them out to friends and family members. And whenever we drop by for a visit, the dogs start to bark. I don't know whether they're happy to see us, or just angry that we didn't let them all stay at our house!

Another time, Marc Anthony invited me to make a cameo appearance on the TV series *Hawthorne*, as DJ Piolín. Jada Pinkett Smith was on of the producers. During the taping of the show, I brought a few listeners along with me so they could see how a television show was made.

As I said, I enjoy film and TV work so much, that all it takes is a quick phone call from a show or movie producer, and I'm ready to sign on, regardless of whether I have to rearrange my schedule, or how exhausted I might be. I feel like a kid again whenever I get one of those calls, or whenever I'm on set. I love making people happy and laugh.

To date, I have made appearances—not just as an extra—in the following films: *Beverly Hills Chihuaha 1, Beverly Hills Chihuahua 3: Viva La Fiesta!, Ice Age 4, The Muppets, 10 Items or Less, Marmaduke, A Day Without a Mexican, The Fluffy Movie: Unity Through Laughter* (with the comedian Gabriel Iglesias) and in TV series like *East Bound & Down* and a documentary called *The Latino List*. There was also a reality show called *Combate Américas*, produced by the Mun2 network and many others.

What I find most important about all these experiences is not only the pleasure it gives me to participate in movies, which is what first attracted me to the world of film and television, but also the never-ending desire to keep learning more and more.

It's true that I've been inspired by many famous people, but I've also learned a lot from and been inspired by those people closest to me, people like my dad, who never stopped fighting to provide us with a better future. People like my grandfather Bartolo, who taught me the importance of generosity toward and solidarity with those in need. People like my mother and mother-in-law, who always knew how to make it, no matter what challenges they faced. And my brother Jorge, who was able—thanks to his own strength, determination, and his faith in God—to rid himself of his dependency on alcohol. And María, who always sees the bright side of things, and who always has words of strength and encouragement that inspire me to be a better person. And all my listeners and all the members of our community who get up every morning, willing to work hard, ready to overcome any obstacles in their path, and determined never to give up. I've learned from all of them, and they inspire me to keep moving forward each and every day.

CHAPTER 30

NEW HORIZONS

Life goes in cycles. Looking back, I realize that this is true. I see many cycles in my life that have come and gone; I see what I've learned from them and where their paths have led me: my life in Mexico, my first jobs here in the United States, the different shows that I've hosted, my life as an undocumented immigrant, and my life as a single man. And at the end of them all, regardless of the uncertainty I've gone through, I've always found a way to keep on doing what I do, and to keep moving forward.

My cycle with Univision—which in 2004 had merged with HBC—came to an end. It didn't happen the way I would have liked it to, surrounded by a controversy that grew out of malicious rumors, misunderstandings, and unfounded accusations—including allegedly having sexually harassed a coworker. Despite the pain that this unfortunate experience caused, the worst thing I could have done at the time would have been to hang my head in defeat. Once again, I had to dig deep inside of me to find the strength and passion to come out and fight for my dreams. And I couldn't have done this without the love and support of María, my children and the other members of my family and all of my listeners who have shown me their support.

Moving to SiriusXM represented a great opportunity to learn from the new developments in technology and thus take advantage of them. From the moment SiriusXM reached out to me, the executives Scott Greenstein and James Meyer and the amazing team I was able to work with—Frank Flores, Tim Sabean, Don Wicklin, David Moreno, Tony Masiello, Jaime Colon, Manny and Marisol—showed me nothing but the highest degree of professionalism. Their facilities are some of the finest I've ever seen, and each broadcasting booth across the country is equipped with the latest technology.

Once the move to SiriusXM was complete, I started planning the new program, making a few changes to improve it while retaining the same basic format as the previous shows, such as the jokes, pranks, family counselors, and—of course—discussions and panels on immigration issues conducted by renowned immigration attorneys.

And we had a very good response among artists, and some of them appeared as guests on the show, including Angélica Vale, Pepe Aguilar, Angélica María, Enrique Iglesias, Oscar de la Hoya, Poncho from Banda El Recodo, El Dasa, Larry Hernández, Noel Torres, Jorge Campos, Eduardo Verástegui, Kate del Castillo, Arolladora Banda El Limón, the fashion designer Mitzy, and the journalist José Díaz-Balart, among many others. In fact, the support from artists was overwhelming right from the start. A real blessing. There's no doubt that God puts the right people in your path with the purpose of helping you find your way again.

One of the first calls we took was from a listener who had already asked for help back when I was at other radio stations, and who was suffering from bipolar disorder. We talked for a bit on the air, and I promised to continue the discussion later. I called him back that night, from my home, and even though it was getting late and my kids wanted me to play with them, I stayed on the line, because I could sense that this was very important for my listener.

This man, who was quite young, told me that he was dealing with a number of problems, that he didn't know how to handle them all, that he started using drugs, and that now things were getting progressively worse. At one point, he told me he had a gun with him, and that he was ready to use it to take his own life. He started to cry, and I cried with him.

"Don't do it," I said. "Come, let's pray together." Then I called my children into the room, though without telling them what exactly was going on. I just told them I had someone on the phone whom I wanted them to pray for. Then I turned my attention back to the caller: "My kids are here with me," I said, "and they want to pray for you too, so you can see how much we love and appreciate you. So don't do it, please. I'm just asking you to trust me enough to talk with me."

We started to pray for him and, again, he began to cry. But gradually, through the prayers, he let go of his desire to commit suicide. I invited him to go to church and to let Jesus into his heart, because that is the only way to truly find a solution to your problems.

And to this very day, I still keep in touch with that listener, and I know that he's doing much better. He never forgets our conversation from that night, and he always asks about how my children are doing.

And there are other stories of courage and struggle. Like the case of a young girl of Mexican descent and member of the U.S. Army who didn't have enough money to pay for college. She sent me an e-mail explaining her situation, and I gave her a call.

"I only had two options," she wrote. "One was that my parents go into debt so that I could study. My mom works as a custodian at the Los Angeles airport, and doesn't make much money, and my dad suffers from diabetes and had to take an early retirement from his job as a truck driver. My other option was to join the army."

The last was the path she ended up choosing.

Such courage, I thought. Some high school students just want to hang out and have fun. But she chose to enlist in the army so she could study, build a career, and help out her family, especially her five-year-old sister and her seventeen-year-old brother.

In her e-mail, she also mentioned she was stationed in Anchorage, Alaska, and she said she wanted to surprise her siblings because they shared a birthday that month, and—even if they couldn't go on the actual date of their birthday—she wanted to take them to Disneyland.

I shared her story with some staff members at Disney, who were struck by her story as well. They gave us complimentary tickets so she and her family could all go, and make her dream come true. And I decided that I wanted to meet them, but I didn't tell them I was coming, so it was a huge surprise for them when we finally all met there at Disneyland.

Another one of the pleasant surprises that I received during this new stage of my career was from Fluffy himself: the comedian Gabriel

Iglesias. It was during his second appearance on the show when he said to me, on the air: "I wanted to tell you that next year I'll be making a movie about my life, and I want you to be in it!"

I was speechless.

"What do you think?" he asked.

"Okay. Absolutely. Of course!" I replied. "It would be an honor!"

I really enjoyed that experience, and learned so much from doing this film with Fluffy, who is also someone who loves to give opportunities to people.

I also interviewed J. R. Martínez, an American soldier born in Louisiana to a Salvadoran mother. He told us his own story of overcoming obstacles and moving on with life when something unexpected happens. While on duty in Iraq, the Humvee he was driving struck an IED. He suffered severe burns to 34 percent of his body, and his recovery took nearly three years and involved over thirty skin graft surgeries. Since then, J.R. has become a motivational speaker; he has worked closely with organizations helping others recover from severe burns and won the thirteenth season of *Dancing with the Stars*. During our interview, I asked him if he'd like us to call his mother and say hello to her. He agreed, so we did. She was thrilled to hear from us, and for the chance to talk to her son.

"Well, now I know what I have to do when I want to get in touch with you, Mom," J.R. joked. "I have to ask Piolín to call you, because you never answer whenever I call!"

But despite how much I enjoyed this experience, after nearly a year, I realized once again that I should look toward new horizons, to find even more effective ways of reaching out to my audience, and to keep on fighting, not only for my own goals, but for the goals of the millions of people in this country who work hard every day in their pursuit of the American dream.

And so I will be back soon to engage with my people on the radio, and I will continue with all of my other everyday activities that I never miss out on. Going to the gym, as I've said, is very important to me. So is coming home and taking my kids to sports practice, or even just to exercise if there are no workouts scheduled for that particular day. That way, when eight o'clock rolls around, I'm ready to go to sleep so I can wake up early, ready for a new day of work. Sometimes it's not always possible to get to bed early because of some prior commitment, but I always try to aim for that time, because being disciplined has always been important to me. And if I don't, I'm exhausted the next day!

To do my morning show, I have to get up by at least three in the morning so I can get to the station by five. So far—ever since I first started working in the radio business—there hasn't been a single day on which I woke up and thought to myself, *Oh no, not another day of work,* because it's something I truly enjoy, and I'm always happy to wake up and start a new day. Once I'm in front of that microphone, I feel a tremendous desire to entertain and lift up the spirits of my people. I've always felt a huge amount of adrenaline pumping through my veins and a deep-seated desire to be there in the broadcast booth. It's as if my body, more so than my mind, knows that this place is where I belong. And those are feelings that I don't usually experience at any other time or place, except when I'm in the studio, on the air.

Displays of appreciation have never failed to appear. For example, once, in late 2013, we got a call from a listener who needed some help: He was living in a room with his family in a very poor section of town, and they didn't have anything to eat. He also told me that he had a daughter with Down syndrome.

"I really don't like to beg," he said, "but my daughter is hungry, and I have no food to give her."

I decided to visit him and bring him some food, and I invited other listeners to do the same. When I finished the show for the day, a colleague and I went to the caller's house. We spoke with him and his family and met his daughter. It was a truly meaningful and emotional encounter.

When we left, I realized that I was pretty hungry myself, and we decided to stop at El Pollo Loco along the way.

"Get whatever you want, bro," I said to my coworker.

While he waited in line, I went to the bathroom to wash my hands. When I came out, my colleague was up at the register. We placed our order and I got ready to pay, but the cashier wouldn't take my money.

"Somebody has already paid for you," she said.

I turned to my colleague and said, "Really? Was it you?"

"Nope, it wasn't me."

"Excuse me, ma'am, but who paid for this?" I asked the cashier. "Is it someone who works here?"

"No," she replied. "It's that gentleman over there on the right."

I turned around and saw him: From his uniform, it appeared to be a man who worked at a tire shop and was taking his lunch break. I walked up to him and asked, "Hey, my brother, why are you paying for our meals?"

"Because I heard you talking to that guy on your show this morning, and so I figured that's why you were here," he replied.

It's gifts like that—the simple acts of kindness and love—that never cease to amaze me.

Two years later, at one of Fluffy's shows in San Jose, the comedian Alfred Robles came up to me and said, "Hey, Piolín, is it true that my brother surprised you and paid for your lunch at El Pollo Loco one day after you went to help out a family out in the middle of nowhere?"

"Yes," I said. I can't believe how small the world really is sometimes.

A similar occurrence happened back in early 2014, when I went out with some friends to eat at a restaurant in South Gate called Las Glorias. After we ate, I got up to go pay, but El Costeño, one of my close friends who also happens to be a comedian, stopped me.

"Nope, this one's on me," he said flatly.

"Not gonna happen, buddy. You paid for dinner last Sunday, so now it's my turn," I replied, just as sternly, but like him, also without malice.

And again I got up and went to pay while the rest of our group headed outside. But then the server came up to me and said, "It's on the house tonight."

"No, ma'am, you don't have to do that," I replied.

"Maybe not, but we're doing it, because we know about all the things you have done to help our community."

"Thank you, really, but . . ."

"And we know what happened," she interrupted, referring to what happened in Univision. I could see the sadness in her eyes. "What they did to you was ugly and unfair. We hope everything works out for you."

Then we hugged, and I had to fight back the tears. I insisted on paying for the bill but she would not accept the tip. She said it was her way of showing her support.

I left there thanking God for another small token of appreciation, because these are people who don't know me personally, only through the radio, and who refuse to believe the lies that have been spread about me. *Wow, God is truly great,* I thought as I walked toward the exit. My eyes were welling up with tears, and when I caught back up with my friends outside, they asked me what had happened. These are the sorts of things that I keep close to my heart, and which I share with my most trusted loved ones.

Not long after that happened, on our way from leaving the studio, María saw a man standing by the side of the street holding up a sign asking for money.

"Eddie, do you have any cash?" she asked.

"No, I don't."

Since she was driving, I reached into the backseat and handed her her purse.

"Here, give him this," she said, pulling out some money.

I rolled down the window and handed it to the man, who was white and middle-aged.

"Piolín?" he asked.

"Yeah, that's me," I said in English.

He reached out and put his hand heavily upon my shoulder. I was taken aback, because I didn't know who he was.

"I don't believe anything they say," he said in English. "You have my support. I know what kind of a person you are."

María and I were dumbstruck for several minutes, until she began to cry.

"Eddie, God sent that person to us," she said. "He was an angel. There are still people with good hearts on this earth. What he said to you . . . we really needed to hear that."

And yes, it's true, that was just what we needed to hear. How could a man who probably didn't speak a word of Spanish know who I was?

How could he know what was happening to my family and me? I was stunned. María was too. I believe that God was speaking to me through him, telling me, *You are my son; do not worry. Everything will be fine.*

Similar things have been happening to me ever since mid-2013. So many people have come up to us to say they support us, they appreciate us, and they keep us in their prayers. I know many people suffered along with me when Univision and I decided to part ways, because my show offered them not only a good time, but it was also a center for information and a network of important contacts within the community. Every time I meet someone who expresses their support, I try to show that I'm relaxed and joke around with them for a bit, but deep down I truly appreciate the gesture.

Whether in person or via the phone, e-mail, Twitter, Facebook, or any other social network, I have received countless messages of solidarity, messages which I consider the most valuable gift that my listeners have ever given to me. One of these messages was from the father of Brian, the boy who needed a heart transplant. I called him up one day to check in on Brian and the rest of the family, and he told me that the harm hadn't been done to me alone, but to everyone who listened to me, to the whole community.

But no matter how hard things may have been, I learned valuable lessons along the way that have made me even stronger. And during an interview with Carmen Dominicci of Telemundo, after I had parted ways with Univision, I talked about this very thing.

"You know what hurts the most," I said. "It's when my older son looked at me and said, 'I can't believe what they did to you. The things they're saying just aren't true.' He had found out about it on the Internet. It was really painful, because I could see the sadness in his eyes. And I said to him, 'You know what, son? It's just another one of life's lessons. Just because somebody claims to be your friend doesn't mean that they truly are. You always have to be careful about that.'"

I wouldn't want him to go through the same sort of thing as me. I wouldn't want anybody to. It was painful not only to me but to my whole family and my listeners. And it hurt especially when my mother called me, and I could hear her crying.

I've felt God's presence throughout all of this, and He has helped me to move forward, to not be defeated. God tells us to bless our enemies, and if it weren't for that powerful message, I would probably be filled with hatred and resentment toward those who would want to harm me. But I don't. I'd rather bless them.

Before we started working with SiriusXM, María and I decided to take a trip with our two sons to the Holy Land. It was a trip we had been planning for several months, since June of 2013, and it was two weeks in different parts of Israel, like Tel Aviv, the Sea of Galilee, the Dead Sea, and Eilat, with a stop at the viewpoint where you can see Egypt, Jordan, and Israel from one lookout, and it would end with four days in Jerusalem.

We walked through the same places where Jesus had walked, and this touched our hearts deeply. We felt a tremendous sense of peace, which was more than welcome after so many tumultuous storms. During that trip, from a spiritual point of view, the Bible became alive for us.

In the Sea of Galilee, we were able to weather the storm in which Jesus told his disciples, *Why are ye fearful, O ye of little faith,* and calmed the surface of the waters upon which he walked. We also visited the Jordan River, where Jesus was baptized by John the Baptist, and there we relived that special moment in the life of Christ. In Cana, we experienced the joy of the first miracle he performed, when he turned water into wine. Today, vendors not only sell wine there, but they also create delicious juices from enormous pomegranates and bake bread.

Lastly, Jerusalem was the key place for us, for the connection we felt there cannot be perceived anywhere else in the world because it's the land on which God chose His name to be inscribed. As we entered the tunnel into Jerusalem, they played a song saying *Welcome home*; we couldn't contain our emotions and we began to weep. Instantly we felt greater unity as a family. Since that trip, every chance we get, we recommend to people that they save up money to visit the Holy Land. If they can only make one trip in their entire lives, we advise them to go there, because it will change their life completely.

• • •

It was also during that intense time that I received some wonderful news. It was November of 2013, and I was told that I had been selected to be inducted into the National Radio Hall of Fame. I would be the first Mexican to be a part of it! And I decided, like I had done on so many other occasions, that I wanted to share this joy with my listeners, so I invited some of them to join me at my table, front and center, right next to the great Larry King. María and I were so happy to see that a number of my fans were able to join me there for the ceremony.

All of them were from Chicago, where the event was being held, and they came from a number of different backgrounds. One of them was an office receptionist, another worked in a warehouse packing toys, another worked in a jewelry store, and the other worked for a car dealership. Upon arrival, we all walked down the red carpet, and we took pictures together during the ceremony, at dinner, and at the after-party.

Along with Larry King, the famous country singer Reba McEntire was also in attendance.

During my speech, I said something like, "I don't know if they're going to regret inviting me here tonight, because I'm the first Mexican to be inducted, and you know how that works here in the United States. . . . First there's one Mexican, and then there's a lot!"

It was without a doubt one of the happiest moments I can remember: the proof that all the sacrifices we made over the years had finally paid off. They had all amounted to something.

When I look into the future, I see myself continuing to fight for my dreams, and putting my faith and support in God and my family. Finally, I will always, always be grateful to my Lord and Savior Jesus Christ for the opportunities and experiences that I have been blessed with.

EPILOGUE

As María and I go over the last few pages of this book, we're remembering the day, perhaps a year ago, when a listener we met on the street told me I should write down everything that has happened to me. I had already been planning on writing this book, and so I kept quiet, knowing that she was right.

Telling my story serves not only to remind me of my past, to allow me to step back and see everything I've done from a distance and to put what I've achieved into perspective, but also to help me to realize that, despite all the highs and lows, I have been blessed throughout my life, and God has always been there for me. But it's just as important to me that I have this chance to tell my story and share everything that I've learned—and that I continue to learn each and every day—in the hopes that you can find some inspiration and achieve your dreams as well.

I also hope that this book will help us all—Latinos and non-Latinos alike—to reconcile whatever differences we may have, to realize that this country is stronger if we stand together, and that we have more to gain if we recognize the value that we all have and that we all bring to this great nation.

While writing this book, I encountered both doubts and certainties. Joys and sorrows. Peace and concern. Thanks to you all, I was able to look back over my life, and rereading the pages reminded me of the principles that guide me and allowed me to reinforce them: faith in God, exercise, solidarity with others, education, and pursuing my dreams. And on the flip side, remembering the past got me thinking about the future.

And even though it's impossible to know what the future may bring—because its path is like the course of a flowing river where some sections run fast, some run deep, some quite peaceful and others torrential—I trust that God, my determination to keep moving forward, and the love of my family will prepare and strengthen me for whatever adventures the future has in store for me.

Recently, a number of people have asked me where I see myself in the next few years. And while I can't predict with any certainty, there are a couple of things I am sure of: I will continue to work to defend the rights of the community, and I will continue to use the best tools that technology puts in my hands to keep in touch with my listeners, wherever they may be.

Don't ever let anybody tell you that you can't achieve your dreams, and no matter what set of circumstances you might find yourself in, don't ever forget why we came: to succeed!

ACKNOWLEDGMENTS

I want to thank God for allowing me to come into this world, and for the opportunities that He has laid in my path, for the breath of life that He gives me each morning when I open my eyes, and for enlightening me to write these pages.

Writing a book, as I've learned these past several months, is a true team effort in which many different hands are involved, and I was blessed with a group of dedicated people whom I relied upon from start to finish.

María, my life partner, thank you for all your devotion, your advice, and your guidance. I would never have been able to complete this without you. Edward and Daniel, thank you both as well, for your detailed comments and for your patience while your dad was focused on writing his memoir. I hope that you find something in these pages that inspires you and motivates you to keep on moving forward.

I would also like to thank my parents for having raised me to work hard and be responsible. And along with my brothers Jorge and Edgar and the rest of my extended family, you were an incredible resource when it came to remembering specific dates and events, no matter what time of the day or night I needed your help. My gratitude to you all is endless. The same is true for my grandparents, Chuy and Cuca, and Bartolo and Lupe, because you also taught me the value of hard work and generosity. The example you set has been invaluable in my own life.

Elizabeth Limón: I don't know what we would have done without your painstaking efforts and your attention to detail and delivery dates for each and every part of this book.

Rudy Franco: thank you for your dedication and for all the years we worked together.

Gary and Claudia Stone: Thank you for bringing us to LA!

Jeff Liberman: Thank you for all your support.

To my listeners: your love and affection and your incredible loyalty have kept me going all these years. If it weren't for all of you, I simply wouldn't have been able to do what I've done.

I would also like to express my enormous gratitude to my former bosses, supervisors, staff members, colleagues, sponsors, engineers, promotional teams, the cleaning staff, and everyone else who put their trust in me and worked side by side with me each and every day. I am also deeply grateful to all the artists and other guests who, over the years, have appeared on my show to help organize and promote our fund-raising events to benefit the needy. I couldn't have done it without you. Thank you for accepting my invitations, for believing in my team and me.

Thank you, Emilio and Gloria Estefan, for always being there, whatever the reason may be. Along with the two of you, I owe an unpayable debt to all of the people with whom I've crossed paths in life and who, through their words, have helped me to learn how to improve myself each and every day.

Ray Garcia: thank you for insisting that I write this book, and for your support all along the way. You were right. To Andrea Montejo and Kim Suarez, my extraordinary editors: your precision, your dedication, and your feedback on how to perfect both the Spanish and English versions of this book was essential. Pablo de la Vega, thank you for helping me organize and assemble all the many pieces of this puzzle. Ezra Fitz, thank you for faithfully capturing and transmitting my voice and my message in English. And to the whole publishing team at Penguin: thank you so much for your care and your attention to all the details.